JIGSAW
the missing piece

GW01424353

by
Terry Jones

To our dear Pat, the
loveliest of friends. Also
in memory of a great buddy
Terry - the 'terrible' Terry
twins on the left wing!
Love
Terry + Ann
X   X

Jigsaw
The Missing Piece
First published 2024

© Terry Jones, 2024

The right of Terry Jones to be identified as the Author of this work has been asserted in accordance with the Copyright, Designs and Patents Act 1988.

All rights reserved. No part of this book may be reprinted or reproduced or utilised in any form or by any electronic, mechanical or other means, no known or hereafter invented, including photocopying and recording, or in any information storage or retrieval system, without permission in writing from the Publishers.

The Holy Bible, New International Version
© 1973, 1978, 1984 by International Bible Society
Used by permission of Zondervan Bible Publishers

ISBN 978-1-80517-972-6

Proofreading: Ann Jones and Sharon Jones
Typesetting and cover design: Sharon Jones
Printed and bound in Great Britain by:
Kingsway CLC Trust, Unit 5, Glendale Ave, Sandycroft, Deeside CH5 2QP

Dedicated

*to my darling wife Ann,
whose partnership, patience and wisdom
has kept me on course,
and the family, friends and strangers
who have consistently listened
to my stories and responded,
'you should write a book!'*

Prologue

JIGSAW

A complex arrangement of unique pieces designed to challenge, frustrate and motivate individuals towards a goal – completion.

Life is not dissimilar. It is challenging, often frustrating, uniquely personal, and forever in need of motivation towards completion. A host of complex, challenging and varied social shapes, cultural patterns and interactive possibilities woven and worked together over time.

For some, the jigsaw is an art form. Pieces carefully separated into colour bands. Others adopt 'shape-patterns' piling similar pieces together. Some dive in with corner pieces and edging while others opt for the formation of scenes - individual cameos that form a segment of the whole picture. The geeks of course choose the hard route, perhaps attempting a clear blue sky or a monochrome sea as their immediate goal. Nothing beats the insertion of the final piece and nothing causes more angst than the missing piece!

Why now? A short glance at the library biography shelf reveals a tendency to write about 'My Life' or 'My Journey' when you are forty or under. For many a superstar athlete it is under thirty, with the occasional music celebrity or footballer under twenty! I shun such works with a passion, not because there may be many a wise quote, insight or reflection contained in the text - it just seems too soon, perhaps fuelled by ego, arrogance, or money. I believe biographies require a reasonable degree of life experience not a few years of fading glory.

For almost twenty-five years, sometimes on multiple occasions, family, friends, and complete strangers have ended a conversation with these words, 'you should write a book.' Year after year I have procrastinated and resisted. Excuses abound. 'My memory is awful. I'm not a diarist or journal keeper. I would exaggerate or lie.' Perhaps most obvious, 'I am just an ordinary guy'.

Now, in my eighty-first year, I finally relented. Three people, over a period of two weeks, early in 2023, ended our conversation, 'you should write a book!' It was time to listen. Clearly, there was enough in the life-story to interest a wide spectrum of listeners who had graciously taken time to engage in conversation. I believe in the power of stories. Repeatedly, it was these cameos of life that evoked the most intense response, often with tears, laughter, and wonderment – occasionally disbelief. I am an avid story-teller. I trust the varied stories here will touch lives across a wide spectrum of experience, both in pain and joy, success, and failure.

Family

I have been married to Ann for over sixty-one years. We met, aged fifteen, at Avenue Baptist Church Youth Club in Westcliff on Sea, Essex. Ann an unofficial 'Essex-girl,' me with a broad scouse accent that defied translation! At seventeen, we had our first date and at eighteen I enlisted in the RAF! Not the ideal scenario for a relationship, but love overcame all obstacles and Ann waited. On the 29th June 1963, aged nineteen, we were married. We have three children, Andrew fifty-eight, Tim fifty-five and Sharon forty-seven. We also lost our first and fourth infant children, Gary and Elizabeth, to congenital heart disease.

Today they may well have survived, given the progress of heart surgery on young babies, but those options were not possible at the time. We have three grandchildren, Ben thirty, Tierney twenty-eight, and Aaron twenty-four.

Interests

- Loitering around and listening to others.
- WWII History.
- Local and Liverpool city history.
- Photography.
- Gardening – lots more than I can cope with!
- Everton FC – don't ask!
- Travel.
- Romance.
- Surprises.
- Cruise Ships.
- Faith.
- Volunteering.
- Helping others find the missing piece!

Website

If you would like to peruse some photos that show a little more of our lives, and reveal the images behind some of these stories, please take a look at our website:

www.jigsawthemissingpiece.com

Contents

1

WWII - BEGINNINGS

On any journey, knowing where you have come from may well aid your ability to map out where you are going. Knowing your history puts life into a context. The context for our beginning was WWII. Both our families moved from London to safer havens in the suburbs. For Ann's family, it was a very short stay in Woking, in preparation for Ann's birth! She duly obliged and was born on March 11th 1944. Two weeks later the family were back in Balham and vulnerable to the devasting Nazi doodlebugs. Ann's dad was a fireman, based at the heart of the blitz and a witness to awful bomb damage and loss of life, including the terrible crush at Balham Underground Station in October 1940. A bomb fell on the road above the station causing a massive crater and damaging a mains water pipe. This flooded the station with a rush of soil and water, and in the ensuing crush sixty-six died and around seventy people were badly injured. Trauma that may have forged Jim's blunt and tough temperament, as well as lifelong issues with his legs, issues which were passed on to Ann from birth. For my family, the move to Watford would last until the end of the war. Just thirteen days after Ann's birth, I was born on March 24th 1944. My thirteen days as a 'toyboy' is written into family folklore!

Distance between our families altered dramatically in July 1945 when my family moved from Watford to Jersey in the Channel Islands. We travelled in a small six-seater De Havilland Dragon Rapide operated by Jersey Airways. As our family was six - Dad, Idwal, Mum, Katherine, three older sisters, Phyllis, Doreen, Beryl, and me, it must have felt like we were VIP arrivals! Considering it was just two months after the liberation of the island, on May 9th 1945, it must have been a daunting prospect to set up home with few home comforts. To augment our bed linen and underwear our mother raided Vice Admiral Friedrich Huffmeier's (German Commandant) empty house on Mount Bingham overlooking Jersey Harbour. Silk sheets were lifted from the bed and a handy pram procured as transport! Evidently the house had not been touched since the German surrender. Whether this was out of disgust, fear, or other reasons is conjecture. The outcome of mum's bravado was knickers for the girls, underpants and a pram for me, and silk-laden beds for all!

Dad was charged with reopening and managing the Home and Colonial grocery store in King Street, St Helier, one of a massive chain of stores stretching across the UK and Ireland. This was no small task given the scarcity of food during the German occupation. Both residents and occupiers suffered terribly from near starvation rations - a situation still requiring significant recovery following the May 9th German surrender. Further folklore was anchored into the family when Dad was reputed to have opened the shop with half a tomato and a rasher of bacon - not too far from the truth. To make ends meet, my three sisters spent hours pickling onions! I, on the other hand, was stuffed into a wooden dumb-waiter and hauled out of sight. Evidently, I was not the most compliant of toddlers!

Jersey, of course, was a wonderful place to grow up. Glorious weather, awesome beaches, crystal clear sea. An Island 'metallic' adventure playground full of discarded German armaments, endless underground infrastructure, and gigantic granite walls. Walls built with slave labour - a significant part of the massive Nazi Atlantic Wall stretching from Norway to the French border with Spain. Almost every bay in Jersey is still protected by these immense structures, built at the cost of hundreds of lives in Jersey and thousands across Europe's coastline.

Meanwhile, now 230 miles away, Ann was also on the move from the flat in Balham to a house in Westcliff on Sea, Essex. Difficulty with walking increasingly became an issue for Ann. With limited paediatric examinations in 1944 a major problem had been missed. After visits to Southend Hospital, resulting in wedged boots, it became clear, over time, that this provision was not the answer. A subsequent visit to Ann's grandparents in Kennington, London, who noticed her hip problems, resulted in a referral to Mr Hindenach, a Polish Consultant Orthopaedic Surgeon at Queen Elizabeth Hospital for Sick Children in Hackney. This visit led to a diagnosis of congenital dislocation of the hips (CDH) with further complications on the left side. Ann's parents were advised that she may not be able to walk. Whilst this was a normal precautionary statement, in 1947 it was infinitely more possible than the present day. Ann, now aged three, spent the next two years in hospital undergoing traction, followed by two major surgeries to correct the abnormality of the left hip. During this time, on May 22nd 1947, Ann, though clearly too young to recall the conversation, received a visit from Princess Elizabeth. The future Queen stopped at Ann's bed and asked the nurse, 'what is wrong with this child and why is she on traction?' I presume an adequate explanation satisfied her Royal Highness.

These days it is hard to imagine that the only permitted visiting was on Wednesday and Sunday afternoons for just one hour! We have occasionally wondered what lasting affect such a lengthy period of hospitalisation, and separation from parents, has had on Ann. In recent years she has struggled, both mentally and emotionally, with hospitals. This from a young child who was desperate to be a nurse! Despite the cautious prognosis, the dedication and skill of Mr Hindenach and his team became evident. Ann had a new found confidence to walk, though the recovery process would continue through her fifth year and keep her from starting school until she was six. Netball and hockey would follow over time - black eye not withstanding on the hockey pitch! At fifteen, Ann left Westborough High School for Girls and moved to Southend Municipal College. Nursing was not possible – secretarial work advisable. She commenced a Royal Society of Arts Pitman's shorthand, typing and bookkeeping course and secured work at the Liverpool Victoria Friendly Society – paying out claims infinitely faster than the present day! At eighteen, she moved to the National Provincial Bank to earn more money in preparation for marriage!

In Jersey, family was on the move once again in 1951. Aged six, my future 'lifetime-nomadic' tag would add a third destination and one that would feature so prominently throughout my life – Liverpool. In typical fashion for Home and Colonial, Dad's promotion to Northern Regional Inspector, and therefore our family's departure from Jersey, was announced with just a week's notice! This presented the family with two major headaches. My eldest sister Phyl's wedding to Alfred LeGoubin, a Jerseyman, and my youngest sister Beryl's school netball championship in Guernsey! Mum had a week to make a wedding dress, two bridesmaid's dresses and a fancy silk outfit for me! Beryl, just thirteen, would travel to Guernsey with her school team, then travel alone by boat to Southampton, then on to Liverpool! We all made the wedding but Beryl was severely sick on the boat crossing to Southampton. Fortunately, a very compassionate and caring soldier looked after her. By the time she reached Liverpool her health had worsened and she was immediately admitted to hospital with a severe rash. Even today it would be ill-advised to allow a thirteen-year-old to travel alone, but with no other option, and a determination not to miss the last and most important annual school tournament, Beryl's grit prevailed.

Within a short time, following our arrival in Liverpool, a house was found at 1 Mayville Road, Allerton, literally a few hundred yards from the 'not yet famous' Penny Lane. As an Inspector, Dad received a company car. A split-screen Black Morris Minor, and later, a super-cool upgrade with a curved one-piece windscreen - 293 AMT. Funny how I can forget almost all else but remember that number. As far as I can recall we were the only car owners in the road and felt rather posh! Dad's remit, as a Regional Inspector, embraced the North of England, North Wales, Isle of Man, and Ireland, with Liverpool as the home base. No mean territory with dozens of Home & Colonial Stores to visit, take stock and train managers. From time to time, he would don a white coat and display his capacity for selling items customers had not come in to buy! He was a master of his trade and extremely persuasive. It was rare for any customer to refuse his 'six sausages for the price of five' with a brown bag of broken biscuits thrown in! Occasionally, I accompanied him on his journeys and spent my time packing small brown sugar bags, patting butter squares, or sorting broken biscuits.

Colwyn Bay was a favourite location as I could pop next door to an amusement arcade. On one memorable visit I put my pocket money into one of those revolving machines that tipped its prizes out with an arm that gradually moved across the base. The prizes were pen-knives! As the arm moved across it stuck! The outcome was exciting and noisy. Every time a knife came round it was pushed into the prize bin. I arrived back at the store with a stack of knives. It was a hard task convincing dad the machine had malfunctioned. One that you would not see in an arcade today!

Shortly after settling in Allerton, I entered Dovedale Road Junior School along with a lad named George Harrison. Like Penny Lane, he was also 'not yet famous'! John

Lennon, you guessed right, 'not yet famous', had left before my time. A few years later I became a choirboy at St Barnabas Church, Penny Lane, complete with red gown, white rufflets, and a monthly half-crown remuneration! Yep, along with the 'not yet famous' Paul McCartney, he who now has a plaque on a pew! It took another forty-five years to make a connection with Ringo Starr when we moved into the Dingle Ward of Toxteth, Liverpool 8, in September 1989. Ringo was born at 9 Madryn Street, Dingle in 1940.

In 1955, the 'nomadic' Jones's moved once again from Allerton to Huyton, a few miles further into the suburbs. A move up the social ladder, from a terrace to a detached bungalow at 1 Swanside Avenue, Huyton. This had been Harold Wilson's constituency since 1950. Fourteen years later, in 1964, he became Prime Minister, then again in 1974. By this time, my middle sister, Doreen, had married George Evans. Previously an WWII RAF Engineer who had spent part of the war servicing Spitfires and Hurricanes in the Egyptian Desert during the Battle of El Alamein. As George was already married, and not divorced when they got together, the union caused considerable pain to the family. Being eleven at the time, I was somewhat oblivious to the difficulties. Whilst the move to Huyton would forge many happy memories for me, it would also throw increasingly dark shadows over our family.

2

SHADOWS

Some secrets in life remain hidden for decades, others rapidly emerge. Despite growing tension and acrimony, my parents managed to hold things together until we arrived in Huyton. With such a large area to cover, Dad was increasingly away from home. Arguments increased over missing money. Given that an Inspector's salary was above the national average, it was a mystery. In time, it emerged that he was in a long-standing adulterous relationship with a Home and Colonial assistant in Colwyn Bay, North Wales. Keeping a mistress was not cheap. At home, the secret was out. Threats of violence and shouting often forced me to flee the house. Hiding, whether in my bedroom or elsewhere, became normal. Emotions were locked away and fears increased.

To add to my misery, I failed the eleven plus exam and started school at Grant Road Secondary Modern - an estate school the wrong side of the tracks for me. Pain increased when a gang from school arrived at our house. The ringleader was a tough customer who head-butted me and kicked me to the ground. It hurt! I recall his name to this day. The police were called and I was driven around the area seeking out the culprits. Suffice to note I was too scared to respond. As a possible release from the pain, and a desire to buy a stack of 'push and go' mini-cars, I filed into our gas meter lock and robbed the stash of shillings! It was obvious, both to parents and police, it was me. The line of new 'push and go' mini cars from the local toy shop was something of a giveaway!

Eventually, things got so bad that mum moved out, with

me in tow. A miserable run-down shop across the city, near Everton FC, with a small area at the rear for beds, became my new home. Tough times all round. To try and make a living, mum would sell blue and white rosettes and do all manner of sewing - hardly enough to survive. Eventually, an unstable reconciliation took place and we moved back home. It was a bittersweet return. Happy to get my room back but terrified about returning to Grant Road. How I survived, let alone learnt anything, is a mystery I can't recall.

Two years on, I miraculously passed the thirteen-plus exam and moved to Hillfoot Hey Grammar School. What relief, as the discipline, atmosphere, and opportunities, not least for football, were immense compared to Grant Road. A paper round gave me enough money to buy a decent bike and fuelled my passion for all things cycling and especially Everton FC. My room was now adorned with Tour de France pictures along with Everton stars. I'm not sure how many Everton stars would feature today as I write and we sit second from bottom in the league! However, just as I was forging good friendships and venturing across the country on bikes with my mates, another 'nomadic' twist and turn emerged.

True to form with the Home and Colonial, it was last minute again. Dad's reputation as an excellent Regional Inspector landed him the top job as Chief Inspector in the London Area. Another hasty move landed us in Southend-on-Sea in June 1959. I had taken my mock O-level exams and moved South before the real thing. Now fifteen, and with a very broad scouse accent, there was no way I was returning to school to face the inevitable barrage of abuse and bullying that would follow. Education was off the agenda and work on it.

3

REDEMPTION

When living in Liverpool, probably aged around twelve, mum contacted an uncle who was a photographer with the Daily Express in Manchester. Knowing my passion for football he arranged to take me on an assignment. A match between Blackpool and Portsmouth. It was the days when photographers lay on the ground either side of the goal. Imagine how important I felt being ushered into the ground and on to the pitch. To meet printing deadlines we left the match before the final whistle and dashed back to the offices in Manchester. I was introduced to film developing, identifying key pictures, printing, and wiring the best black and white pictures to London for the Sunday papers. As a young lad, with hormones stirring, it was my first introduction to semi-naked young ladies whose pictures adorned the offices and machine rooms! I left with a distinct desire to be a photographer!

Now, at fifteen, without a single qualification, I had to begin at the bottom. I soon found work with Albany Laundry, delivering brown parcels of washed and ironed laundry to homes, shops, and factories. It was routine and boring, but I enjoyed the travel, stacking the parcels in order and keeping fit as I delivered the goods. Threepenny pieces were still legal currency and I remember the day, on our morning coffee break, when I tried my luck in the café slot machine. Several pieces in, I hit the jackpot and watched in wonder as the coins pounded the metal tray. Every eye in the café turned towards the noise of the win! I can't recall whether the cry went up, 'drinks are on the Albany lad!'

One personal issue was my intense loneliness. I had no

school contacts, no mates to hang out with. Often, I would end the day walking the amusement arcades on Southend seafront. The turning point came when mum randomly asked a guy on the street whether he knew of any youth clubs in the area. She had stumbled across John Jackson, one of the volunteer workers at Avenue Baptist Church Youth Club! The club had a dedicated facility. A detached wooden bungalow equipped with full size snooker table, darts, music room, lounge, tuck shop, and a married couple who patiently oversaw around forty club members. We also had access to table tennis and badminton in the church halls. Perhaps the scouse accent wasn't too bad after all, as I was accepted warmly into the vibrant life of 'Carey House'. I am grateful to John Jackson for taking me under his wing and teaching me the deft art of badminton. Many years later it would pay off well in the RAF, along with football, table tennis and snooker! Another impact in my life was the Christian witness of many of the young people. I saw in their lives something that was clearly missing in mine – a missing piece of the jigsaw of life.

Revelation came one evening in the middle of communion. I had no idea what communion meant, but Pam, my girlfriend at the time, invited me to stay for the communion service. All around me were young and old celebrating their faith in Jesus and remembering the love, mercy and forgiveness Jesus Christ made possible by his life, death, and resurrection. I became deeply troubled, and wanted to escape quickly, but somehow knew I was being convicted of my need to seek forgiveness and call on Jesus to be my Lord and Saviour. When I eventually came out of the church building, the wrestle inside was so real. My first reaction was to shout at Pam, 'why did you take me in there?' Her wisdom was to suggest I seek out our Minister, Rev George Thompson Brake. After a battle within, I turned up at his office. I must have sounded strange, 'I don't know why I'm here,' but he knew. Very simply, from the Bible,

George shared the gospel. The good news of God's love for me, and the reason Jesus was born into the world. I knelt down, and in the best prayer I could muster asked Jesus to forgive my sin and be Lord and Saviour of my life. No stars appeared. No divine voice from heaven. No fuss, just the first step in a lifelong journey of discipleship and faith, with all its twists and turns. The Bible however is very clear. 'If you confess with your mouth that Jesus is Lord and believe in your heart that God raised him from the dead you will be saved.' Romans chapter 10 verse 9. If you have never opened a Bible, it contains 66 books. 39 in the Old Testament and 27 in the New Testament. Where I have written texts from the Bible, I always put the book first followed by the chapter then verse. Please don't give up here!

Nothing appeared to change much but I recall my sister Phyl writing and saying 'your letters have changed!' It was a real encouragement, and a reminder that Christian faith is a marathon journey of discovery, transformation, and small steps along the way. One small, but significant and important step, was my public confession of Christian faith. I had witnessed others being baptised as believers in Jesus and knew that it was important for me to take that further step in becoming a disciple – a follower of Jesus. In Acts chapter 2 verse 41 we read, 'Those who accepted his message were baptised.' They believed first, in response to the Word of God spoken to them, then, as a sign they had truly believed, they were baptised.

In a parallel universe, Ann also began that same journey of faith. The youth would meet in Carey House after the evening service. Ann, and her boyfriend David, were planning a walk after the service rather than staying with the youth. On the stairs out of church John Jackson, the same youth leader my mum had spoken to, asked if they were going to the youth gathering - a timely moment.

A moment that changed the direction of Ann's life. The Minister, George Thompson Brake, was sharing his Christian journey - David and Ann were deeply touched. Ann describes it as 'only me in the room.' The walk home together was strangely silent as they reflected on the message. Ann asked David, 'did something happen to you tonight?' 'Yes', was the reply, a simple indication that the Spirit of God had used George's testimony to speak into the lives of two teenagers.

When Ann arrived home, that special moment at the Youth Club was cut short by Ann's Dad, 'Go to the off licence and get me some ciggies.' Ann was used to that regular errand for Dad, but somehow it felt wrong that evening. However, the seed was sown. A few months later both David and Ann confessed their faith publicly in Believer's Baptism. Ann had joined the youth club in 1959, before I arrived from Liverpool, and was well liked. So liked, she was voted the first Youth Club President in 1960 and her picture hung in the club lounge. A year later I became the second President and our pictures faced each other before our first date! A marriage was being made in heaven as we gazed at each other on earth! There were only ever two Youth Presidents before the bungalow was demolished to make way for apartments. We both deny any responsibility for the demise of Carey House!

The marriage prepared in heaven appeared on the earth via the breakdown of both our teen relationships. David was giving money to Ann to save for an engagement ring. When he asked for the money back, to buy an overcoat, Ann knew the relationship was over. Pam also was facing pressure from home. She had joined a Baptist Youth Club but her parents' Christian faith was earthed in a much more conservative journey and they were not overly happy she was going out with a scouser! When she started dating a guy two year's older, it must have raised serious concerns and tripled their prayers! Pam duly ended our relationship! Two 'free' seventeen-year-old teens were now in the youth 'availability' crowd. It took me a couple of months to ask Ann for a date in January 1962. More to the point, I announced among a small group of friends in the youth club music room, 'I'm taking Ann to the pictures on Saturday!' It was news to Ann that I had a keen interest! She said 'yes' and the first seed of love was sown and quickly blossomed.

Back in the world of work, my ambition was still to be a photographer. I had enrolled for a course in shorthand and typing, alongside photography, at Southend Municipal College, not long after taking the Albany job. However, I had a passion for all things sport, and wanted to move on from the mundane laundry work. I spotted an advert in the local paper for a Sports Shop assistant in Leigh-on-Sea, a few miles outside Southend. An interview was offered and within a few days I was selected. The elderly owner was a brilliant teacher and I soon excelled at stringing tennis and badminton racquets, repairing cricket bats and, something of a speciality, making sea and fresh water fishing rods. Selling all manner of fishing tackle enhanced my people skills and introduced me to the art of fishing in local freshwater venues as well as in the sea off Southend Pier. It was so satisfying to absorb the training and know I had skills in serving others and responding to their needs. Meanwhile, Ann's investment in secretarial skills was also serving others in the Liverpool Victoria Insurance office in Southend. She was so pleased to get her first job and to work with a helpful manager and staff.

The first test of our blossoming relationship was my emerging plans. Although I was happy at Leigh Sports and, unbeknown to me being considered as assistant manager in a new store the boss was opening, photography remained my paramount goal. While working through my course at the Municipal College, I began writing to newspapers seeking a photography apprenticeship or other role – not a single reply! Just when it appeared there was little hope, a breakthrough came. An advert in the local paper read, 'Photographers needed in the Royal Air Force.' I could hardly contain my excitement at the possibility of finally achieving my goal. I also felt very disloyal, given my emotions, as the paper was left by my boss on the Sports Shop counter! He had trained me for eighteen months and clearly hoped I might serve him for many years!

However, an advert response is not acceptance. I filled in the application and was invited to attend an interview at the RAF recruiting office in Holborn, Central London. I was extremely nervous, given my lack of school certificates. Perhaps my football story with my uncle, several years earlier, struck a chord with the Officer, as well as my efforts to gain a photography certificate. Suffice to say I passed the exam questions and was duly invited to sign on in the photography branch - initially for nine years, with options for twelve in the future. My pride and elation were incredible.

Now I was faced with how Ann would react. I must have let it slip at youth club before telling her. To compound the mistake, it was her ex-boyfriend who announced the news that I was joining the RAF! Mercifully, she was not overly shocked. I asked her whether she would wait and her answer was straightforward - 'yes I will.' Love had not only blossomed, so had loyalty and patient commitment. A commitment that would get us through trial and tragedy in the future.

4

ROYAL AIR FORCE

Just weeks after my acceptance into the RAF, I was on my way to RAF Bridgenorth in Shropshire for eight weeks square-bashing. Having been a scout for several years I had an inkling of discipline and a general understanding of pioneering, living under canvas with others, and map reading. I had also done lengthy bike trips with a gang from school in Liverpool which involved several stays in youth hostels. Those stays gave me an awareness of life in a billet! I settled well but soon missed Ann.

The primary goal at Bridgenorth was to survive the brutal elements, embrace discipline, forge a team, and make sure you complete the course and pass out with flying colours. The reality of failing was always present. Little tricks made it easier to complete the basic training; ironing leather pimples off the toecap of boots enabled the cap to shine with spit and polish; fashioning stiff lengths of hardboard to enhance the edges of your bed-pack; remembering never to put the muzzle of your rifle into the ground; ensuring you were always in a straight line on parade and above all, respecting your troop sergeant and corporal who held the power over completion or failure!

During the eight-week training we had one break for home leave – Easter 1962. On Thursday April 19th I arrived at Ann's home to much-needed hugs and kisses. We were both excited after a month apart, but also somewhat nervous. I was gearing up to ask Ann's dad if I could marry his daughter! As Jim was not the easiest person to get on with, Ann and her mum retreated to the kitchen as I entered the lounge. No grilling. No lengthy discussion. A 'yes' sealed the short conversation, followed by negotiation on the proposed date of the wedding. Ann's mum wanted us to wait until September 1963, Ann wanted Easter '63. We compromised and went for June 29th! Now that the marriage date was settled, it was time for the engagement! On Saturday April 21st we headed for the H. Samuel store on Southend High St and, with my meagre savings of eight pounds, purchased a gold ring with three small diamonds. It was the happiest moment of our lives. Given our youth, at eighteen, along with past family baggage and unhappiness, we were told it wouldn't last! On paper that was statistically likely.

All too soon duty called. Ann accompanied me to the station to say goodbye. A trait that developed over the next year when she would travel up to Liverpool Street Station with me, then take the train back to Southend. Anything to grab as much time as possible – a long goodbye!

Over the next four weeks we tackled map reading, were let loose in the countryside to test our survival skills and, most scary, given bullets for rifle and machine-gun. It was live-firing time on the range. Having a steady hand, unaffected by heavy drinking, I managed to tot up a good score and gained my marksman badge. You have been warned! The final weeks focused on refining the passing-out drill routine and ensuring all our kit was in perfect condition.

Completion was now on our radar with the passing out parade. Ann would be coming with my mum. A daunting prospect given her constant and determined efforts to end our relationship. Ann was blissfully unaware of the challenging cross-country journey from Southend in Essex to Kinver Edge in Shropshire. Trying to find a house, without an address, whilst walking up a rugged country path in total darkness, with mum declaring 'I don't know if this is the road or the way,' tested patience to the limit!

By divine guidance, and a minor miracle, they eventually knocked at my Aunties house! One more addition to family folklore!

It was a perfect final day at Bridgenorth. Warm sunshine and a clear blue sky. Ann in a lovely candy-stripe dress was, according to my drill instructor Sgt Jackson, 'the most excited and animated person in the crowd!' The platoon was sharp, so sharp we gained top marks and the highest score recorded at a passing out parade! It was an immense relief and a tribute to the instructors who bullied us all the way but brought out the best. Hugs all round and some lengthy kisses for my fiancé.

5

TRADE TRAINING

If I needed further resolve and grit, then my trade training posting would provide it in bucket loads. As the newly created Photography II course, at RAF Wellesbourne Mountford in Warwickshire, didn't start until September, I would serve time as a rookie elsewhere. Following a week off in Southend, I made my way to RAF West Raynham in Norfolk, eleven miles from civilisation in Kings Lynn! Manageable in summer but, unbeknown to me at the time, the country was heading for the severest winter in many decades - the endless snow storms of '62-63. The months on station dragged on with very little work for me, being a rookie without portfolio. Every menial job was passed down, but I learned how to tough out the hard times and persevere with mind-numbing tasks, such as chipping ice from the runway. Another vital lesson stored away for the challenges ahead.

Countless love letters to Ann would fill my evenings as I looked forward to weekends together and catching up with friends from Avenue Baptist Youth Club. With little money, hitch-hiking to Kings Lynn, then down the A11 to Southend was the priority. In the days when uniforms were still allowed outside the base, it was relatively easy to thumb a lift though at times it was a long haul to make it to Southend before darkness! It also had its dangers. I was picked up once by a driver in a Rolls-Royce. My best 'hitch' ever, but my worst nightmare when he began to talk, breathing pure alcohol into my lungs. I took the first opportunity to say 'thanks' and exit the vehicle!

Occasionally, Ann would spend the weekend with her

grandparents in Wokingham, Berkshire. Cross-country hiking is never recommended but love conquers all! Determined not to miss a moment with my beloved, I set out from West Raynham one Friday afternoon at 4pm. At 1am, I made it to Sandhurst Road, just out of Wokingham. The road was straight and long. No street lights, pitch-black, and lined on both sides with very tall poplar trees that doubled as ghosts. I had only ever visited grandad's bungalow once – in daylight. This was to be a dark, late-night adventure. Try as I might, I could not find 'Cleavers' as it was impossible to see the signs without light. As I began to despair, I saw a small light in the distance heading my way. A sign of hope. However, as I began to wave the cyclist down, his intention was to get past me at all cost. The dance of death began! He swerved, I moved, he swerved back, I moved back. It was perfectly understandable. Who in their right mind, meeting a shadowy figure walking in the middle of the road at 1am in the morning, would casually stop?

Despite his desperate lunge to avoid me, I managed to persuade him I was an innocent teenager. The uniform probably helped! He could not direct me to 'Cleavers' but parted with a priceless box of matches. Within a few minutes I was striking a match at the ancient wooden sign of 'Cleavers.' Now, just the matter of discerning which window to tap, in the hope it was where Ann was staying, and I could kip on the sofa. She had no idea I had decided, at the last minute, to make the trip! I crept around the bungalow, decided on a likely window-pane, and knocked. It turned out to be my future mother-in-law! Bless her, she handled a potentially dangerous and scary moment with wisdom and discernment. She knew the power of love! I was ushered in, a couch prepared and a drink supplied. In the morning, she woke Ann and explained that an unexpected guest had arrived in the middle of the night! Suffice to say, it was worth every effort, and I got back to

29

base in time not to be charged with being AWOL (absent without leave).

September finally arrived and, as I first thought, I would leave the wilds of West Raynham for relative comfort in the scenic delights of the West Midlands. How wrong could I have been. Wellesbourne Mountford opened in 1941 and was constructed in the typical Class A airfield design. The main unit to use the airfield was No. 22 RAF Operational Training Unit, flying Vickers Wellingtons and Avro Ansons for RAF Bomber Command from April 1941. Though it was no longer a flying station in 1962, very little had changed with respect to living accommodation. The billets were long wooden structures housing around thirty recruits and heated by two coal burners. The School of Photography had been there since 1948. I was soon to discover the downside of trade training in a WWII environment. From late December to March 1963, severe snow storms, blizzards and plummeting temperatures resulted in the coldest winter since 1895! Inside the billet, RAF Greatcoats were worn throughout the night and grown men took shifts to keep the stoves alight. The wash room water supply and fire buckets were frozen solid. In the day we shivered our way through the training. It was something of a miracle to get home to Southend for Christmas and begin the countdown to marriage on June 29th.

Having completed the newly-crafted Photography II course in February '63, I held my breath as I received my next posting. The shock was palpable. I was posted back to West Raynham! Never trust the RAF when they ask you to select your favoured postings. My hope was to be down South near to Ann, especially with marriage on the horizon. A return to Norfolk was certainly not on my radar, not least as the 'Big Freeze' showed no signs of abating. However, when you sign on you go where you are sent. My first task was pure déjà vu - chipping ice off the runway - for days on end! I had arrived back at West Raynham with a range of fresh photographic knowledge but very little real experience on the ground. I was soon to realise how limited my capacity with a camera would be at this stage of my career. Although I suspect, as a rookie, my colleagues in the photo section were keen to play a practical joke when the occasion arose.

Within a few weeks of my arrival at West Raynham, hope was on the horizon. I received news of a cross-posting to RAF Wyton in Cambridgeshire. A V-Bomber base with Valiants and Victors, Canberras and Comets. I was ecstatic. Not only would I be nearer Ann, but civilisation, with Cambridge just fifteen miles away. One primary task remained before my exodus to Wyton. 85 Squadron, Gloster Javelins, were disbanding and the station temporarily closing. My task was to sit on top of a Land-Rover and take pictures of the squadron as they prepared to depart on mass. It was possibly joke-time, with a fully expected outcome from my colleagues in the photo section!

I was given an almost impossible task. The photo department had state of the art Leica and Twin Lens Rollieflex cameras - I was handed an MPP S92. A technically good camera but totally unsuited for movement. It was the equivalent of giving me a Mini to compete in a Formula One race. Focusing was bad enough with a sturdy tripod but hand-held it was a nightmare. A round rack-screw to move the bellows and focus, with a 5x4 inch negative plate to push into the back for one exposure! Suffice to say, almost every shot was out of focus. I imagine my department Sgt signed the work sheet - 'may not make it as a photographer!' It took another ten years before I was trusted with a decent camera in my final posting at Strike Command HQ RAF High Wycombe.

Finally, after two difficult postings to Norfolk, I was on my way to RAF Wyton. The contrast with West Raynham was immense; superb sports facilities, modern accommodation, buzzing with aircraft, a large photographic unit, easy access to transport and a vibrant social life. As a keen sportsman, I expected to fare well in terms of time off for training and matches, both badminton and football. As I excelled at badminton and, to a slightly lesser degree football, I was always in the frame for station teams. Later, badminton would feature in the RAF Championships. How well John Jackson had nurtured my emerging skill back in my youth club days. Never underestimate the value of mentoring young people in their youth.

In terms of my work, the contrast between West Raynham and Wyton was vast. To put it bluntly, I was a spare-part at West Raynham, with little or no use for photographers, whereas Wyton was teeming with photographic activity. 543 Squadron, Vickers Valiant V-Bombers, were equipped with up to eight F.52 cameras with 36 or 48 inch (91 or 122cm) focal length lenses. These would either be fixed straight down or a fan arrangement to give horizon to horizon coverage. There was also provision for vertically mounted F.49 'survey' cameras with 6inch (15cm) lens and fixed rear bomb-bay mountings for oblique imagery. As well as the Cold War reconnaissance role, 543 were tasked with major survey sorties across the world. Each camera would have 500 feet of film, 9x9 inch per negative. A week-long survey might end up with 3000 feet of film from each of the eight cameras, totalling 24,000 feet!

On return to Wyton the cassettes would be collected from the aircraft and the film developed in multiple tanks. Each tank had rollers that fed the film through the whole development process - an operation often fraught with complications, such as film breakage in the tanks or a fault in the processing machine resulting in stoppage of the film flow. This could end up with severe over-development and a very expensive survey operation compromised. The first sign of a problem was a halt in the film-flow, the rods and rollers that controlled the flow would start rising in the tanks. This was swiftly followed by a rise in blood pressure and a degree of panic! If the film had been severed it was critical that a fast repair took place. No mean task, whilst ensuring all the rods were kept down in the tanks! I have certainly panicked a few times in the darkroom!

In 1963, 4 Handley Page Victors, fitted with yellow 'Astor' reconnaissance radar, together with passive sensors, were used to equip a secretive unit, the Radar Reconnaissance Flight, attached to 543 squadron. 58 Squadron Canberras, also with a photo reconnaissance role, completed the trio serviced by the photographic unit. Together they formed part of the Joint Air Reconnaissance Intelligence Centre (JARIC} along with RAF Brampton, just 6 miles away. Wyton's primary function, as part of JARIC, was to collect and document a photographic record of enemy targets required for the defence of the country during wartime. Exciting times for a young teenage recruit.

6

MARRIAGE

The timing of my posting to Wyton was perfect. It was just three months before our wedding at Avenue Baptist Church, Westcliff-on-Sea, Essex on June 29th 1963. Ann was working at the National Provincial Bank in Southend and was initially steeling herself to live in the wilds of Norfolk. Now we were looking forward to exploring the delights of Cambridge and spending time looking for a flat. We set aside just one day to find a home! Contrary to hunting for a rental apartment today, we quickly found the perfect location - a first floor flat, near to the River Cam with its scenic beauty and walks. Later in our stay, the landlord asked if we would move to the second floor. As we had a very comfortable sofa, we asked if the sofa could come with us! He agreed and we happily moved into a flat that also had access to a flat roof with room for sunbathing! We had embarked on a lifetime of amazing provision of homes. A journey of 'faith before sight' that would be our mantra, and experience, right up to the present day with our wonderful 'faith' provision of a retirement home. A varied, challenging and faith-filled story still way in the future!

For around twenty-five years, the title of this book was set in stone, 'Four houses in Henley-on-Thames and a Semi in Toxteth' (Henley spoken with a posh accent and Toxteth with pure scouse)! The small strapline underneath was, 'It will never sell!' The title changed to 'Jigsaw' just prior to completing the book as it suddenly struck me as a way of saving ink and infinitely more understandable, though the first title is utterly true and will occupy several lines later in the book!

We cannot underline enough just how amazing has been our home provision. Miraculous may sound so presumptuous but I will leave you to discern for yourself as our journey unfolds. Alongside home provision we would also experience timely work for Ann – always at the right time and place. When the accountant at the National Provincial Bank in Southend heard she was getting married, and moving to Cambridge, he immediately asked her whether she had considered a transfer – something Ann didn't know was possible. Following our wedding she would walk straight into a new role as secretary to the Branch Manager in St Andrew's Street, Cambridge. As he was also treasurer for the local Samaritans Branch, she could add that role to her CV! In fact, she was the only admin staff member in the bank so was technically secretary for the whole branch!

Preparation for our wedding had its fair share of trials. At one point, Ann's dad threatened to withdraw his consent and not walk her up the aisle. My mum, who was making the bridesmaids' dresses, changed the colour without telling Ann! At nineteen, we were considered too young for marriage. 'It will never last' was a familiar refrain. Despite the battles, we persevered, rode the disappointments, and looked forward to marriage, honeymoon and settling into our nicely furnished flat at 35 De Freville Avenue, Cambridge.

What a relief to finally make it to June 29th. I had toyed with wearing my Number One RAF Dress Uniform, but with the lowest of ranks it appeared far too presumptuous! A white 'Blanco' belt and gloves would have been rather smart though! We were delighted to have Ann's elderly grandparents present. It was the first wedding of a grandchild they had been able to attend as they both worked in their Ironmongery store in Kennington, London, until selling up in their late seventies. Both Youth Club and the RAF gave us trusted and close friends. Rick and Vivian Owen, who had been a wonderful example to me in youth club, Rick being my best man. Pam Rivers, whose timely prompting to speak to our Minister led to a confession of faith in Jesus, was there with boyfriend David (not the David who bought the overcoat!) Ann had three bridesmaids; her cousin Mavis and my eldest sister Phyllis's two daughters Denise and Jackie. They had flown over from Jersey the day before but arrived at Ann's home less than an hour before the service! Waiting for their arrival caused a degree of panic as to whether they would be dressed in time. Ann's mum said she should go without them! Ann responded, 'no I won't!' She had previously told her mum to 'leave me in bed if it's raining.' Raining it was, but by the time she reached the church, complete with all three bridesmaids, the sun was shining. As she walked down the aisle her face shone. She was a picture of beauty in her five-pound homemade white brocade dress. Dad put his threats aside and let his daughter go! I received her with gratefulness, joy, and a heart full of love.

Following the service, we gathered at Westcliff Hotel for the reception. Compared to the thousands spent today, the total bill for forty guests was seventy-five pounds - a bill we had to pay ourselves. Young as we were, we survived the occasion and made our way to Southend Airport for our flight to Jersey and our honeymoon. Whilst I had flown twice, in a De Haviland Rapide and De Haviland Comet, this was Ann's first flight. Instead of the Jersey Airlines turbo-prop we were led to a WWII workhorse - a Douglas Dakota DC4! Entering by the rear door you were very aware of the acute angle as you boarded and looked upward towards the cockpit. Ann was more nervous about the flight than the wedding, however, the flight was fine, but it was somewhat strange for me to land back on the island where I had grown up as a toddler.

For Ann it was her first for everything. Wedding, flight, stay in a hotel, island holiday and, more daunting than expected, which cutlery to use for melon! We landed at 8pm in the evening and took a taxi to the Hotel de France. Ann was excited but overwhelmed by the biggest hotel in Jersey. It was around 9pm when we sat down for evening dinner. Just one other couple were present - across the other side of the restaurant. It meant neither of us could check what cutlery to use and when. The melon duly arrived and we decided to work 'outside-in' as posh people do. It turned out to be the fish knife and fork! When the waiter returned, he told us about the dessert spoon and, if we had used it, he would have replaced it. Nowhere to hide!

Jersey did not disappoint. It took Ann about a day to fall in love with this beautiful island. An island that would feature so much in our future and be filled with so many of our relatives. I was excited about taking her to every bay, courtesy of the ancient 'Tantivy' coaches – they are still running! One place has been our life-long favourite, Corbiere Lighthouse situated on a rugged rock promontory on the West Coast. Today our house is filled with a range of photos and art depicting the many hues of this most stunning of locations.

Jersey is an eclectic paradise. The rugged North Coast with small bays and stunning vistas across to Normandy on the French Coast. On the West, five-mile St Quen's Bay with Atlantic rollers, hidden German defence works and sandy bluffs. On the South, the wide sweep of St Aubin's Bay with its awesome beach protected by a massive granite wall spanning the capital St Helier to St Aubin's Harbour. The majestic Elizabeth Castle, with its WWII DUKWS (amphibious transport) ferrying tourists to and from the shore, situated just outside Jersey Harbour. In the East, the magnificent Gorey Castle, perched high above the harbour, and around the dotted bays back to St Helier - a treacherous coastline that has claimed both ships and lives.

The flavour of France is everywhere - in local families, farms, sign posts and Jersey-French dialect. The mark of the Germans features across the island in gigantic granite walls protecting bays, rusting and renewed armaments and numerous tourist attractions depicting the periods of occupation throughout the centuries. Who could not fall for this Island of stunning contrasts and varied history.

Time spent with family was precious, full of joy-filled memories, but duty always calls. Fortunately, our return flight to Southend was a little more comfortable in a turbo-prop. Following a night with Ann's folks, we made our way to Cambridge and settled into our new home. As I made my first fifteen-mile journey to RAF Wyton, Ann bussed or cycled to the centre of Cambridge and the challenge waiting at her new bank position in St Andrew's Street.

A close shave occurred one morning on the way to Wyton, when following a car towing a sizeable yacht. I noticed the yacht was moving slightly towards the back of the trailer and mentioned it to my driver. A short way along I said, 'that yacht could catch the wind and rise off the trailer.' No sooner had I spoken than the yacht reared into the air and turned over, eventually crashing over us and into a side ditch! One of many potentially catastrophic motoring fails that stretch over the years. Just wait till I get to Germany, go windsurfing in Staines and take a dramatic U-turn in Oregon!

Whilst we enjoyed our new marital status, home, and work, our embryonic Christian faith began to wane. We searched for a spiritual home but the Baptist Church was so different from Avenue; a common factor for many Christians when moving home and seeking a new church. My RAF friends were all reasonably heavy drinkers and it didn't take long before we were hosting a party in the flat or attending another elsewhere. Our youthful faith was tested and found wanting.

In June 1964 we returned to our special 'Jersey-Isle' retracing many of our '63 memories. We were so grateful for my sister Phyl and brother-in-law Alfred's hospitality but failed to appreciate how costly it was for them. We had no savings and little spare cash, so very little was offered to cover our stay - something I do regret with the hindsight of passing years. My sister was always glad to have us, join us on the beach, with nieces Jackie and Denise, and generally model what it meant to be a faithful Christian disciple. Through the years, Phyl's daughters Denise and Jackie, along with husbands Mick and Bob, and son Ray with his wife Lin, have perfectly modelled and mirrored Alfred and Phyl's generous hospitality by offering their homes in Jersey – thank you all.

Alfred introduced us to float and spin-fishing off Egypt, a somewhat treacherous hillside on the rugged North Coast. The trek down the hillside was always scary but the fishing, for rock-wrasse, mackerel, and bass, was always exciting. Hooking a sizeable mackerel, on a heavyweight spinner, was an enjoyable fight. On the culinary front, seabass is one of the tastiest meals around, though Ann was never happy to watch the gutting process!

It was always a sad moment leaving Jersey, and usually accompanied by tears, especially when leaving by boat and passing Corbiere Lighthouse.

7

DARK DAYS

Just three months after returning from holiday, in September 1964, I received news of a three-year posting to RAF Gutersloh in Northern Germany. Ann also received news that she was pregnant! We were thrilled but somewhat daunted, given the timing. I duly flew ahead of Ann as I needed to find accommodation. At 20 years of age the RAF did not recognise our marriage for accommodation purposes, as you had to be 21!

Gutersloh was the most northerly flying station in Germany and in an area where Hitler's youth movement had been especially active. Given that we were arriving less than twenty years after the war, with memories still somewhat raw, it was hardly surprising that we were not always welcome. Unfortunately, I made the mistake of securing accommodation in the wrong village. The army detachment at Gutersloh had experienced problems in 1963. Their response was to pay a visit to Harsewinkel, leaving a degree of damage to property, and anger and bitterness among the residents. Setting up home in a small apartment was not good news. We were spat at, refused service in local shops, and generally despised. To add to our woes, when Ann arrived, winter was setting in.

To make ends meet she took a mind-numbing job at Voisins, a German towel factory. Her day consisted of cutting spare cotton off towels. The regime was intensely strict; talking to other English or foreign workers was verboten - perhaps a small ironic payback for war memories. Ann often commented on the strict routine of the German women when travelling to work on the short train journey from

Harsewinkel to Gutersloh. They would perch on the edge of the seat so as not to crease their coats or spoil their hair by leaning back against the seat. We both noticed how disciplined and regimented they were when confronted by German men in uniform, whether train guards, bus drivers or policemen. There was an element of fear in their behaviour. A reminder of the mass obedience to Hitler a couple of decades earlier.

On the base I was assigned to 4 Squadron 'Hawker Hunters', one of two fighter/reconnaissance squadrons, 'Shiny 2' being the other. Intense rivalry sparked a stream of banter and comparison. In addition to the ageing 'Hunters,' 19 Squadron English Electric Lightnings arrived some months after my posting. The noise level on station increased dramatically! Photo work was minimal on the Lightnings as their only equipment was a small forward facing gunnery camera. Nevertheless, compared to the Hunter, it was always fun climbing into the cockpit to reload the gunnery camera, and ear-splitting when the two after-burners were screaming on take-off.

The photographic section personnel were split into two roles, the photo processing rooms in the hanger and the 'Line.' The 'Line' was situated away from the hanger and staffed by one or two members of the trades responsible for preparing and seeing the aircraft off safely. The 'Hunter' was equipped with three F45 5X4 inch film cameras, one on each side of the nose cone and one at the front. In the cockpit was a small gunnery camera for checking hits should the guns be fired. My job was to ensure the camera cassettes were loaded with film and unloaded on return.

As photographers had the least amount of work, we were charged with supporting all other trades; we parked eight aircraft overnight, cleaned them when required, pulled them from the hanger, strapped pilots in, checked their ejector seat pins were out and, most dangerous, crawled under the plane to extinguish 'start-up' exhaust flames with a fireproof glove! It was always a scary procedure, especially on a blow-back. Finally, we would see each aircraft off the stand and spend the next two to three hours waiting for their return. It was an excellent time to play football, clean and service cars, share banter and pretend we were special by driving the squadron Land Rover, with 4 Squadron logo, around the base.

As Ann's pregnancy developed it became clear that we needed to move away from Harsewinkel. The thought of Ann alone in a small apartment, caring for a child in a hostile environment, would have been a terrible strain on Ann, and our relationship. We chose to look at Spexard, a village about 10 miles the other side of the base. A German family of six offered us a few rooms with a shared bathroom. Not ideal, but all we could afford. We often wonder how on earth we survived. Timing the bathroom was a lottery. Using more than one ring on the cooker blew the house fuse. Whilst the wife was supportive, especially as Ann's pregnancy moved on, the husband was a heavy drinker and occasionally had eyes on Ann.

On April 24th 1964 our first child, Gary, was born in Munster Army Hospital. We had no car. The thirty-six mile journey was dependent on friends and the availability of RAF transport. At three days old, Ann became concerned at Gary's sleepiness and poor feeding. At the time the Army Hospital was not renowned for compassionate care. If you are in the Army, you get on with things and move on. Unknown to Ann, Gary had been taken from the maternity ward and placed in an incubator due to a collapsed lung. A week later Ann was taken into the sister's office, where an Army Consultant Paediatrician was waiting. In a very casual and callous manner he told Ann that Gary was seriously ill with a heart defect and not expected to live.

However, if he did live for three months, he would be transferred to England. Our best option, he said, was to go home and, basically, 'forget about him!' At that point he left the room! The Sister then informed Ann, she could contact me to come and take her home. Gary would remain at the hospital.

Ann went back, alone, to her room. A room with no privacy but shared with other mothers. When I arrived, she took me into the bathroom and told me that Gary was not expected to live - no sympathy, counselling, or care, not even the offer of a cup of tea. Military life can be that brutal.

A few days later, we were asked if we would like to take Gary home. We clearly did want him home and responded straight away. Some days later we awoke to find Gary had died in the night. We were far from God and lost in our grief and loss. Yet, even in those moments the Spirit of God was beginning a fresh work in our lives. As I cried 'why' a voice within responded 'you are far from me but I will draw you back.'

Our first contact with an RAF Doctor revealed a significantly more compassionate and concerned response than in Munster. He was very angry that the Army Consultant had not informed him that he had a very sick baby under his care. When I returned to work, Squadron Leader Smith, 4 Squadron Commanding Officer, expressed his condolences and concern. If I had mentioned the seriousness of Gary's condition, he said, 'I would have immediately requested a flight home.' Hindsight is wonderful but I guess it underlined the difference between brutal reality and compassionate understanding.

Alongside this more comforting empathy, our close friends, Terry and Pat Burgon, who had been at Wyton with us, invited us to stay at their home. They shared our loss and offered breathing space to come to terms with grief. As a young and still somewhat immature twenty-two, I found myself yearning to make love to Ann. Maybe a strange desire to replace Gary as soon as possible. I knew little about the emotional differences between men and women. Whilst I wanted physical closeness to counter my inner grief, Ann needed emotional reassurance and comfort. She had carried and given birth to life over nine months. Her body had prepared for caring, feeding, and nurturing a young baby, and now, like countless other mothers, that awesome joy had been extinguished. Men tend to feel responsible for loss, having fertilised life. Women feel the pain of loss having carried that life for up to nine months.

The funeral details were taken out of our hands and left to the Army to organise. We, with our dear friends Terry and Pat, travelled seventy miles to Hanover Military Cemetery. The Padre led a short and meaningless service, following which just Terry Burgon and myself attended the burial while Pat stayed with Ann. Whether this was military protocol or just the effect of grief, I cannot recall, but it remains a painful memory.

8

RECOVERY

All too soon I was back on duty and facing a six-week separation from Ann. The squadron were leaving in a matter of weeks for the Dutch Air Force Base at Leeuwarden in Northern Holland. The timing was not good for either of us, but especially Ann. Following Gary's death, we had the opportunity to take a break before the squadron departed. A visit home to Ann's parents was the obvious choice but Ann could not face it. Perhaps it was too painful to confront the issue of grief or simply too painful to meet the family without a child. Instead, I rang my eldest sister Phyllis, in Jersey, asking if we could stay for two weeks. I knew Phyllis would be a gentle and practical support for Ann. It was this space that Ann needed. Phyllis, and husband Alfred, were caretakers of a small Methodist Chapel in the north of the island. They gladly opened their small home at the rear of the Chapel, even though they had three children – Ray, Denise, and Jackie. Once again, we had little spare money to contribute for hospitality. Years later we realised what a sacrifice they made for us to stay, not least at a time of family sadness.

One important issue occupied our minds during the holiday; where Ann should stay on our return to base. I was not keen to leave her alone in Germany, not least because of the uncertain behaviour of our German landlord. Just a couple of days before we were due back at base, we experienced an amazing provision, one which began a renewal of our faith. We were about to discover how personal, detailed, and practical God is when we seek his guidance and will. A discovery that would cement a pattern for our future.

As we shared our dilemma with Phyllis, she suggested Ann stay in Jersey. Phyllis lived out her faith in Jesus in very practical and generous ways. Even though she knew we had no money to offer in support, she offered her home. Ann immediately pointed out she would have to support herself if she was to stay. We agreed to make that possible. On our final day in Jersey, we began by visiting an employment agency in St Helier. What might be the chance of a temporary secretarial job for just six weeks? The agency assistant was slightly stunned when we asked the question. She replied with a degree of incredulity, 'We have just received a request for a secretary, for six weeks, to cover a medical emergency!' Coincidence, or divine timing in answer to prayer?'

The States of Jersey had commissioned a new power station at Mount Bingham, overlooking the harbour. The secretary to the Chief Engineer was going into hospital and he needed a replacement, quickly! The timing was perfect. Ann's shorthand-typing skills and experience landed her the post. We could not have been happier, though parting would be painful. I was not prepared for how frustrating the journey back to Gutersloh would be.

The flight from Jersey to Heathrow was straightforward. At Heathrow, the timing between my onward flight to Dusseldorf was short and I ended up racing between terminals. No opportunity for a drink. I was now beginning to build up a thirst but needed to protect my limited spare cash. The flight from Heathrow to Dusseldorf offered no refreshment and I was now desperate to quench my thirst. I had arranged for my buddy, Terry Burgon, to pick me up at the airport. A cool German beer together was now uppermost in my mind before the journey to Gutersloh. Little did I know the agony would go on for many hours into the night.

Search as I may, there was no sign of Terry. No way of contact. Instead of thirst, my mind now focused on getting back to Gutersloh, 99 miles away. I managed to find a bus to Dusseldorf train station, and booked a ticket to Gutersloh – so I thought! My wallet was almost empty. When I checked the departure board, the timing farce continued unabated. I literally had to run once again and just made it in time. Now, with a burning thirst, I headed for the toilet; no taps, just a short pipe bent over a bowl. I could not believe it. I searched everywhere, but no way to access water! I had not long been back in my seat when a very large passenger opposite me opened his small leather case and brought out a bottle of beer! Talk about torture. I was mentally willing this guy to offer me a bottle - he didn't and I could not ask! All I could think about was the bar outside Gutersloh Station and spending my last few Marks on a cold beer. I was unprepared for the next twist.

As I viewed the landscape, I knew we ought to be slowing down. Instead, I stood horrified as we sped past the Gutersloh signs. In my haste at Dusseldorf, I had forgotten to check that the Berlin train stopped at Gutersloh! My emotions, on leaving Ann, were already shaky. Now they were wrecked. I swopped an intensity of thirst for a nightmare scenario of uncertainty. If Berlin was the next stop I was in serious trouble. No money to get back and, as I was due on duty the next day, a possible charge for being absent without leave. The farce had turned into a nightmare.

I knew that Bielefeld was 20 miles from Gutersloh and offered, possibly, the last option for a stop. My spiritual renewal had tentatively begun but I was suddenly a professional at prayer! As we approached Bielefeld, and slowed, my relief was palpable. Thankfully the train stopped and I was swift to alight. It was now past midnight and I just needed to get back to Gutersloh. I was relieved to find a taxi outside but soon realised, when discovering the fare, that I didn't have enough Marks – plastic cards were in the future. Little did I know there would be one more twist to the nightmare.

After a degree of haggling, and help from a German who spoke English, we agreed on the last of my cash plus wristwatch. My plan was to head for Terry's house, hope he had not made the trip to Dusseldorf, and pray he was amiable enough to get up in the middle of the night and loan me twenty marks! After all, we had been the best of buddies for three years. I arrived at the house after a slightly difficult moment when the driver wondered why I was taking him down a very dark farm track at 1.30am! At one point I thought he was going to bail out and leave me stranded. Terry's blue Peugeot was outside which gave me hope. However, after a period of knocking, either Terry was away, unwilling to answer or dead to the world. As the driver was getting more nervous, I decided it would be wise to take off my watch. Just at the point of handing it, and the cash, over to the driver, the door opened. Terry was clearly agitated and, when I asked if he could loan me twenty Marks he closed the door! I was too shocked, and tired, to knock again. As I handed over the dual fare, Terry opened the door and said he would get the money. I paid the incredulous driver and he duly dropped me at home. No doubt he was relieved to be on his way back to Bielefeld. I, on the other hand, put my mouth under the tap and gulped water. I had not had a drop to drink since leaving Jersey!

What on earth happened on Terry's doorstep? I met him at work the next day. Regarding the no-show at Dusseldorf, he had simply forgotten when I was returning! Mobiles were the future and there was no phone in Terry's house. A pigeon might have been handy! Regarding the door-episode, you could not make it up. Terry's wife, Pat, had gone to a friend's house earlier in the evening for a party. He expected her home by midnight. By 1.00am he is beside himself with worry as to where Pat is. Around 1.30am I knock on the door. Terry opens the door expecting Pat! Instead, it's me asking for money in the middle of the night! In due course Pat arrived home, explaining why she was so late. She had been listening to another wife pouring out her troubles! We remained life-long friends.

9

HEALING

Just two days after I left Jersey, and preparing to move with 4 Squadron to Leeuvarden, Ann began work as secretary to the Chief Engineer responsible for overseeing the new Jersey Power Station. A thirty-minute bus journey across the island, from the rugged North Coast to St Helier, finishing with a steep climb up Mt Bingham. Given the Consultant's initial diagnosis that Ann, then age three, might not be able to walk, this was no mean feat. A testimony to the skill of her surgeon, Mr Hindenach, in 1947. To help Ann navigate the daily journey, brother-in-law Alfred rescued a 49cc moped from his garage, gave it a service and suggested Ann ride to work. She had grown up sitting between dad and mum on a Royal Enfield, so was familiar with motor bikes. This provision gave Ann the freedom and joy of navigating some of the Island's beauty. Another blessing was the provision of fresh lobster sandwiches for her lunch. Alfred kept a couple of lobster pots in the sea off Egypt. Whilst Alfred descended as if on a Sunday stroll, we clung to the cliff whenever we accompanied him on fishing trips. It is hard to imagine Ann climbing such a dangerous cliff but she has never shied away from a challenge. In later years, even in a wheelchair, with passers-by scratching their heads and pondering, 'how did she get up here or down there?'

Ann absolutely hates snakes. As a young child she was out walking with her uncle on her grandfather's sandy land in Berkshire when Uncle Vernon pointed to adders curled up on a bank. At the sound of humans, they slithered away. As Ann watched them disappear, not knowing where they might emerge, she freaked out and ran back to the house.

Now at work in Jersey, she certainly had not expected to experience a closer call. The engineer's site consisted of two cabins. One day, as Ann walked between the cabins, she looked down and froze. She had a snake between her feet! Panic trumped fear as she stepped over it, followed by a swift appeal to the engineers to ensure it was gone. As the snake slithered off not a single guy moved!

Engineers also featured in a funny incident when Ann's moped failed to start one evening. A group gathered around the small, and simple machine, attempting to rescue a damsel in distress. After some time, having failed to spark the moped or determine the issue, they simply stood and looked - that look of men who lift the bonnet of their car, hoping to ascertain a problem but have no idea what is causing it. Eventually Ann phoned Alfred and he made his way over. On arrival he took out the spark plug, wiped it clean, replaced it, and hey-presto it fired into life. Ann made her way home. The engineers quietly retreated! They were building a large power station but a small spark plug was beyond their expertise!

The time in Jersey was hugely helpful in beginning to heal Ann's grief, and assure me she was in good hands. My sister's solid Christian faith, prayer support and practical kindness helped to turn Ann's heart back to the Saviour she had accepted six years earlier. In asking Ann to stay, space to heal was provided. The island's stunning beauty lifted her spirit and the miraculous timing of work revealed a God concerned with material as well as spiritual need. A future life of faith was being nurtured, both in Jersey and Germany.

In Holland, I was immersed in the daily routine of squadron sorties to the Dutch firing zones. Each gun pack consisted of cannon tipped with different colours. An old Meteor aircraft would tow a large flag some distance behind, whilst the Hawker Hunter pilots fired their four cannons. The goal was to hit the target flag! On return the photographers would process the camera footage and the team would assess each pilot's accuracy. From my scant memory, not too many 'hits' were registered. However, nobody hit the Meteor!

At the weekend, I joined my mates on various camping trips to the islands off Holland's North Coast. Being in a group shielded me from processing the loss of Gary. My natural tendency, perhaps fuelled by family breakdown, was to bury my feelings. Military life tended to instil an attitude of stoic acceptance – 'just deal with it and move on' was the military mantra. As one of the Medical Officers had advised, following Gary's death, 'go home and have another baby.' There was no counselling provision, just a blunt mentality of distance. Instead of facing and vocalising pain, I did what I had always done – I buried it.

10

TRANSFORMATION

As the weeks passed in Holland and Jersey so the eagerness to be back together filled our days. Ann duly completed her assignment at the emerging power station and I returned with the squadron to Gutersloh. Contrary to the feeling when Gary died, Ann now felt able to visit her parents in Essex before returning from Heathrow to Dusseldorf. This time my buddy Terry was in place when needed, ferrying me to an emotional meeting with Ann at Dusseldorf Airport and the onward journey back to Gutersloh. Thirst would not feature in the journey!

Now at home and alone, it was important that Ann found work. Another wonderful, timely provision occurred. The Station admin office had a vacancy for a typist and Ann landed the post. It was below her qualifications as a secretary but she was grateful for the work. However, just weeks later she was transferred as secretary to the Station Housing Officer, Squadron Leader Shepherd. An unexpected and rapid promotion! Instead of isolation at the towel factory she was now surrounded by the buzz of an office. Not long after settling in, a Corporal, John Austin, popped into the office enquiring whether anyone would like to receive 'Daily Bread' - a helpful booklet with daily Bible readings and practical application. Ann said 'yes please' and an invitation to an evening meal, with John and his wife Estelle, swiftly followed. Curry was on the menu. John loved hot curry. Neither of us had ever tasted curry! The outcome was predictable. I dived in, trying to be a model guest, a few minutes later I was paying the price. Nobody told me that water would exacerbate the burning, both inside my mouth and over my face! I gave in with half a plate remaining. Estelle told me not to worry as John would have it for breakfast in the morning!

A further step in our renewal of faith was taking place as John and Estelle made us welcome in their home and invited us to attend a SASRA meeting. (Soldiers and Airmen's Scripture Reader's Association) – a Royal Charter Mission Association to the Armed Forces. Weekly Bible Studies soon enabled us to grow as Christian disciples. It was also inspiring to attend larger meetings with SASRA members from other Army and Air Force stations, as well as occasional Navy personnel. Listening to men and women sharing their journey of faith in Jesus fuelled our praise, prayer, and passion to share our own faith with our colleagues. It also ignited our prayers for another baby. In August 1965 Ann suspected she might be pregnant again. Three months later this was confirmed. Inevitably, it was a mixture of grateful excitement and a little nervous anticipation, given the memory of Gary's death.

Just thirteen months after Gary's death, we were back in Munster Army Hospital. Due to Ann's height, at four foot ten, and Gary's congenital heart problems, the hospital wanted Ann in ahead of the birth. Rather than sitting around in the hospital, I drove her to Munster Zoo. It might have been a serious mistake as Ann fell flat on her stomach exiting the car! Happily, she survived without injury. It would have been a bonus had it induced immediate labour, but she bounces well! Three days later, on May 10th 1966, Ann was induced and Andrew Glyn Jones was born, weighing in at 7Ibs 8ozs, bonny and perfectly healthy. Sadly, Army regulations also applied to RAF families so I was not permitted at the birth. Despite this, our past sadness and grief were replaced with joy and relief. Our prayer for another child was answered.

A significant step, which enabled us to gain a degree of

freedom from the confines of our small rooms, was the purchase of our first car. A stunning, second-hand, 1962 US export VW Beetle; over-riders, white-wall tyres, and a red paint job second to none. When chipped, you could see the incredible depth of paint layers. I may be biased, but I doubt there was a better model ever produced. A very helpful Sergeant not only sold us the car but took me through the 'learner' process so I could drive it! Within a couple of months, we were able to explore much wider surroundings.

One of our first visits was to the Mohne Dam, one of the three dams attacked in the 617 Squadron 'Dam-Buster' raids that helped to shorten WWII. Our most frightening and moving outing, with John and Estelle, was to the Bergen-Belsen Concentration Camp. Our immediate impression was one of eerie-desolation, silence, and heart wrenching disbelief. No trees, no colour, no bird-song, simply huge mounds, and stark plaques. 'Here lie ten-thousand or five-thousand tot' (dead). Some thirty-five thousand human beings from many different nations, mostly Jewish, were murdered and crudely buried at Belsen. Many were simply left to die in heaps. A further twenty-eight thousand died in the weeks after liberation on 15th April 1945. The silence in the camp was reflected in the silence of our car as we made our way home to Gutersloh. We were not to know of the drama ahead.

It was one of those summer days full of vacillation. Should we stop for a swim or not? Eventually we saw a sign for the Blau Sea, a large lake half-way home. We parked and sat a few feet from the edge of the water, still pondering whether to swim, whilst Ann remained in the car to feed Andrew. There was just one other person in the water, apparently making his way to an island in the middle of the lake. Around half way to the island I noticed his hands were held high and he was waving frantically. I turned to

John and said, 'I think he's in trouble.' However, as we ran to the edge of the lake, he appeared to be making further strokes and we returned to the girls. Seconds later, as we kept our eyes on him, he was clearly in trouble. I immediately ditched my wallet and shoes, and dived in. As I made my way, hampered by clothing, I could see his head bobbing up and down and hoped he could hang on. I recall lifting my arms, just a few feet away, and seeing him disappear. Even though I reached the spot within seconds, there was no sign of him. The water was very dark so impossible to see anything. I dived and moved my hands around, trying to touch his body, but he had already gone. Eventually, when all hope had passed, I swam back to the bank and changed my sodden clothes.

An hour later the young man's body was retrieved by German Police divers. He was well built and in his late teens/early twenties. Like so many young people he had suffered cold water shock, an all too familiar scenario that takes so many lives every year. It was a day we shall never forget. The horrendous memories associated with genocide and the loss of a single life in tragic circumstances. On reflection, I realised I might also have died that day. I had a little life-saving knowledge but, given the panic of a drowning muscle-bound young man, he might well have taken me down with him. We were all glad to get home. The memories, however, remain vivid to this day.

The potential of early death also came closer to home on two further occasions when I was driving home from shifts on the Squadron's night-flying sorties. Both were seconds from disaster and, as I reflect today, both may well have been accompanied by angels! They were 'what if' moments in life. In Spexard, we lived just off the Berlin Auto-Bahn. If we wanted testimony to the speed of the Auto-Bahn we only had to walk along our road and observe the wrecks in the scrap yard. Cars where the front or back seats, or both, were caked in blood. Engines rammed into the boot and cars whose make was almost unidentifiable. It was frightening.

On my first close encounter with death, I decided to take a short cut on a small section of the Auto-Bahn to avoid the centre of Spexard. Whether in haste or tiredness, I missed the right entry point, ended up negotiating several spirals, and moved on to the Auto-Bahn - the wrong way! I was immediately confronted with flashing lights and loud horns. To my horror, I was heading towards a fleet of cars racing towards me at speed and I was within feet of being corralled in by the safety barriers. My only exit was to swerve rapidly to my left and career down a steep bank. At the bottom I held my breath and lifted my soul in thanksgiving. Not only might I have died, but taken many others with me. My penance was an hour's hefty bumping of the car to get all four wheels back on the ground. I had stopped in a sharp dip in the bank and needed traction to get up the other side and on to the right spiral! When home, I had also paid for my error when I noticed the two VW Beetle exhaust pipes were bent upwards, as if they also had offered a speedy prayer!

My second brush with death was equally scary and involved a few yards of rapid discernment and action. I had turned out of the station and turned left and on the right side of the road. I was taking a colleague back, after a night-flying shift on the line, but heading away from home in Spexard. His home was round a bend at the end of the Station perimeter. I turned right into a farm track, dropped him off and proceeded back, in pitch-black darkness. As I turned left on to the main road, I automatically adopted a UK mindset and stayed left! One bend and I was heading down the long straight road alongside the RAF Station. I accelerated accordingly. The problem was a car in the distance, on my side of the road! Several thoughts raced through my mind. 'He will move over soon.' 'It's late and he may be drunk.' As our cars drew ever closer, another more sinister thought dominated, 'It's an auto suicide!' Strange as it may seem, I cannot recall ever slowing down. Until the moment of impending collision, I was certain he would move over – to the right side of the road! Literally feet from impact, I swerved to the left and, mercifully, he also swerved left. Any other combination would have been lethal. Had I realised, at the last minute, that I was on the wrong side and swerved right, I would have hit him. Had he decided to swerve right at the last minute, which he was perfectly in the right to do, he would have hit me. We both chose the wrong, but, as it happened the right course of action! Fifty yards down the road, and still on the left, I woke up and realised I was on the wrong side of the road. He had stopped, no doubt breathing heavily. I ran back, and in the best German possible repented of my sin and asked his forgiveness! He was laughing as I did so! Perhaps the potent German lager helped! Such 'what if' moments are salutary and invoke, or should invoke, reflection. What if I had been killed or had killed someone else? What if my life was over in the blink of an eye? Where would my eternal spirit be going? What legacy would I have left in my brief sojourn on earth? What was the purpose for my life?

A clip in the film 'About Schmidt' (2002) has always impacted my reflection. Jack Nicholson (Warren Schmidt) is retired, alone, and on tour in his RV Campervan. After several weeks away he is returning home and reflecting on the impact of his life. 'What have I done that has made a difference to anyone … anyone at all?' 'Nothing' is his estimation. He pushes the door on arrival, moving a host of letters behind the door. He picks up the bundle and tosses it on the table. Tired, and somewhat depressed, he moves away from the table, but spots the familiar sight of an airmail letter from ChildReach. He sits at the table and opens the letter. It is a letter from an orphanage Sister in

Tanzania who writes to Warren about his supported child, Ndugu. Warren is a kind of foster-father to him. As he reads the thank you letter, and opens a coloured, 'stick-people' picture from Ndugu, depicting Warren holding Ndugu's hand, tears begin to flow. He realises he has made a difference in at least one life.

Where have I made a difference to someone else's life? What legacy will I have left when I die? What motivates me every morning? Is there a missing piece in my life's jigsaw?

11

ROLL ON - ROLL OFF

Three months after Andrew's birth we were beginning to lose our early apprehension of ever sleeping through the night. Peace and routine settled at home and the flashbacks of Gary's lifeless body gave way to assurance and joy. We were now eager to plan a holiday. After some scanty research we discovered an advertisement for a small 'roll on-roll off' ferry linking France to Jersey. We decided to drive across Germany and France then take the St Malo ferry, Duchess de Normandie, to Jersey. Duchess de Normandie was a grand name so we trusted the advert which highlighted 'roll on-roll off.' We were soon to discover just how deceptive adverts can be!

We shudder even now when recounting how thoughtlessly reckless we were. Andrew was just three months old and spent the journey in the boot of our VW Beetle, just behind the back seat and above the engine! We also had military jerry-cans filled with petrol. UK forces in Germany were issued with petrol coupons. By filling up in Germany we were able to save significantly on our fuel costs. To add to my youthful zeal, I drove two days and one night without sleep! Finally, when reaching a plateau overlooking St Malo harbour, and a very tight schedule to catch the ferry, I had to stop. I promptly fell asleep at the wheel! Little did I know the danger awaiting a few miles away.

The 'roll on-roll off' promise in the brochure, turned out to be a deck platform able to take one car at a time. The problem was the tide. The platform worked if the boat was lower than the quay - it wasn't! The tide was high and the hydraulic platform was above the quay! The unique French resolution was two planks of wood. Each plank had a curled metal lip on one end that rested on the side-rail of the boat. The other end simply rested at an acute angle on the quay. The trick was to line the car up with the planks, slam the accelerator down and land on the deck by sheer velocity! A reasonable ask if the sea is calm. St Malo harbour was not calm. The outcome was comical but deadly serious. Every few seconds the boat would move away from the quay and the planks would be carried to the edge of the dockside! On enquiry, we discovered that two cars had been back and forth to Jersey and Guernsey without being offloaded. After weighing the dilemma, I insisted the crew removed one of the cars before I attempted a semi-suicidal leap on to the deck. In typical Gallic fashion my plea was ignored and I was instructed to line up and make my move as the ferry was due to sail. Ann lifted Andrew out of the car and stood on the dockside as there was no way I was risking their safety. On the deck a crew member was slowly lifting his palms to indicate my gentle arrival on deck. I was not settling for 'gentle', I lined up the wheels, revved the engine violently, then slammed my foot down on the accelerator. Velocity would triumph. The crew member swerved out of my path as I landed mid-ships. He was not amused at my attempt to break the speed-limit!

However, the fun had just begun as I parked up on the uncovered deck. Once out of the harbour, the four flimsy wooden 'cheese-blocks' that had been placed under the wheels promptly disappeared along the ship! We were now sat in the car, holding it down on a small outside deck! The only car that made it on board, now accompanying the two already stuck there from previous voyages because the tide was too high to use the lift! Our thoughts now turned to Jersey Harbour. Would the tide favour the use of the hydraulic platform or leave us stranded above the quay? To quicken our prayers, the flat-bottomed, aptly named in Jersey, 'Smokey-Joe,' a glorified tugboat, began to rock from side to side, producing a motion like no other we had experienced.

Half way to Jersey, I made the mistake of searching below deck for a coffee. The so-called café turned out to be a small square hole in a tiny room filled with French peasant workers on route to Jersey for potato picking. To add to the rocky ambiance, each peasant appeared to be dragging tobacco from a fat Gauloises cigarette – a French favourite. I made my way through the fog with a degree of caution. On arrival at the hole, I was met by a scruffy old man whose face was framed by the square wood of a small opening. Like his countrymen, and women, an oversized fag hung out of the side of his mouth and he had a look that spoke of being irritated by my presence. I retreated in haste with our black soup-like coffees.

On return to Ann, she expressed her concern over the stability of the car. Left alone, she had struggled to hold all four wheels on the deck! My extra weight was sufficient to stabilise the situation. By now, both of us were feeling decidedly groggy, yet Andrew, in his small compartment over the engine, appeared to be tranquil. He had travelled hundreds of miles blissfully ignorant of the potential dangers.

Relief was near as we navigated the rocky East Coast and headed into calmer waters on the approach to St Helier. Fortunately, the tide was low and the under-used lift would finally disembark cars safely. Further relief for Ann was the sight of my sister Phyllis on the quay to greet us. For Phyllis, it was not an auspicious first-meeting with her nephew. As Ann handed him, more accurately dumped him in Phyl's lap, he promptly threw up all over her! As ever, she took it with grace and calm. A demeanour she displayed throughout her life - a serenity and smile that was infectious.

From the very beginning, on our honeymoon, Ann had fallen in love with Jersey. The perfect beaches, crystal-clear sea, narrow country lanes, Jersey brown cows, granite farms and rocky coastline with Cornish-like coves. Now, we were able to explore even more of this sun-kissed Isle and deepen our family relationships. We often reminisce over long hot days, when we would linger on the beach well into the evening. It was as if such days were guaranteed then but not so much now. Being sun-lovers, it didn't take long for our tan to emerge. On a Jersey beach even the wind tans! Having our car, we were not limited by the 'Tantivy' bus timetable. Every bay was explored with new curiosity, adding to our knowledge of the island and our joy over its beauty and constant surprises. Once again it was time to leave our beloved Isle.

Our minds were now filled with the state of the tide, both at Jersey and St Malo harbours. Mercifully, both tides were perfect and we had a seamless drive on and off the hydraulic lift. One frightening 'plank' experience was more than enough! From tides our attention turned to fuel. Each of our jerry-cans were filled with 'low-cost' Jersey petrol, but not enough to make it into Germany. Our scarce resources were down to a few Francs and we needed to cross into Germany to use our precious petrol coupons. The drive through France was without trauma, but we were constantly praying about our diminishing fuel. When the fuel gauge was clearly showing empty, and the last of the cans drained, I pulled into a French petrol station, counted our final Francs into the attendant's hand and, with a series of hand gestures and a modicum of French, received a few litres of fuel. From that moment on, conservation was paramount. We were still some miles from the border and the gauge had been firmly fixed on empty for some time. Every decline in the road was a chance to switch off the engine, coast as far as we could, pray for traffic lights to be on green and make the border. Eventually, we believed our trusty VW Beetle was running on air! Never has a border station sign made us so excited! We made it back into Germany, and, perhaps through sheer relief, or excitement, I managed to drive right past the first petrol station! A quick U-turn, fill the tank in exchange for coupons, and our last leg to Gutersloh.

As we settled back down at home, it was also the final leg of our three-year posting in Germany. It had been a time of sadness and loss, followed by restoration and joy. Many of the key lessons of life had been birthed within us, waiting for application in the years to come; how to cope with death and grief when emotionally immature; overcoming obstacles and issues in marriage; living with meagre resources; working hard at routine, and often, boring jobs; building a Christian faith that is authentic, practical, and life-changing. These, and many more, were stepping stones towards a later calling to Christian Ministry and Mission. In our marriage we discovered a resilience and perseverance emerging out of trials as we sought to work at relationship, forgiveness, and life's priorities. Germany had been a tough training ground for a young married couple. There were times when the strain pointed towards break-down but our growing faith stood the test.

Though I had been driving in Europe for over a year, and made a journey home to the UK shortly after taking my test in Germany, it was vital I passed the UK driving test before arriving back permanently. I had one more trip home to see family, before leaving Germany, so booked a test in Southend. It was a surreal moment. I drove to the test centre in Leigh-on-Sea, put my 'L' plates on the car and proceeded with the test. Sadly, I was clearly far too confident and failed! Driving with one hand, and the other hanging down out of the window, obviously didn't impress the examiner - just joking. As the examiner said goodbye, I removed my 'L' plates and waved to him as I drove away!

I would now be under pressure when we returned home. If I didn't pass, I would not be allowed to drive away with a cheeky smile!

As 1967 arrived, and our final ten months in Germany loomed large, 4 Squadron faced a tragic loss. I was on 'line duty' on January 23rd. As usual, the serviceable aircraft were towed from the hangar and positioned on the line. All trades would be active with final checks, fuelling, arming, and signing the log book. Your signature indicated all checks were satisfactory and the plane safe to fly. If there was an accident, all trades would head on mass to the line hut and swarm around the log book hastily checking they had signed!

We had just one non-commissioned pilot on the squadron, Master Pilot 'Ginger' Ratcliffe, the highest rank and equivalent to Warrant Officer. 'Ginger,' along with other pilots, arrived to check the log and inspect the aircraft. When complete, it was our role to strap the pilot in, remove and reveal the ejector seat pin and show it to the pilot. Once complete we would ensure all equipment was stored away and wait for the pilot to indicate 'start-up.' Once the engine was started, and the scary flame put out, we would get the thumbs up and wave the plane off the stand. Sorties would last several hours, which gave us time to have a break, though often we were called to other duties, such as cleaning the aircraft still in the hangar or tasks in the photo section and, most challenging, clearing snow off the runway.

As we waited for the aircraft to return, we received the news that 'Ginger' had crashed and been killed. The details were sketchy at first, but eventually we learnt he had encountered very low cloud and flown into a hillside near Kassel, West Germany. Ironically, ten years previously in May 1957, he was flying a Hawker Hunter and encountered engine failure. He tried to eject but the canopy would not jettison. Spotting a likely beach at Baltrum Island, Northern Germany, he made a safe landing even though the port wheel failed to come down. The plane stopped just short of the water, with an incoming tide. In a valiant effort to save the plane, Ginger commandeered a herd of horses from an adjacent farm and attempted to drag the plane back up the beach! Sadly, his efforts failed, the tide won and the plane was eventually retrieved and scrapped. This time, tragically, he was killed instantaneously. The wreckage was transported back to the station and loosely assembled piece by piece in the hangar. One abiding image was part of Ginger's flying suit with his flight manual still perfectly intact. I would go on to print those manuals in later years.

It would not be the last crash I would witness. Gutersloh would occasionally host aircraft from other Air Forces. The Lockheed F104 Starfighter, nicknamed the 'Flying Coffin', was one of the most frequent. On this occasion, things didn't go to plan. We heard a screaming noise and saw a German F104 circling the Station. Clearly the throttle was wide open as the plane descended towards the runway. Unfortunately, the young pilot chose the wrong end of the runway. The arrester cables were up and his wheels were also up! The plane careered through the wires and flopped on to the runway. In a very rapid manoeuvre, the pilot leapt out of the cockpit and was caught by a quick-thinking fireman! In the end the arrester wires probably saved his life, as crashing straight into the runway at speed, with no undercarriage, might well have been fatal.

Now it was time for yet another move and a new horizon.

12

LITHOGRAPHY

Our new posting, in October 1967, was to No 1 AIDU (Aeronautical Information Documents Unit) RAF Northolt - the oldest RAF base and the longest continuous use of any RAF airfield. During WWII it was a front-line base with Polish Squadrons (302/303) equipped with Spitfires and Hurricanes, 303 Squadron being the highest scoring of the RAF's 66 squadrons involved in the Battle of Britain. It was now home to 32 Squadron operating VIP and general air transport roles. In 1995 the squadron merged with the Queen's Flight, from RAF Benson, incorporating 'Royal' into its name.

Our much-loved Beetle was still immaculate and, shortly after arriving at Northolt, attracted the attention of a Sergeant. So impressed by the condition, he said, 'Whenever you move again, or want to sell, please contact me.' He would wait two years. But for now, it would be firmly in our possession, along with many memories. Fortunately, I did pass my driving test this time.

Since joining the RAF in 1962, Northolt would be my second posting without any work on aircraft. For the next two years I would pick up new, offset-printing skills. Rotaprint R20's would be my daily work-station. This was a completely new venture, as the photo training course at RAF Wellsbourne Mountford did not cover lithography. The unit bread and butter, was the printing of flying manuals for pilots; booklets that slipped into a flying-suit and gave the pilot information on all airports and procedures for landing. I soon became competent at mastering the whole R20 process; the preparation of 3M metal sheets with the information to be printed and fitted to the machine, followed by the inking of the rollers, stacking of paper and operation of the press. Various factors, such as humidity, heat, quality of paper, consistency of ink, and the sharp eyes of the operator, all contributed to an efficient end-product. Possibly the most frustrating element, especially if not spotted quickly, was any foreign element on the rubber ink pad that caused an indentation. If you trusted your machine, left it running and went to brew a tea, and a small object, such as a hard slip of paper was pressed into the ink roller, you could return to dozens of wasted ink-splatted sheets. The machine was then shut down, all ink-rollers removed and thoroughly cleaned, and the wasted sheets ditched. Constant attention was paramount.

The most pressing need was a home. After a short perusal of vacant houses, we managed to secure a three-bed terrace in Hayes, a short journey away from the base. To our delight, we were just around the corner from Grange Park Baptist Church. For the first time since joining the RAF we would be worshipping in a local church. It was a further step in anchoring our faith, growing in discipleship, and forming new friendships. We settled quickly, appreciated the warmth of welcome, and benefitted from the pastoral care of their Minister John Eccleston.

On the family front we received a surprise! Ann hurt her coccyx on the wooden arm of a lounge chair. It was so sore she had to visit our GP. After a few questions, he asked if she could be pregnant. 'No' was the reply. A rapid test, according to the GP, proved otherwise! He was wrong, but a month later Ann really was pregnant! Eight months later, on December 4th 1968, our third son Tim was born in Hillingdon Hospital, weighing in at 6Ibs 10oz. It was still the norm that fathers were not present at the birth. However, it was so quick I would never have made it!

A year later, it was another 'first' for us - an impending move into RAF housing. After six years, we finally accumulated enough points to qualify for a house on the base. The move would alleviate travel expenses, connect us with service families and, in time, open an opportunity to begin a Sunday School on site. Christian faith can easily become an 'insular' experience and lifestyle. We were keen to earth our faith practically, beyond the confines of a church building. The RAF were also keen to promote and support any endeavour that served the needs of its families. Northolt had a very small station-compliment so it was never to be a large work. However, it was warmly received on the station and a wonderful apprenticeship that would prepare us well for significant Youth and Sunday School work in the future. Three dramas would unfold over the coming year. The first, a small but very embarrassing mistake. The second a shock followed by extreme relief. The third an extremely distressing accident.

Mistake

A Sunday-School meeting was planned for a house across the square from ours. I had to pick another teacher up from home so went straight to the meeting, parking outside. When finished, someone else offered to take the teacher home. I forgot all about the car at the front of the house and walked home via the back door. Ann was up early in the morning, drew the curtains, and exclaimed, 'our car has gone.' Once dressed, I raced to the station Military Police and reported the theft. I was distraught that our beautiful VW Beetle had gone - our first car, and one that had forged so many memories. Following the MP visit, the local police were informed and a meeting arranged. It was while the police were taking notes that the light went on. Suddenly I knew where the car was - the other side of the estate square! I apologised to the police, who then advised me to visit the Military Police once I had retrieved the vehicle.

One more apology followed and, no doubt, left the MP's discussing a Senior Aircraftman who was two sandwiches short of a picnic!

Shock

Early in 1969 we had news of another posting, but one we had not been expecting. A one-year 'unaccompanied' tour to a sandspit in the Middle East! It was a huge blow to both of us, not least with Tim just a few months old. Several months passed as I awaited confirmation of my location. Just as we were coming to terms with this unexpected shock, we received further news that my one-year posting had been cancelled and replaced with a three-year 'accompanied' posting to Cyprus in July! Our relief, thanksgiving and joy overflowed. We were not to know it at the time, but it would be a huge leap forward in Christian service, faith, and discipleship. God was about to prepare us thoroughly for our calling to Ministry and Mission.

Distressing accident

We had packed and despatched all our crates to Cyprus, when the third drama unfolded just a few yards from the back of our house. Ann was looking after a friend's children for the day when a couple of Andrew's little friends knocked for him to go out and play. Against her better judgement she allowed him to go on a borrowed trike. Within a few minutes there was thunderous knocking on the back door. A neighbour, in a state of distress, informed Ann that Andrew had been knocked over by an RAF lorry backing up the road. The driver then appeared, carrying Andrew. His eyes were closed and his body limp. On taking him into her arms, Ann realised his left femur was broken. We lived just across the road from the RAF medical centre so Ann carried him over and an ambulance was called. A lengthy stay in Mount Vernon Hospital ensued, with Andrew on traction. To add injury to our distress, the RAF stated that it was the trike that had broken his femur not the lorry! The lorry merely hit the trike which was then pressed into Andrew's leg – the inanimate trike was to blame! However, regulations stated clearly, that when reversing an RAF lorry there should be a person directing the manoeuvre. This was not the case, as the driver was alone. With a little more courage and wisdom, we should have pursued the case. The only compensation was a new trike for our neighbour's child.

13

CYPRUS

After several months delay, the journey to Cyprus finally took place in October 1969 with Andrew barely walking and Tim only ten months old. Whilst we had qualified for a base-house at Northolt, we were now competing with hundreds more personnel at RAF Episkopi and Akrotiri. Our goal was a rental property in Limassol, 18 miles from JARIC (Joint Air Reconnaissance Intelligence Centre) at Episkopi, the first of my two postings from 1969-1972. Following two nights in a hotel we began our search, aided by the RAF Housing Office. As forces personnel were constantly completing their tour, and returning to the UK, rental properties were abundant. Very quickly we found a bungalow that met our needs. A typical Greek arrangement whereby a house is built for a future marriage in the family then rented until required. We were relieved to move in, settle the boys down and unpack our crates. Sadly, our crates were rain damaged before transit then, on arrival in Cyprus, stored outside in the heat awaiting our delayed arrival! The combination of rain followed by intense sun had caused significant damage to clothing, including Ann's lovingly-knitted Arran jumper for me. As I removed it from the crate, it literally fell apart in my hands. Music was also off the table as our record collection was welded together! Mercifully, all else was intact or could be prised apart!

It was now time to report for duty at Episkopi - my third 'non-flying' station. JARIC was similar to the photo-section at RAF Wyton but infinitely more secretive. It was populated with a large contingent of photographers, cartographers, intelligence, and other trades. Multiple processing and printing operations were it's bread and butter, including international land surveys and intelligence gathering across the Middle East.

It was good to link up with colleagues from previous stations and make new friends. It was also encouraging to see the significant range of sports on offer. I had progressed to County standard in Badminton, and played football for section and station teams. The prospect of Wednesdays off, to represent the Station at either sport, was an exciting possibility. JARIC also had an annual round-robin tournament including tennis, table-tennis, badminton, and squash, which enabled me to pick up some small trophies.

As Episkopi was a thirty-minute journey, at 6.30am in the morning for a 7-1pm shift, I purchased a small, cheap, and very old BMW. It was nothing like the posh brand today but just about puffed its way to work. The journey was spectacular, bay after bay of azure blue sea and sky. Occasionally, I would leave home early and pull over in one of the bays simply to admire the view, reflect, and pray. As a family we soon settled into a routine. In the summer, I was home by 1.30pm. Ann would be ready with the boys and we would make our way to Ladies Mile, a long sandy beach adjacent to RAF Akrotiri. Cars could be parked a few feet from the edge of the water and the boys would crawl in and out of the shallow, warm, and safe crystal clear sea.

One painful memory still lingers large - our very first excursion to the beach. It was perfect weather for 'Brits' but not locals, whose season ended very abruptly when the temperature dipped below twenty-five degrees! We arrived at the beach but even 'Brits 'were absent. This seemed strange, given the cloudless sky and perfectly calm and warm sea. I soon discovered the dangers of a quiet beach and sea. As I ran into the sea, for my first taste of the Mediterranean, I felt a sharp pin-prick in my foot.

Within seconds, the pain increased dramatically. It was agony in the water but hell out of it. Neither of us knew what was happening. With my rapidly swelling foot we both became afraid of the consequences, not least whether I had trodden on something lethal! The beach was totally empty and Ann could not drive. I was camped in the water writhing in pain. Never have I been more relieved to see an approaching car, especially with a driver who responded to our SOS hand signals! He wasn't sure what had happened, but immediately whisked me off to the Station Medical Centre. Meanwhile, Ann was left wondering whether she would see me again!

It turned out that I had stepped on a weever fish. When the sea is calm, they move inshore and camp at the water's edge. Here they bury themselves in the sand, leaving a sharp poisonous tip protruding. With a few tablets, and a dose of appropriate cream, plus the Dr's assurance the pain would decrease in a couple of hours, I was returned to a much-relieved Ann. The lesson was clear. Always disturb the sand prior to wading into the water when it is like glass and no one else is around!

Just two months after arriving in Cyprus, disaster struck a swathe of Limassol. A vicious tornado swept in from the sea, carving a mile-wide path of destruction across RAF Akrotiri and the town centre. As the tornado swept in, we were driving to the Forces Medical Centre in town as Andrew required treatment for measles. Unbeknown to us we were driving towards the tornado which had already caused a lot of damage and was now heading back out to sea. The sky was eerily dark, the wind much stronger than when we left home and the threat of lightning very real. Within minutes of arriving at the centre, and in with the doctor, a nurse ran into the office and began to shout, 'get ready for casualties, there has been a tornado.' The doctor, with a degree of haste, told us how to treat Andrew and we made a swift exit. As we were leaving the centre a man walked in covered in blood, explaining briefly his experience. He had been driving in the path of the tornado and his car had been completely overturned, every window smashed, then landed back on four wheels! Realising there would be casualties, requiring many ambulances, he chose to drive the car to the Medical Centre. It was a wise decision as he was the first casualty to be seen.

When we arrived home, I thought about members of our Christian family in Limassol who were living near the path of the tornado and may require help. I promptly headed back towards town in the car. Discovering the main road was blocked I turned off to find another route. The sky was now pitch black and all street and traffic lights out. As I followed behind another car, the sky lit up with a massive bolt of forked lightning. I gasped, looked to my left, and by the time I had returned my eyes to the road the car in front had stopped dead. I smashed straight into his boot, lurched up and hit my head on the windscreen before settling back into my seat somewhat stunned.

Though commonplace, I was amazed by the locals 'beat-shop' response. Almost every stretch of road had a smattering of small garages, equipped with a Land Rover and designed to respond super-fast to an accident. First on scene gets the prize. I had hardly assessed my bruised and aching head when the first of two 'Rovers' arrived. The first driver attached a chain to the front of the vehicle and started negotiating the terms of removal! 'We give you car. You no pay insurance. Car ready tomorrow.' Any vague promise to get an agreement. No sooner had the first negotiation started than a second team were attaching a chain to the back of the car whilst shouting their own 'better deal' through the open car window! All this with an increasingly sore head! In the end, the cheap BMW was declared a write-off and I arrived back home on foot to tell

Ann the sorry tale. As for the friends I had ventured out to help, they had suffered damage to windows but thankfully were safe. No sooner had the tornado arrived, than it swept back out to sea, leaving a trail of destruction in its wake.

Finding another car was now paramount. Our prayer was answered quickly, as a family from the SASRA meeting, David and Linda Molden, were returning home and offered us their ageing Triumph Herald at a very reasonable price. A double blessing was my promotion to Corporal which gave us extra money. So much so, that the Scripture Reader (Forces Missionary) Victor Leinster, suggested I trade in the Triumph for a new Datsun. My answer was immediate, 'I could not afford a new car.' He suggested I visit the Datsun dealer. Nothing ventured, nothing gained, so I paid a visit to the garage. In my mind I was expecting an offer around £150 towards a Datsun Sunny costing £650. My faith was obviously lacking as the salesman immediately offered £450 and would probably have gone to £500 if I had bartered! I accepted straight away and picked up a new Blue Datsun a few days later.

14
LOVING SERVICE

One of the most wonderful things about being a Christian is watching, over the years, how a living God puts the pieces in place. Cyprus would equip us well for the journey ahead. Our life revolved around the Scripture Reader's home, with its large basement, and the ministry and mission that flowed from the forces personnel who attended worship, prayer, and Bible study meetings. At times weekends were just hectic, without doubt, preparing us for the future.

Saturday afternoon it was youth work on the beach, followed by tea together with the youth. In the evening, the labour-intensive work of visiting the local school and carting hundreds of heavy wooden chairs from three levels of classrooms into the downstairs hall - three 'fold-up chairs' on each arm! It seemed as if we had three years of permanent ridges up our forearms! Little was I to know it was an invaluable apprenticeship for two future churches requiring constant chair movement! On the Sunday morning around four-hundred children would be collected for Sunday School! At around 8am, often in temperatures already at eighty degrees plus, we would have escort duty on a fleet of Turkish buses. Hundreds of children would be collected from homes, cafes, pubs - yes at 8am - with some waiting at designated spots on the street.

It was a military operation run with precision, passion, and lots of love. Some of the kids came from tough Army homes and were rough and ready, but many amazed us by completing a whole range of Emmaus Bible studies, gaining average marks between 90-100%! Certificates were presented regularly with gold, silver, bronze, and blue stars.

Children who completed the whole set of studies would be presented with a Bible. What I would give today to meet some of those children and see what impact our investment had made in their lives. However, what a joy it was then to see young lives transformed by prayer, studying the Bible, and believing in Jesus Christ.

Once the School was finished, some of the chairs were left for the afternoon Gospel Service and the rest returned upstairs! The bus escorts of course were spared hard labour, but not the sweat of boarding non-air-conditioned buses with midday temperatures regularly over one hundred degrees! As soon as everything was packed and the escorts returned, it was straight to communion in the SASRA home. Back then, being a largely 'Brethren' community, it was called 'The Breaking of Bread.' So much for a day of rest, but it was never a burden. No sooner had we finished sharing, than it was home for lunch and back at the hall for the 3pm 'Gospel' service. Ludicrous now, but then it was expected that men would wear ties and women hats, in searing heat! To add to this - almost comical attire - mini-skirts were in! At the midweek prayer meeting, women would be expected to wear hats, whilst nothing was said with regards to short mini-skirts! Religious legalism is a hard taskmaster.

To cap 'manic-Sunday', we returned the remaining chairs upstairs and joined together for a 'Fellowship Tea'. Following tea, the younger children were taken home and Dad or Mum would return just in time for the evening Bible study followed by singing! It may appear as a heavy commitment of constant work throughout the whole weekend. For us it was an investment in hundreds of young lives and families, and a character-building routine that would stand us in good stead for future work. There were of course, memorable times of rest and recreation, both on the beautiful sun-kissed beaches, in the crystal clear azure blue sea, and up in the invigorating air of the Troodos mountains where we would enjoy our annual camps and fellowship outings. Famagusta and Coral Bay were our favourite day destination and holiday spots, with their fabulous sandy beaches, warm glass-like crystal clear sea and, largely, unspoilt coastlines. When Ann's mum visited, she would have us up very early in the morning at Famagusta for the pre-breakfast swim! It's hard to imagine today, that resorts such as Coral Bay and Ayia Napa were pristine beaches then, usually with just one melon stall! In all our three years, only one red-hot day, at Coral Bay, were we forced to leave the beach. As the Greek-Turkish conflict had not yet kicked off, occasionally we would go to the stunning Kyrenia Mountains and beaches in the North of the Island. Even though these were times of recreation, we would sometimes gather children on the beach and do an impromptu holiday club - sometimes, we only have one opportunity to pass on the Good News.

15

CHANGE AND TRAGEDY

One very memorable day was the arrival of a juggernaut outside our bungalow. We had asked our landlord whether he would consider a change from private rental to RAF hiring. The living arrangement would then come under military administration. It was agreed and a date fixed for the removal of everything from the bungalow, apart from white goods. Everything was then returned to the landlord. In eight years of service, we had never needed to equip our homes with furniture. Now we were about to receive a completely new home. Everything from carpets to curtains, settees and beds, cutlery to crockery, cupboards and all else to complete a home. Everything was brand new in our chosen style and colours – though both were somewhat limited! Ann is a very much a home-maker. She simply stood in amazement as the stores team emptied the lorry contents into our empty bungalow. In true military fashion, everything was counted in and anything with a chip or scratch replaced. On 'marching-out,' when finally completing our three years, everything had to be accounted for, the home left spotless and charges made for any damage! I am pleased to report that, when we left, it was spotless and we were not charged a cent!

One of the most dramatic and heart-breaking moments, during my time at Episkopi, was a horrendous crash. I was on my way to work, early in the morning, when I rounded a bend and was confronted by bodies and screaming. A large construction lorry had ripped down the side of a local bus packed with workers. Given the scene, I, and other station staff, had missed the crash by minutes. Bodies had been thrown across the road and into a roadside ditch. Others were stacked in the door well of the bus with blood everywhere. Those who had survived, and scrambled from the jagged side of the bus, were cut, dazed, wailing, and screaming. The scene was horrific. Slowly we were instructed to drive past and leave the road open for police and ambulances. As a young boy, I had witnessed the body of a man who drowned in the River Mersey. Then, in Germany, at the Blau Sea, the young adult drowned and his body recovered by the German Police Divers. This accident would leave another indelible mark on my mind - so clear I can picture it fully to this day, along with those other tragedies.

Halfway through my tour at Episkopi, I was surprised with an unexpected posting. It would be a cross-posting to RAF Akrotiri, on the Akrotiri Peninsula, eleven miles from RAF Episkopi and a short journey from our home in Limassol. Lightnings, Canberras, and other visiting aircraft were already served by the photo-section. However, in 1970, after the RAF had received the first Phantom Jets in 1969, a new portacabin photographic facility was required to service the Phantoms with their latest camera technology. I was part of the team servicing the installation. Although I would miss the spectacular journey along the coast to Episkopi, it would be a dream posting for our final eighteen months in Cyprus. The benefits were significant. I could drive along Ladies Mile beach and access the station via the beach entrance. It was a move back to a flying station - we both like aircraft! It would also be an introduction to the latest processing and printing techniques and a move away from the limited routines of manning a large processing and printing facility. There was also an unexpected bonus at lunchtime. A small group would exit the controlled sixty-eight degrees portacabins into one hundred degrees plus. Literally yards from our complex were deep pools of crystal-clear water, linked to the sea. For the best part of an hour, we would snorkel, swim, and sunbathe before returning to the cool cabins. These 'photo-boys' were the most tanned on the station! In many ways, Cyprus was a three-year working holiday!

Gradually, but significantly, we grew in our faith, and our passion to share the Good News of Jesus love, grace, and mercy. Some of the most memorable and encouraging meetings were the joint gatherings with Christians from Cyprus and Lebanon. These would be attended by friends from all three armed-services as well as Christians from local churches. 'Testimony' was a key part of these gatherings as we were encouraged to share our story of faith - occasionally in the time it took for a match to burn down! A lesson for those times of witness that are fleeting. Listening to the range of stories was a reminder that God is uniquely personal. Some stories were intensely dramatic, others a long journey of discovery.

'Bottle Bill's' story remains vivid in my mind and was not unusual. Bill was a soldier in the Queen's Own Scottish Borderers, a tough regiment known for its drinking culture. To access their barracks at a weekend, as I had done in Germany, you walked over piles of empty bottles. Bill's nickname revealed his addiction. When based in Singapore, suffering from acute alcoholism and non-stop shaking, an Army doctor informed him that his life was in danger. If he didn't stop drinking, he had around six months to live. He was repatriated to the UK and admitted to an Army hospital. In hospital he remembered a Scripture Reader visiting his barracks and sharing the good news of Jesus love, forgiveness, and new life. As Bill recalled the Scripture Readers' visit in Singapore, the Holy Spirit convicted Bill of his need of a Saviour. He responded to the inner voice, knelt at his bedside, and prayed for forgiveness and help, asking Jesus to be his Saviour and Lord. When he woke the next morning, his hands were still and he had found peace with God. He made a full recovery and became a missionary with the Glasgow City Mission, and later a Pastor in the North of Scotland.

Being a Christian in the forces was never easy. Several times I have been, as far as I could ascertain, the lone Christian on a Station, Squadron detachment or daily work assignment. Weekends away were always tough. On a detachment to Crete, I shared a room with a Sergeant who would drink heavily over the weekend and return plastered late in the evening. It was impossible to sleep or talk sensibly. Mockery and cynicism were sometimes around. However, I kept the faith and witnessed whenever I had an opportunity. Who knows the fruit of such moments. Much of the time, we simply sow a seed that others may add to their own story. Every so often we are allowed the joy of knowing our labour has not been in vain as we hear the testimony of lives changed by faith in Jesus Christ.

16

FAITH

One of the most important aspects of Christian life, that would equip us so well for our future, had been indelibly forged via the servicing of the Sunday School. I toyed with 'Faith' as the second, possible, title for this book, as 'Faith' has been a cornerstone of our lifelong spiritual journey. 'Faith' not in terms of a religious badge, but in terms of trusting the Lord for what cannot be seen.

The treasurer, for our Youth and Sunday School work, was completing his tour of duty and the need arose for a replacement. The Scripture Reader, Victor Leinster, asked if I would take over. I agreed and, shortly after, received the monthly Turkish Bus bill of £76.50, not a small sum in 1970. My first test of faith had arrived. Faith is described in the Bible as 'the evidence of things not seen' - Hebrews chapter 11 verse 1. Compared to the bill, there was very little in the kitty! The Turks had a strict policy, no payment on time - no buses. A murmur of panic entered my mind. We were a relatively small Christian group and the bill was large! We and the group prayed. On the final day for payment, I witnessed a minor miracle – all we needed was in the account. Relief and thanksgiving were in equal measure. This miracle has been endlessly repeated over years, not simply for money, but houses, land, woodlands, restaurant, playgroup, holidays, cars, church buildings and much more. However, 'walking by faith, not sight' began with a Turkish bus bill! If you have survived reading to this point, I can promise a rollercoaster journey ahead.

Cyprus also afforded increasing opportunities to lead prayer meetings, prepare bible studies and speak at Christian events. Gradually, I became aware of the still small voice of the Holy Spirit prompting me to consider my future. Ten years of service would be completed when leaving Cyprus, giving us two years left to serve. We began to pray about our future. I could consider signing up for the full twenty-two years, something that was tempting at the time, or complete my twelve and leave. When I enquired about signing on, I was told that the photographic trade was closed and I could not be considered for an extension! The door was now firmly shut and another was slightly ajar. Such moments focus both the mind and prayer. An adventure in discernment and guidance was on the horizon.

Among family folklore are Ann's driving adventures. Her first attempt bordered on comical, though it could have been serious. I had taken her out in our Datsun Sunny. She was doing well as we motored along a flat and straight road out of Limassol. In the distance I noticed a police checkpoint. Nothing fancy with bars or bollards, just a couple of Cypriot Police waving cars down. As we approached, one policeman started to wave us through. As Ann accelerated slightly, he must have spotted the 'L' plate and made a swift move to the middle of the road. He held up his hand literally yards from the accelerating Datsun! I yelled 'brake' and Ann stopped - with the policeman's hands touching the bonnet! I wound the window down and told him, politely, how dangerous his move was. He could have been awkward and officious, but shrugged it off.

My documents were checked and he stepped aside. Ann was clearly nervous from the first incident, so waited for the policeman to wave her forward. As she started to move, a very typical Greek reunion occurred. A Cypriot friend of the policeman, passing in the other direction, drew to a halt and shouted to his friend – our indecisive, overzealous officer. Excited to greet his mate, or relative, he immediately walked in front of the moving Datsun and ended up sprawled across the bonnet! I put my head in my hands. He took a step back and waved Ann forward as if this was his normal daily experience! A hundred yards down the road, and somewhat shaken, Ann decided she needed to stop, get out, and let me drive. A wise move given her scare. The only woman, completely innocent, to knock the same policeman down twice – well nearly! Family folklore had a comical addition!

To add to our family folklore, and evoke much laughter from family and friends, Ann also recalls that every time she tried to pass her driving test, now in one of our VW Beetles, she got pregnant and had to curtail her lessons! Ann became far too large to fit behind the wheel – twice! (Just take care if you own a VW Beetle as they clearly have the power to invoke a virgin birth, or should I say, Volkswagen birth)!

All too soon our three year posting, in this paradise of an isle, was ending and, just before leaving, we received confirmation that Ann was pregnant with our fourth child – this time our Datsun Sunny was to blame! My final posting would be to RAF High Wycombe 'Strike Command Headquarters' - my fourth, non-flying station. Most RAF personnel, who had spent a tour in Cyprus, would endorse our own assessment that it was the best posting in the world. In fact, it was swiftly becoming the 'only' overseas posting. The world had shrunk as far as RAF bases were concerned. Just Germany and Cyprus left, with the oddities scattered on sandspits in the Middle East and the icy Falklands. Short-term detachments and war-zones were now the order of the day. It had been a privilege to sign up when the world was open but sad to be ending with limited options. In a way, it was also helpful in discerning the decision to leave after twelve years. I wasn't to know, at this juncture, that my 'closed' trade group would open up again prior to my leaving the RAF, thus giving me an option to extend my service. However, a sealed and settled new vocation was on the horizon. We left the 'sunshine-isle' with grateful hearts but also tears! The sight of a few donkeys, as we lifted off the runway, was enough to move our emotions!

17

JOYS AND TRIALS

As RAF High Wycombe loomed large, some of the most awesome, incredible, and heartbreaking jigsaw pieces were about to be inserted in our lives. The High Wycombe area is an area of outer-London, so we began our house search in Marlow, a few miles further out. It turned out to be even more affluent! After visiting a good number of estate agents, we realised it would be an almost impossible house-hunt, as they appeared to have nothing in the RAF 'Hiring' price bracket. Growing increasingly tired, we shortened our time with agents by staying at half-open doors and waiting for a swift, and increasingly expected, reply - 'no nothing available.' However, we were surprised when one agent, a Mr Deacon, invited us in and introduced himself – Mr Deacon was a Deacon at Marlow Baptist Church! Faith was about to become sight.

He showed us a vacant bungalow in Henley on Thames belonging to a Squadron Leader. I knew of Henley, only from its historic venue for the Henley Regatta, a world-famous rowing event that began in 1839. If I was concerned about 'affluence' I was now entering the major league. Nevertheless, as fellow Christian Baptists, the offer from Mr Deacon had a fragrance of divine guidance. We arranged a time to visit Elizabeth Road, fell in love with the home, and location, and held our breath regarding the rental. It was, amazingly, within the RAF guidelines. Our first of four homes in Henley was settled, the remainder would be 'faith-moves' with even more extraordinary stories, although, Mr Deacon, the Deacon, fits the bill well!

A bungalow was a helpful move for Ann, as she was

beginning to show signs of wear in her hips. Not yet critical, but hints of what was to come. Andrew was now six and Tim almost four. Andrew had begun his schooling, a year earlier, at Berengaria Forces School in Limassol Cyprus. Henley was a complete change for him, and us. He was attending a very progressive school that we found undisciplined and chaotic. Tim would join Andrew a year later. Fortunately, they would both move schools following my demob from the RAF and a new home.

Around six months after moving to Henley on April 8th 1973, and after three boys, Elizabeth was born at the Royal Berkshire Hospital in Reading. The joy of a baby girl was short lived. She was taken straight to the intensive care ward with breathing problems. After some hours, and no news, Ann asked if she could see Elizabeth. The Ward Sister agreed and, as Ann entered the ICU, the Ward Sister took her aside and mentioned that Elizabeth had problems. Ann immediately said, 'is it her heart?' 'Yes' was the answer and 'a transfer to Hammersmith Heart Hospital is being arranged.' Within thirty minutes, I had completed a rapid journey from Henley to Reading, and prayed quietly for God's peace for us both. When we lost Gary, we were both immature Christians and far away from Christian life and help. All we could do was cry out in our pain and fire the inevitable 'why' questions to God. Now we could draw on the reassurance of God's presence, peace, and hope, even if the outcome was as expected – a short life. In time, fellow believers, from Henley Baptist Church, would hold us up in their prayers and rally round with practical help.

As Ann needed to stay in Reading and recover from the birth, I was alone in the ambulance to Hammersmith. The blue-light journey, with Elizabeth in a special incubator aiding her breathing, was hard. On arrival at Hammersmith, I was met by a team of specialists and Elizabeth was taken for tests. The tests confirmed the initial diagnosis at Royal

Berkshire Hospital. In layman's terms, the main arteries were reversed, with blood flowing back on itself. She was being kept alive by a bridge that remained open rather than closing. When it was clear that nothing could be done for Elizabeth immediately, as she would need to be twelve weeks old, she was transferred to Battle Hospital in Reading where we would be able to visit her without lengthy journeys.

Three days after my journey to Hammersmith, Ann was released from hospital in Reading. She was not allowed to travel home with me, but placed in a bus with mothers taking their baby home. Little consideration was given to a mother deeply concerned for the life of her child. Sadly, it was almost a carbon copy of our experience in Munster Army Hospital but not expected here at home with the NHS. Ann endured every stop, as each mother and baby left the bus. Finally, she was alone to carry her pain home. Three weeks later, we received the phone call that Elizabeth had died.

Our response was far more positive than we could possibly have imagined. In comparison to the emptiness, pain and loneliness surrounding Gary's death, we had an inner peace, an assurance from Scripture, and hope for the future. The Spirit of God responded to our, and our friends, prayers and we knew a healing peace within. 'The peace that transcends all understanding', Philippians chapter 4 verse 7. That peace came from our relationship with Jesus. 'He Himself is our peace', Ephesians chapter 2 verse 14. Our assurance came from verses in 2 Corinthians chapter 1 verses 3-4: 'Praise be to the God and Father of our Lord Jesus Christ, the Father of compassion and the God of all comfort, who comforts us in all our troubles, so that we can comfort those in any trouble with the comfort we ourselves receive from God.' Notice the exchange here – we are comforted, so we may comfort others in need.

Just a week after losing Elizabeth, Ann heard of a neighbour who had lost her baby with the cord around its neck. She was able to visit and empathise with our neighbour's loss. We also found hope. 'We have this hope, as an anchor for our soul, firm and secure', Hebrews chapter 6 verse 19. Humanly, we were hurting and grieving, yet the 'anchor' held. We could transform our sorrow and grief into comfort for others. Something we would need to do many times in the future.

One of our deepest regrets, in burying Elizabeth, was the absence of our sons, Andrew and Tim. At that time, we felt they were too young to be at the funeral. This was a big mistake. Andrew, especially, had held her tiny hands and was enthralled as he saw her in Ann's arms. Now, she had gone and he was not part of the process of letting go and grieving.

Following Elizabeth's death, our GP visited for a post-mortem consultation. The link between Gary and Elizabeth was clear, both dying from congenital heart disease. The guidance from Dr Dudeney was clear. Any future children would have a 50% chance of CHD. He suggested we both took preventative measures not to have any more children. We took his advice carefully, but also began to pray - our prayers would last three and a half years!

18

TRANSITION

My first days at RAF High Wycombe were slightly disorientating as the photo section was small-scale compared to my previous postings. Just a handful of photographers to service the requirements of high-ranking officers and Public Relations requirements. It was somewhat novel for me, as I had not handled a camera since the fateful assignment at West Raynham with an ancient hand-held S92 camera with bellows and plates! Now I was faced with modern Leicas and Nikons - colour film instead of black and white! As the only member of the section with a steady hand, I majored on tinting 35mm negatives for top-brass presentations and the occasional PR role. Once our presentations were complete, they would be delivered by hand to the appropriate department and officer.

As an NCO, it would not be common to form a friendship with an officer. So, on one of my deliveries, I was surprised to enter the office of a decorated Squadron Leader Pilot, and notice, along the complete edge of his desk, a bible text and a pack of bible tracts – small booklets explaining how to become a Christian. It was easy to begin a conversation around our Christian faith. I believe Tim Cripps was the youngest ever test-pilot at the Empire Test School, Royal Aircraft Establishment, Farnborough. Both his, and his wife's fathers were extremely high-ranking Army Officers. Tim might have expected to rise through the ranks into the top tier of the RAF. However, one issue was made very clear to him by his Group Captain boss - if he refused to remove his text and tracts from his office table, he would not be recommended for promotion. Political correctness ahead of its time or mild persecution?

Eventually, Tim chose to resign his commission and become a school teacher in Sussex. It was a privilege to have prayed with him on a regular basis, and to learn from his earnest desire to 'Seek first the Kingdom of God and His righteousness' Matthew chapter 6 verse 33. When Jesus, and His will, is first in our lives we must expect opposition.

Shortly after arrival in Henley, we paid our first visit to Henley Baptist Church. It was strange to swop from a basement fellowship in Cyprus, and a three-year investment in consistent youth and mission activity, to sitting in a pew without portfolio! However, we were warmly welcomed and soon found opportunity to preach, share in prayer and bible study groups, and invest in youth work. One memorable youth mission was the 'Smokey Zone' Coffee Bar in the Church Hall. For appropriate ambiance, our mission team hung copious amounts of hessian across the hall. Our wooden RAF removal crates were painted over, followed by Ann's creative suggestion that we decorate them with brick wallpaper to give them a chimney look. To complete the atmosphere, we scoured the town for old chimney pots which were then inserted on top of the crates. Dim lights were added to create a foggy effect, and a music group completed a trendy scene. Posters and leaflets were distributed through the town, inviting teenagers to the mission week. Each night a team of older volunteers served coffee and drinks to a full house and our mission team sat on tables with the youth. It was low-key relationship building as we shared our faith and invited the teens to our youth club. A short epilogue completed the evening with Christian tracts passed on to the teens. It is rarely wise to count numbers and assume we made a significant impact, but we planted truth into young minds, assured that the Holy Spirit continues the work of conviction and conversion.

As the months passed, we began to pray in earnest about our future. The call to Christian Ministry, labelled 'full-time' - though all Christian service is full-time - was the burning desire of my heart. I began the process of seeking insight from friends, Pastors, and our regional Baptist Superintendent. The guidance was positive, supportive, and practical. It was also, at times, very confusing and distracting. Having become a Christian in a Baptist Church, it seemed logical to consider a Baptist Training College, as any football player would logically assume he should train where the team trained. If Baptist Ministry was my 'calling' then that is where I should be trained. However, when I mentioned colleges to friends, an array of disparate comments followed, 'Too charismatic, too liberal, too Calvinistic' and so on. I realised I needed clear personal guidance and prayed I would have peace about where I would be trained. After careful and prayerful consideration, I approached Spurgeon's College, a famous ministerial training college in South Norwood, London, founded by 'The Prince of Preachers' Charles Haddon Spurgeon. My interview didn't go quite as planned. I was told I needed to gain some qualifications. Having left school at fifteen, and refused to go back when moving from the North to the South, I had no qualifications.

My response was petty and ill-informed. A reaction, as a mature adult with over ten years military experience and a lot of evangelical passion, to the request for more education. Why would I need such qualifications? Didn't they appreciate my spirituality, experience, and application of faith over the past ten years in a tough environment? Surely it was about my spiritual gifting? Little did I know how God would redeem lost education for my benefit and the rigours of seeking to be a fruitful Christian Minister over the next thirty-five years. I left Spurgeon's with a chip on my shoulder, determined to find a college that would not put such a premium on secular qualifications. Though are any qualifications merely secular? After a period of calming down, I took a dose of humility and decided to take five 'O' levels whilst still in the RAF. Once complete, I took a further dose of humility and returned to Spurgeon's for another interview. By this time, the previous principal, Dr George Beasley Murray had retired, and a new principal Dr Raymond Brown appointed. This time my interview was far more relaxed. Ray Brown had a similar background to mine and clearly understood my limitations, but also my potential. I was duly invited to enter college some six months after leaving the RAF in March 1974. I had work to do!

In the RAF we had moved 13 times in 12 years. What we needed now, especially for our boys, was a period of stability. Only a fool, would contemplate that stability in Henley-on-Thames! Without any significant savings we would be looking at seemingly impossible house rental rates. Even a tent rental would be beyond us. In fact, you would be hard pressed to get a sewer for £60-80 a month. Yet, once again we would see how 'faith is the evidence of things not seen.' God is pretty cool at putting the right pieces in place at the right time. We would discover over our lifetime, that 'timing' is everything.

The first miracle provision came six months prior to leaving the RAF. A couple around the corner from our home, who we had never met, heard about our need, and knocked on our door. They asked whether we would consider house-sitting their home! They were heading out to Kenya for a year, working for Kenco (Kenya Coffee Company), and were keen to leave their home in safe hands. How did they know we were safe hands? Had they caught just a fragrance of our compassion and concern for others when losing Elizabeth? Were they friends with the family we visited who had lost their baby? All we knew is we needed a home and, as we prayed, God provided through this couple. We were delighted to agree. It was a clear indication of the rightness of staying in Henley and the certainty of divine care for us as a family. It was a joy to share this answer to prayer with our Christian family at Henley Baptist Church who had been regularly praying for us. Now we had the stability we needed, knowing we would vacate our hiring on demob and move into our 'Kenco' home the very next day. The second 'faith' provision of a new home was complete. Two, even more amazing home provisions, would follow in due course, hence the original book title!

19

NEW HORIZONS

After twelve years, nine RAF Stations, two three-year overseas tours in Germany and Cyprus, and thirteen homes, on April 4th 1974 I put on my uniform for the last time. With a few exceptions, it had been an amazing journey. A young, immature lad had been forged into a man, wonderfully supported, encouraged, and partnered by my devoted wife Ann. The tough moments had strengthened our marriage and refined our faith. The disciplines had fashioned character and taught us much about perseverance, grit, resilience, and commitment. We learned how to live with little income, trust divine provision, adapt to changing circumstances, and appreciate simple pleasures. We valued friendship, triumphed over tragedy, and were determined not to waste our lives. All would equip us well for a complete change of direction.

My pressing priority now, was to discern how to support our family for the next six months, prior to commencing four years ministerial training at Spurgeon's College in London. I needed a short-term job. Little did I know I was about to embark on the most dirty, boring, mind-numbing, and challenging six months of work since my laundry-van days at the age of fifteen! On the plus side, it would also be an opportunity to earth my faith in another testing environment, observe life in a factory, and surprise forty engineers by staying the course when no other 'toilet' employee had lasted more than a matter of weeks.

I was signed on at Baker-Perkins in Twyford, a few miles from Henley. A company making biscuit handling machines. My job description featured; cleaning the toilets and washbasins three times a day after forty engineers had washed their grease-laden hands and visited the loos. Removing copious amounts of swarf from the lathes and depositing it in skips. Sweeping the floor regularly to avoid loose metal becoming a hazard and, in true military fashion, anything else I was told to do! It was a learning experience I would never forget, and one that equipped me in ways I would never have imagined.

After passing the four-week milestone, and ensuring the toilets and basins were gleaming after every attack of filthy grease, some of the engineers became inquisitive. They had not seen such pristine washrooms for years! I began to loiter at their lathes and along the assembly line. Little by little I learnt their stories and they began to hear of mine. I asked the boss if I could leave tracts in the toilets! Men don't easily open up in public, but I discovered they would look at tracts whilst sitting on the loo! I shared my testimony and managed to converse with most of the engineers. On one occasion I met Cyril. A mountain of a man from the West Indies. Cyril was a Christian who taught me 'there are higher heights and deeper depths.' At the time I had little clue what he was talking about but his smile penetrated my lack of insight, almost as if he was thinking - 'you will one day!' That day would be four years hence.

As I gained the respect of the men, I explored how best to use those moments between shifts when there was a lull in my routine. I asked if I could help with grinding off small pieces of protruding metal on the machines and was duly handed a sizeable grinder. I noticed how long it took some men to find a drill in a large box where every conceivable piece of equipment was thrown. This gave me an opportunity to help, and confuse most of them! I drilled holes in pieces of wood and inserted drills. It was the days of plastic tape 'press-outs' from a small machine. You turned a dial, which had letters and numbers, pressed the required letters, and your plastic strip emerged, ready to stick. By each hole I put the drill size and was proud of the finished article! However, I could not believe how long it took for men, who had been scrabbling in laden boxes trying to find the right drill, to accept they could look at the wooden innovations and find a 1" drill in a fraction of the time it had previously taken! Maybe they enjoyed lingering at the drill-box while chatting about football to their mates. Maybe such an innovation was a step too far and they preferred the chaotic tool box! It's easy to forget what a challenge 'change' can be - in a tight knit factory or a church!

In preparation for college, I was required to read up on basic Greek and Hebrew! At lunch, I would sit with the engineers, wading through the assignments. Their incredulity knew no bounds. A bog-cleaner wrestling with Greek. I could hardly wade through a comic, never mind Greek! However, I persevered, ploughed on, and generally plodded my way through JW Wenham's 'Basic Elements of New Testament Greek.' Forget the Hebrew, I was already mired in the Greek! However, I prayed a very direct prayer as I began my studies. 'Lord, help me go as far as you want.' After missing out on my O Levels at Grammar School, I was keen to redeem as much education as possible. Par for the course, it would be another surprise as I stretched my brain cells way beyond my early expectations.

One of the more humorous episodes at Baker-Perkins was the testing of the biscuit handling machines once the build was complete. Hundreds of biscuits were fed into one end, simulating the process from baking to packaging. Finely tuned 'biscuit-grabbers' required exact tolerance, but a newly completed machine rarely played the game. The result was absolute chaos as the out of sync grabbers fired the biscuits into the air and across the workshop floor. Everything was halted as the engineers worked to refine the grabbers. I, on the other hand, set about clearing up hundreds of wasted and broken biscuits! It was even more chaotic and hilarious when we fed the machine chocolate biscuits! As a chocaholic, it was my chance to gorge on broken chocolate digestives!

As my leaving date approached, I was ready to move on, but I would carry with me the many lessons I had learned and the good wishes of the engineers and managers. The need for endurance, stickability and patience, especially in tough times, was birthed firmly in my mind. It would serve me well in the years to come. The importance of loitering and listening featured consistently over those six months. It would occur time and time again in the future. The humility to clean toilets and make them shine, taught me to be a servant not a star. Sweeping floors would accompany all my years of ministry. Two keys undergirded so much of my time at Baker-Perkins - hard work and completion.

Completion is a value I treasure because it so often requires hard work and patience. It also requires 'detail'. A lot of that was clearly instilled in me in the RAF, but I was determined to hone that throughout my life. If detail is lacking, it is not necessarily you that is affected, it is those other people who need it to function well. A few people have said to me 'I don't do detail,' to which I have generally responded, 'it will come back to bite you.' In the end, it is others who need your detail. If it is consistently lacking, especially when vital issues are at stake, those people will eventually become frustrated and question your integrity. I had wrestled with the 'practice' of Christian life and service, now I had to wrestle with the theology behind the practice, but in the meantime, houses would occupy prayer and faith once again.

20

BADGEMORE

A few months before leaving my job at Baker-Perkins, I asked our church friends to pray about another new home for us in Henley. Our very kind 'Kenco' family would be returning from their year in Kenya, early in September, so we would need to vacate their home in August. As we prayed, an elderly couple in the congregation were considering retirement. The small-holding they ran, a couple of miles outside of Henley, was proving difficult to maintain. The house was a very large brick and flint property, divided into two separate homes and surrounded by acres of farm land and Henley Golf Club. A relative of our friends had been living in the house next door but had recently died, leaving the house empty. When our friends realised the urgency of our situation, they approached us and offered the empty, but fully furnished, property! As they outlined the lay out, all we could do was stand rather open-mouthed, especially when they mentioned the tennis court and large lawn!

Two key issues occupied our minds and prayers at this point. The finance required both for college fees and another home. I had applied to Oxford County Council for a grant and was awaiting a reply. If all went well, I had calculated that we could afford £10 a week maximum for rental. We had no idea what the house at Badgemore would cost, but offering £10 a week would surely be an insult! Ann had a part-time job as subscription manager for the British Journal of Sociology, with book publishers Routledge, Keegan, and Paul, but her wage would not cover our weekly bills. In a mixture of excitement, trepidation, and faith, we paid a visit to Badgemore. It was so beautiful, and ideal for us and our boys. They would have acres of space, not just in the garden but adventuring into the woods and fields beyond. Our third 'miracle' home was about to materialise, but not easily. When our tour was complete, with hearts racing a little, we asked about the rental - it would be £12 per week! A difference of £2 appears so small today, but at that time, still without any certainty regarding a grant, it might have appeared reckless. We wanted to act with integrity and honesty alongside faith, so suggested we pray for a week and then let them know our answer. A week later, we had this verse regarding guidance from Colossians chapter 3 verse 15, 'The peace that Christ gives is to guide you in the decisions you make; for it is to this peace that God has called you together in the one body.' We had peace, returned to our friends, and committed ourselves to paying the extra £2. Our trial had begun, in more ways than one!

Shortly after moving in, we received news that the grant application had been turned down! Our test of faith, which had begun three years previously in Cyprus, when seeking to pay the bus bill on time, was once again on trial. The issue for Oxford CC was the 'place' of study. They were questioning why I was doing my studies at a Baptist Training College in London whilst living in Oxfordshire. It was logical for us, that becoming a Baptist Minister required training in a Baptist College, just as playing for Everton required attending the Everton training academy. (After 70 years supporting Everton, I sometimes wonder whether they have a training ground!)

The reply from Oxford CC was not only a blow for us, but also raised a question mark over our 'faith' commitment to our friends. We had no savings, or other source of income. I immediately asked the church in Henley to pray, and informed the college Principal, Dr Raymond Brown. He responded immediately, assuring us of his prayers and a college letter to Oxford CC. As we prayed, God moved.

Over a six-week period, around 11pm every other Friday, an envelope was discreetly slipped through our letter-box. It contained a verse from the Bible, wrapped around £30! Enough to meet our needs. Six weeks later, a letter from the College Principal, along with my reasoning in a separate letter, convinced the Council of the rightness of my case. The best news of all was the amount granted. It was twice what I had calculated and expected. Not only extra money for a mature, married student, but an allowance due to living away from home during the week! Faith in what could not be seen, had once again been honoured. 'My God shall supply ALL your need, according to HIS riches in glory' was not, and would not, be an empty promise. It strengthened my belief that the Lord would constantly ask us to walk by faith, not sight. Our £12 'faith-promise' to our friends was well and truly exceeded. Ephesians chapter 3 verse 20 was written large over our move to Badgemore, 'Now to him who is able to do immeasurably more than all we ask or imagine… ' It would be our story, in more miraculous ways, for the next forty-five years.

21

SPURGEON'S COLLEGE

Whilst the decision to stay in Henley, and nurture stability in the family, would consistently prove right, it would also result in a dramatic change in our married life. Ann would experience a significantly extra workload. The boys would be without their dad. Most weeks I would be away living in college with a clear focus on study, whilst Ann focused on family, work, home, shopping, meals, washing and the commute to school! It was clearly an unequal partnership, but one undergirded by love, sacrifice, and a commitment to prepare well for Christian ministry and service in the years ahead. Without any shadow of doubt, I would never have survived college, study, or any extra college requirements, such as weekend travel and preaching, without Ann's devotion, partnership, prayer, and sheer hard work. She was such an amazing, courageous, wise, strong, and beautiful person. This was the lady, aged three, whose parents were told 'she may never be able to walk'! A lot of pain, hospitalisations, surgery, and limitations were ahead, but for now she was holding everything together!

It didn't take long in college to realise I was amongst a number of gifted, scholarly, intelligent and able colleagues. Some were post graduates, with one or more degrees, others had mission experience abroad and a few had excelled in language studies. Oxbridge graduates were well represented. Academically, I felt well out of my depth and my early results in Hebrew and Greek certainly reflected this. My response was to pay a visit to Dr Brown and plead with him to drop me from the Hebrew class. With 7% in my first Greek test, I needed only one language challenge. His reply was simple, just keep going! I appreciated his confidence in me and began an apprenticeship in 'plodding.' Whilst I would never become a linguist, I plodded and slowly improved.

My biggest regret was the amount of time spent in my room. I was determined to take everything I could from the learning process and, in some measure, redeem the education I had lost at fifteen. The negative side was the loss of wider friendships and social life. As a mature, married student, returning home each weekend, it was never easy to fit fully into college life. Fortunately, I did form a small number of close friendships, some of which remain to this day. It was also tough on Ann. Most of the married students either lived in college or in local accommodation. Wives were able to join in much of college life and attend gatherings organised by Dr Brown's wife Christine. These times would have furnished Ann with practical and theological insights into Christian ministry as well as being a wife and mother. Also, those times would have allowed her to forge deeper friendships within the group. As it was, Ann was only able to make a couple of Christmas events during my four years.

One precious opportunity for prayer was to share with a couple who, after years of trying and many tests, had been told categorically by physicians, 'you will not be able to have children.' They ended up having five! It reminds me that God's word is always the last word. Time and again, both in ministry and life, I have been told 'you can't do that' or 'it will never work.' Many of the stories already told, and those that will emerge later, will reveal just how central and important God's 'last word' has been for us.

I entered college on the Diploma course. That was my goal, and certainly my expectation for the next three years prior to the final Pastoral Studies year. To my surprise, after several months, and a gradual improvement in languages and essays, I was invited into Dr Brown's office and offered a switch to a BA degree. I had plodded enough to convince the faculty I could handle it! It was both scary but also encouraging. Part of the irony was the ability to cope with Greek and Hebrew and to be one of just four students who went on to complete the Hebrew classes! To be frank and honest, I did it by rote not academic ability. Others would perfect their languages. I would rely on the Greek and Hebrew lexicons! I did, however, appreciate some of the mistakes that could be avoided, when preaching, by having a cursory knowledge of the biblical text in both languages.

As for my petty responses in my college interviews, 'why do I need qualifications,' it became clear, that without taking those 5 O Levels in the RAF, I would not have been eligible to move to the degree course. University requirements today would not have disbarred me, but at the time it was mandatory. How grateful I was for the timely push from George Beasley Murray to 'go away and get some O Levels.' I also learned that degrees are not given away. Hard work, perseverance, and determined application are vital. As I got on with the job, often burning the midnight oil, my initial prayer, 'Lord, help me to go as far as you want to take me.' was being answered way beyond my expectations. I did fall apart in the final Greek exam, much to my embarrassment, with lengthy sighs which must have annoyed those around me. I came out of the exam convinced I had blown the whole three-years work. In the end I scraped an honours degree; not the sort that propels you into the academic fast-lane, but it was my best effort and I was proud of the outcome. I did, however, get to shake Prince Charles hand at an investiture ceremony. As I stopped to receive the roll, he leaned forward and said, 'where the hell is Spurgeon's College?' I offered a tour but he never replied! Now it was a case of completing my Pastoral Studies year, which would not be straightforward.

22

ASHFORD BAPTIST CHURCH

In my first year at college (Sep '74-Sep '75), I had a placement with the Rev Brian Hankins at Tyndale Baptist Church, Reading. Whilst this was important and helpful for a student, it added further pressure for Ann. Instead of having all weekends free to help her, and share with the boys, I was now committed to certain Sundays at Tyndale. If I was preaching, I would often spend part of Saturday, either preparing or refining my message. Such are the extra pressures that belong to married students with a family and away from home each week. In the second year (Sept '75 - 'Sep '76), the pressures increased significantly as I was assigned to Ashford Baptist Church in Middlesex, a church without a Minister. Both first and second years were standard practice at Spurgeon's College. Alongside another Minister in the first year, on your own in the second. Now it would not be occasional, but regular Sunday visits. Both preaching and pastoral visiting would increase, along with further pressures for the family. However, whenever we could, we travelled as a family and earthed ourselves in the life of ABC.

Ashford would turn out to be an amazing year, followed by an unexpected invitation. An elderly part-time Pastor, Dennis Boulter, had quietly nurtured a congregation of around forty members, along with a faithful diaconate. He had laid a solid foundation for growth. I was the apprentice stepping into his shoes and learning along the way. My year featured every pastoral situation possible; conversions, baptisms, dedications, weddings, preaching, funerals, pastoral care and visitation, counselling, regular leader's meetings, outings, and mistakes! Throughout the year there was steady growth, both in new members and spiritual hunger. I could not have asked for a better student-pastorate. The church had adopted our family and we were blessed with new friends. My preaching developed accordingly and I loved the opportunity to visit homes, hospitals, and some work places. At the end of year, I received a bolt from the blue when the Church Secretary, David Hayes, took me aside and asked whether I would consider being their Pastor! My immediate response was to chuckle quietly, followed by, 'I have almost two more years left at college. Be assured I will certainly pray about your kind invitation when seeking a church during my final year.' Health warning – never pre-empt or underestimate what God wants to do, and especially His timing. A major change was nearer than I expected.

Three months into the New Year (March '77), a Girls' Brigade weekend was due at ABC and I was invited, along with all the family, to be the guest speaker. The church had large Girls' and Boys' Brigades with a passionate and experienced team of leaders. There was a display and prize-giving on the Saturday, at which I would present the prizes, and on Sunday I would preach. We had been away from ABC for six months since the completion of the Student Pastorate in September '76. It didn't take us long to realise just how much we had missed everyone. The welcome was like a home-coming! Sunday only reinforced our sense of belonging to this lovely church family. At the end of the evening service, I had a deep conviction that the Holy Spirit was at work. I recalled the invitation from the leadership back in Sep '76, 'we would like you to be our Pastor,' and my light-hearted response and chuckle, 'I have almost two years left at college and will pray about ABC when leaving.' Now here I was, wrestling with a conviction that the Holy Spirit was moving way ahead of my timing. At the conclusion of the weekend, I sought out the secretary, David Hayes, and said, 'David, I don't know what is happening, will you pray for a month and we will do the same.' He agreed and we left it there.

As we prayed and questioned, 'Lord, do you want me at ABC?' God spoke clearly from Joshua chapter 1 verse 6, 'Be strong and very courageous, you are the man to lead these people …'.

The clarity was undeniable and confirmed when we met the leaders a month later. We both had peace that God had brought us together. What I needed now was the blessing of the London Baptist Superintendent and my College Principal Dr Raymond Brown! Was I too naive? It is only during the last year of college that we would receive guidance regarding settlement in a church. I, on the other hand, am half-way through my third year of four! I am also fully convinced that all we, and the church, need to do is pray, listen to the Holy Spirit, and discern the will of God. How simple and straightforward can it be? Whilst I had become a Christian in a Baptist Church, I had spent twelve years in the RAF with Christians from a whole spectrum of denominations and none. I had no idea what the protocol was for settlement in a Baptist Church. My first step was to tell Dr Brown I had been invited to accept the pastorate at ABC and, with Ann's blessing, we had accepted the invitation and would take up the post! Alongside the pastorate, I would complete my degree and pastoral studies year.

Ray's first words, following the details of my call, were, 'have you talked to the London Superintendent?' Clearly, I didn't know the Baptist system! I'm not even sure I knew who the London Superintendent was, let alone consult him! At that moment of revelation, I was so grateful for Ray's gracious response. He discerned that my call was unusual, at this point in my training, but certainly not impossible. He was a man of great faith, learning and insight. To know he was so supportive, was a great encouragement and a model for any Minister. Despite my attempt to re-write ministerial regulations, Rev Douglas Sparkes, the London Baptist Superintendent, was equally gracious, endorsing our call and outlining the future process with respect to ordination and induction at Ashford Baptist Church. The dye was cast and we began conversations with ABC regarding a home and the balance of time between my pastoral studies year at college and church commitments.

23

CHALLENGE AND CHANGE

The challenge was to get Ann through the driving test. Reminders of past explanations about family folklore rose to the surface again from Ann. 'Every time I learn to drive, I get pregnant and can't fit into the seat!' As far as we could tell she was not pregnant at this point, which was just as well as her lessons were in a Mini! It was handy for me to pop in the car on a Monday morning and drive to college, but it was foolish to have our car all week in London while Ann struggled on her moped. Friends at church were supportive in getting our boys to and from school, but Ann needed to have more flexibility and freedom. Not least because she was now able to take more paid work and, with a car at home, would be able to drive the boys to school and on to work. Unlike me, Ann sailed through the driving test first time and our second VW Beetle was now in Ann's hands. To reach college, I would now switch to a coach from Henley to Victoria Coach Station, train to South Norwood and a healthy walk to South Norwood Hill.

As that change occurred so another was in the wings. Our 'landlord' friends and neighbours at Badgemore were struggling with their health and contemplating selling the house we were in! It was a tough blow as we had hoped to be settled there until I finished college. Once again, our faith would be tested and prayer increased. As ever, I asked the church to pray with us and for us. We had two very close friends, Percy and Wyn Wiltshire, who had taken us under their wing from the moment we arrived in Henley. They were people of wisdom, faith, prayer, and generosity, often inviting us on their motor boat for trips on the Thames and filling the gaps in our financial shortfall. With little money to spend on outings, these trips were so special for us. When static, we fished from the boat with homemade rods and simple tackle. It was great fun and occasionally we caught more than the guys along the bank!

A very special blessing for me, as I write, is the memory-making projects at Badgemore that Andy and Tim still remember with fondness. Despite the intense pressure associated with college training, I built a wooden fort and a Subbuteo stadium with stands and floodlights. The fort sides took many hours of sawing small wooden dowels to stick on hardboard. It had a drawbridge and walkways for soldiers which I had painted by hand. For an extremely poor DIY guy it was special to produce something that the boys loved and used. Equally, the Subbuteo stadium doubled as an exercise pitch for Scooby our footballing budgie! His tragic demise will feature shortly!

Progress regarding another home was also fostered by Percy and Wyn. They mentioned that the house next door to theirs, in the centre of town, was empty and being fully renovated throughout. The owner was a Reuters Correspondent working in Tehran. Wyn suggested to Percy that he inquire about a possible rental. Several weeks later, as our deadline for moving approached, we still had no news. Once more I asked the church to pray earnestly for a home. Percy had been procrastinating over the inquiry and Wyn was prompted, by our further appeal, to give him a spiritual kick up the backside! However, sometimes patience, even procrastination, is rewarded with right timing. At least that is what Percy would say! It was the right time. As Percy knocked on the house, the builders responded and explained the situation. The owners lived in Iran, so they could not answer his question regarding rental. As Percy turned back home, amazingly, the owners were walking down the road. They had returned from Tehran to view the building work! Percy explained the urgency and, after a short conversation, they agreed right away! Our fourth 'miracle' home was sealed on the pavement of Queen's Street in a matter of minutes! Amazingly, whilst the owners could easily have quadrupled our rent at Badgemore, they agreed on £12! We would lose our lawn and tennis court but would have the beautiful River Thames and park just round the corner!

One major issue was furniture. For the last fourteen years, ever since we were married, we had lived in furnished accommodation. Our new four storey home in Queen's Street was completely empty! Between them, Ann's Mum and Auntie provided a selection of tables, cupboards, and beds. The folks from church added four three-piece suites! Others filled in the gaps until we had a workable home. As well as the exciting adventures for our boys along the river, we had three rooms in the cellar, perfectly finished and centrally heated! It became more a boy's den than a man cave and the boys loved it. We moved in and gave thanks to God for yet another Henley home - our last before moving to our first pastorate and manse. Adding to our blessings, Percy and Wyn's motor boat was near which meant that trips along the Thames would be offered at short notice! Their close presence also furnished us with a shoulder to lean on when tears or troubles were near.

Next door, Stuart and Pam, welcomed us with flowers and introduced our boys to their children, who were of similar age. Stuart and Pam had an interesting story. They were potters and painters, the last of the 'Flower Power' generation. They were down to their last few pounds and unsure of the future. After consideration, they took a punt with their last few pounds and bought a lump of clay. Their goal was to model little bears named 'Ursa Minor' and enter a competition. The first prize was a Design Centre label. Although various shapes, the bears would measure around two inches high and one inch wide. The clay was fired and the bears hand painted. Some of the brushes had one hair! When they had a dozen different bears, Stuart made a little wooden triangular home to house them in small cubby holes. This would complete their competition entry - they won! So began an amazing journey of selling. Gradually, at craft fairs the bears were the stars and they regularly sold out. The range featured wedding couples, choir pieces - with very small notes on song sheets - firemen, policemen, football and cricket teams and anything they were requested to produce. Commissions arrived from International Cricket, Baseball and Rugby Teams who wanted the whole squad on a plaque! Every bear had to be perfectly balanced. Imagine balancing a musician's trombone without the bear falling over! Just one problem occurred. They began their pricing far too low. It was difficult to raise their prices, other than in small increments. A bear costing three pounds could not be doubled overnight. In a very short time Ursa Minor bears became internationally sought after. One request stood out in Stuart's huge pile of letters. It was from the Disney Corporation in the US asking for 20,000 bears! Stuart wrote back, explaining that each bear takes many hours to produce, not least in the delicate painting required. Stuart and Pam were the only production line! Disney had not appreciated the work involved and all Stuart and Pam could do was laugh and file the request. They were also receiving many letters pleading for surgery on their bears! 'My Doctor Bear has lost his stethoscope.' 'The trumpet has gone missing from a band player.' 'A footballer has lost a boot! 'Please can you mend our bear' was the cry of many a letter! The bears were robust, but handling or dropping had its setbacks!

We are proud to report that we have a mini-house full of 'Ursa Minors,' including a black and white striped robber with a swag bag which was banned in California! We also received anniversary and birthday gifts with the appropriate number between two bears. Many years after moving on,

Stuart and Pam remembered our 40th wedding anniversary and surprised us with two bears flanking the number 40. We are still in touch and require no bear surgery!

Scooby was my pride and joy. A green budgie able to play Subbuteo at a frantic pace. His capacity to score stunning goals was legendary. When bored, he would simply pick up the goal and run. It's a long and painful story, with an echo of impending divorce! A student at college had two aged Jack Russell dogs; Toppi the heavier and Tina somewhat smaller. For years they had a strict daily routine, including long walks morning and evening, and were set in their ways. Derek was on his way to language study in Belgium and needed a home for the dogs. He put a request out and, being a dog lover, I hinted that we might be able to help. However, when I suggested the possibility to Ann, it was a definite 'no!' Several weeks later, Derek's deadline was fast approaching. In an act of sheer madness, I suggested we take them on a trial basis. The boys were excited - Ann was not! I had not considered the implications for her. Ann was working part-time, she had two boys and was in the early stages of pregnancy and her hips were painful. All week I would be at college and she would have two dogs requiring long walks. Disaster loomed, on all fronts!

The first signs of conflict took place in the hallway. It appears that Tina was more sickly than Derek had revealed. The result was a tussle between Toppi and Tina - the heavier dog bullying the lightweight. Ann's task in the morning was impossible. She had to hold the two dogs apart, shuffle along the hall and open the front door, all with increasing signs of hip degeneration. Instead of a long walk, it was a short trot down the road and back. Strangely, once out in the road, they trotted alongside each other like close friends! Further signs of looming disaster appeared at the breakfast table. Scooby would fly down and share a bowl of cornflakes. The dog's eyes would widen as they traced Scooby's flight. Ann sensed a crisis and warned me that the dogs would get Scooby. In typical male fashion I dismissed the warning.

Following Ann's wise warning, I was away in Worcester with a mission team from college. It was a very difficult mission, in a church praying for change but held to ransom by a stubborn Superintendent. Midweek was a free day but the team felt it right to give the morning to prayer. A terse five word letter arrived from Ann, 'Toppi has achieved her aim.' My immediate impression was that Toppi had attacked Tina and Tina was dead! In a way, I felt relief. Ann would only have one dog to look after! Given the terse letter, I said to the team that I should go home but wanted to pray first for guidance. I tried to imagine Ann cleaning up a bloodied and dying dog. I opened my Bible reading and read the first line, 'your wisest course of action is to do as Moses did, stand still and see the salvation of your God.' I could not have received clearer guidance. No wonder the Bible is the most comprehensive manual for living our lives with wisdom, clarity, and fulfilment.

All the team knew was that the prayer time on that day would set the agenda for the remaining days of our mission. I was the team leader, and preacher for the last Sunday. Prayer would go on without me, but it didn't feel right to abandon the team at a crucial time. That first line in my devotions gave me the guidance I needed. 'Stand still and see the salvation of your God.' I obeyed and returned to the team, declaring 'I am not going home,' followed by sharing the devotional for that day! A colleague, and good friend, Joel Benjamin immediately responded, 'let the dead bury their dead.' He was sure I should stay in Worcester.

On Sunday, we finished the mission with heavy hearts. Many of those who attended during the week had been blessed, but the hold and resistance to change was solid from the Superintendent. It would take eighteen months to see a breakthrough. The sudden, and unexpected death of the Church Superintendent resulted in a huge change in the life and future of the church. Many of those who had left, following the mission, returned. A young student took on the pastorate and the church saw rapid growth - so rapid that they moved into a local school to accommodate the growth. During that tough eighteen months, I received letters from some of those who had left. They shared their heartache over one person's ironclad hold over a church which was showing such hopeful promise of growth. It took a death to bring new life. It was as if God was saying 'I want my church back.'

I returned home with a degree of uncertainty as to how Ann and the boys had coped with the loss of Tina. Imagine my distress when I was greeted by two dogs and no budgie! When Ann wrote, 'Toppi has achieved her aim' my immediate thought was that the heavier dog had killed the lighter. Instead, Toppi had killed Scooby! It was so swift. Scooby's tail, while munching corn flakes at breakfast, had flicked over the edge of the table. In one rapid move, Toppi pounced and grabbed the budgie. The boys screamed, Ann shouted, and the budgie was dropped. As Ann picked up Scooby there was no obvious damage, sadly, the famous 'Subbuteo star' died in her hand. Now it was my turn to lament his demise and apologise to Ann.

We often mention this episode as being the nearest to divorce. I had acted with reckless disregard for Ann's workload, wishes, health, and safety. I had also lost a great pet and nearly broke the boys' hearts. The moral of the story is 'agreement.' If you are not in agreement - be warned! Not all unilateral decisions end in disaster, but it's a happier home when, together, you have peace about a decision. I contacted Derek in Belgium requesting he return and take the dogs back. We met, briefly, in a London

Park and, almost in a clandestine exchange, passed the offending dogs over and promptly drove away with a sigh of relief and no divorce proceedings!

24

PRAYER, PROMISE AND MIRACLE

As Autumn emerged in 1976, Ann began to suffer with increased hip pain. We had been praying about the wisdom of having another baby since Elizabeth died in 1973. Given the increased pain, Ann shared, 'it's now or never' if she was to carry another child for nine months. We needed clear guidance, assurance, and the peace that guides us in decisions we make, described in Colossians chapter 34 verse 15 as, 'The peace that Christ gives is to guide you in the decisions you make; for it is to this peace that God has called you …' Increasingly, in our Christian discipleship, we learned the importance of this peace, not least in the major decisions in life. We set aside a day to pray, specifically with one question in mind, 'is it wise to proceed in having another child?' We contacted family, friends and fellow Christians asking that they remember us in prayer on that day. The promise we received was very simple and assuring. John chapter 4 verse 59, 'Your child shall live.' The Greek word used is 'pais' which covers both son or daughter. Naturally, our hope was that, if Ann conceived, it might be a daughter! As Ann has never had any problems conceiving, it was no surprise when she announced she was pregnant in November 1976 - no cars were involved! We were deeply thankful for answered prayer, but it would not be an easy journey.

My challenge at college was to finish my degree. Given my school history, this was no mean feat. My thesis was around 20,000 words and my grammar was largely scouse based! I was tackling 'Nouthetic Counselling' based on Dr Jay Adams ground breaking book 'Competent to Counsel.' He was best known as the founder of the modern Biblical

Counselling movement and strongly opposed to secular psychology in the counselling rooms of Pastors and Christian laypersons. 'Nouthetic' is a combination of the Greek 'nous' (reasonable mind) and 'tithemi' (to set or put in place). The core of Adams' counselling ministry was the importance of placing into the mind biblical truth. This is not the place to delve more deeply into Adams' work, but suffice to note 'other counselling approaches are available' - not least that of the renowned Dr Paul Tournier.

For me, it was a major triumph to finish my thesis, scrape through the final exams and redeem a little of the education I had lost when leaving my grammar school in Liverpool. I was grateful to be stretched and become more aware of the discipline needed to maintain the rigours of pastoral ministry. Education can also be infectious. Having faced a significant educational challenge, and achieved way beyond my expectations, my appetite would grow in the future.

Yet another move was on our radar. The congregation at ABC had been earnest in prayer and faith, as they sought a home, but also acutely sensitive to Ann's disability needs. Her left hip was deteriorating and, though she would hang on for a further four years, a major operation was inevitable. Her consultant at Nuffield Orthopaedic Hospital in Oxford, Mr Goodfellow, was eager not to operate until necessary, but always had her best, long-term, interests at heart. He was especially concerned for the longevity of a hip replacement when in her mid-thirties. The lifespan of a new hip, at the time, was around fifteen years. As Ann's condition was complicated, it might mean a replacement in the future could not be guaranteed. Mr Goodfellow mentioned, at a later date,' I hope this replacement hip never needs a revision.' Ann was also eager not to enter hospital, facing a complicated hip operation and long recovery so near to our 5th baby's birth, which was due on July 4th 1977.

Given our history, having lost two children, the doctors at the Royal Berkshire Hospital were keen to have her in early. Ann was desperate for a natural birth and was given three days grace before inducing her. 'Natural' however was not to be and the induction began on the morning of July 7th. It was then the light went on. If all was well, our yet nameless baby would be born on 7.7.77 - a perfect biblical number!

On the morning of the 7th, I was preparing my breakfast and looked out of the kitchen window. There was no manicured garden or lawn, simply the waste from an extensive renovation, which had not yet been removed. I could not believe what I was seeing. In the centre of the garden was a pile of brick and earth much higher than the surrounding debris. About a foot high, and straight as a dye, was a perfect rose rising through the rubble! I had not even seen a weed, given the pile of debris, let alone a beautiful pale pink rose in that wasteland! It was a powerful assurance to me that God had provided this rose in a truly wonderful way. A rose doesn't appear overnight. Maybe I had never looked at that spot before and therefore missed any growth, but for me, either way, it was a sign and symbol of God's provision, against the odds, for our daughter's wellbeing and future. We would name her Sharon, picking up on the verse with that name in Song of Solomon chapter 2 verse 1. We still have that pressed rose forty-seven years later.

At the Royal Berks it was touch and go regarding the 7th, as Ann toughed it out until 9.45pm when Sharon finally appeared, weighing in at 7lbs 13oz. After three boys and the loss of a baby girl, our joy was complete. That joy would soon be tempered as another trial was waiting in the wings.

Shortly after Sharon's birth, a paediatrician, Dr Richardson, arrived at Ann's bed. She explained to Ann that there was a problem as Sharon was turning yellow - not blue. It was not the heart but an unknown blood issue, later diagnosed as an ABO incompatibility. A complete blood exchange was needed lasting around six hours. Although off duty at midnight, Dr Richardson stayed through the night to oversee the complicated procedure. Early in the morning, she reported to Ann that the procedure had gone well and it would be a week before we would know the outcome. On the way, God had plans for a miracle!

Suffice to say that our prayer support from family, friends and churches was set in motion. One very special, and unexpected, prayer was from the MSS (Medical Secret Service) a group of four Christian doctors who visited Ann's ward to share their prayer support. Sadly, it was rest time on the ward and the very efficient Sister refused them entry! They stood outside, found a pencil and blood test card, then wrote on the back, 'This is where the higher medical service takes over. Called to see you during rest hour. Banned from seeing you! Dr Andrews, Dr A. Richardson, Dr Willis, and myself, are all praying for the family. Look up! More reinforcements coming. Dr S.A. Richardson.' This small, plain, scribbled note on the back of a medical card, is just about the most precious possession we have. Not worth a dime, but priceless. As I write, tears are flowing and thanksgiving is bursting out.

After just two days under ultra violet light, and five ahead of the diagnosis timeline report, a miracle took place in the special care ward. At the end of feeding, the sister took Sharon in her arms, looked at Ann, and said, 'We don't know what's happened, but Sharon has made a miraculous (her word) recovery, would you like to take her back to the ward?' Well, I think we might say 'yes please!' Before we left the ward, we were told that a paediatrician had visited to check out Sharon's hips. The outcome was predictable but minor compared to what we had already faced. As expected, given Ann's hip deformities at birth, Sharon was identical. Her left hip socket had not formed, so the femur was unstable, and her right hip 'clicky.'

On the house front, we launched out again in faith, knowing Ashford would be stretched to pay us. They had also moved in faith with respect to a manse. Some funds were available but a hefty mortgage would be needed. Whilst Ann was still in hospital, recovering from Sharon's birth, we received news that the church had found a bungalow! Not only were they highly sought after, given the proximity of Heathrow Airport and a swift train journey to London, but a very expensive commitment for around forty church members. Faith, allied to prayer, would feature once again as we and the church looked forward to serving together. It was a new venture on both sides - my first pastorate and their first full-time Pastor.

Just three months after Sharon was born, we said goodbye to the last of our miracle homes in Henley. It had been an incredible journey and one that had cemented our life of faith, forged close relationships, and deepened our trust in Jesus as Lord and Saviour of our lives. Our new bungalow was such a contrast to our four storey town house in Queen Street, Henley. There were four bedrooms so all three kids had their own space. Initially, Andy and Tim shared a room so it was Concorde wallpaper on one side and football on the other. Later, Andy would inherit the prized 'dorma' room and Tim would take the smallest, leaving room for Sharon in the middle of the house. Ann and I would inhabit a front room bedroom. A dedicated office was earmarked at the back, overlooking a sizeable garden, with a handy garage for all the stuff that garages hold! With space for two cars at the front, it was a wonderful provision – prayerfully, thoughtfully, and carefully provided.

Early highlights included Concorde viewing for all the family in a field just off the end of the Heathrow runway. Jam sandwiches were generally the order of the day. The spectacular take-off was ear-splitting but never to be missed! Later, as our church organist Ian Kirby was a Concorde flight engineer, we would be treated to a tour of the hangar and an escorted tour of both Concorde and a 747 Jumbo Jet. The comfort difference between the two aircraft was dramatic; a slim, tight cabin and cockpit on the Concorde and room to swing a cat on the 747! Sadly, no free tickets to the States were on offer! One of the quirky facts about Ian was that he drove to work in a three-wheeler Reliant - a la Del-Boy - then climbed into a Concorde cockpit and flew at Mach 2 – 1,522 mph!

The challenge of dual commitments, to both church and college, inevitably resulted in competing loyalties. As ABC was growing rapidly, with all the pastoral care required, it was College that suffered. I was aware of the importance of my Pastoral Studies year and honouring College, but also acutely aware of neglecting our children, juggling church commitments, and supporting Ann. I was also wrestling with the real Terry! College had instilled an image of the omnipotent, all-conquering Pastor available to everyone, every day, at all hours. Capable of leading, preparing the whole service and preaching twice on a Sunday with a midweek Bible Study. Preparation in the mornings and pastoral visits in the afternoon, not forgetting baptism, discipleship, and marriage classes! I had no time to miss the early signs of breakdown.

Coupled with the ministerial false image, I was also to blame. I considered myself super-holy, clearly holier than God! I was made to conquer the world – single handed! I started collecting masks; legalistic actions to cover for weaknesses, mistakes, and inadequacies. I recall a lecturer suggesting we were to be out of our slippers by 8am in case anyone called and saw us unprepared for the day's work. Jeans were considered inappropriate. Football was not kosher on a Sunday, when we also removed the budgie's - a new one, Sunshine - swing. No enjoyment allowed on Sundays! When 'holy' people came to dinner or tea, Christian music would welcome them. All designed to impress the guests and cast a ray of holiness. As for sex on the sofa…! As time wore on so the masks increased and the chains of religious and legalistic falsehood gripped tighter. I could survive intact for now but the bubble would begin to burst, not in a catastrophic explosion but over a period of years.

My biggest regret during these early years was the time I was missing with our boys, Andrew and Tim. Andrew was heading for his teenage years. The time when physical, emotional, and relational needs are colliding. A time when a sensitive and understanding Dad is most needed. In my own teenage years my dad was never there. I had no model to emulate and it showed. The demands of the church family swamped my commitment to my own family. Andrew suffered the most and the gap between us would widen with each year. Added to that pressure, he was a Pastor's kid, expected to conform and obey his parents. Behaving perfectly was mandatory. Attending church and wearing the right clothes was vital for dad's image not his - leg warmers were the precursors to WW3! It took a lot of pain, perseverance, time, love, and forgiveness, to mend the bridges I had never crossed.

25

COMPLETION AND PROPHECY

As 1978 dawned, preparations were in hand for my ordination at Henley-on-Thames BC on June 3rd and induction at Ashford (Middlesex) BC on June 24th. We were grateful for the support of Dr Raymond Brown (College Principal) and Rev Frank Payne (Pastor at Henley BC) who officiated at my ordination. Ray spoke on 2 Thessalonians chapter 2 verses 16-17, 'May our Lord Jesus Christ himself and God our Father, who loved us and, in his grace gave us unfailing courage and a firm hope, encourage you and strengthen you to always do and say what is good.' I trust I have been as obedient as possible, given the frailty of my humanity!

Just three weeks later, Rev Douglas Sparkes (General London Supt.) and Dr Bruce Milne (Spurgeon's College Theology Lecturer) officiated at my ABC induction. It is a joy to reflect here and be reminded that both Ray Brown and Douglas Sparkes were the two brothers in Christ who encouraged and supported me when I began an unconventional settlement at ABC, much earlier than expected!

At the induction, Dr Bruce Milne spoke, in his gentle Scottish lilt, on, 'wat's it all for' - the calling and years of preparation, the hard times and doubts, the sacrifices and prayers, the preaching and service - 'wat's it all for?' With a timely pause, Bruce waited as we wrestled with the answer - 'Aye … the glory of God … the glory of God.' Not self, not celebrity, not accolades and awards, but 'the glory of God.' What Minister or Church could ever say that has always been the goal?

With that inspiring message, my time at college and subsequent ordination and induction were over. After the BA Degree, my Diploma in Pastoral Theology crowned four years of intense learning, important challenges and changes in theological understanding, and a gradual move from self-righteousness to freedom in Jesus. The pastoral apprenticeship would continue in earnest – more challenges, changes and mysteries were on the horizon.

After several months of treatment, it was clear that Sharon's hip problems remained and we would need a referral to Mr Goodfellow's Clinic at the Nuffield Orthopaedic Hospital in Oxford. As he was Ann's consultant, we were assured she was in good hands. Following x-rays, the outcome was clear, she would need traction then frog plaster for three months. This procedure involved encasing her from the chest to her toes! To get around, the hospital provided a glorified skateboard! Sharon was placed on top and honed the practice of pushing herself around! One special occasion, during this time of hospitalisation, was a request from Mr Goodfellow to use Ann and Sharon as examples of congenital defects across generations. Orthopaedic consultants along with student physiotherapists and radiographers from across the world had gathered at the Nuffield for a conference. Mr Goodfellow was eager to point out the specifics relating to both Ann's historic problems and Sharon's present ones. Ann agreed, and she and Sharon were wheeled on the platform together. Sharon soon became the star of the show as she was so cute and happy twisting around on her traction! My 'star' was her mum!

We were so grateful for the specialist care that a dedicated orthopaedic hospital afforded, not least in the guidance given for protecting plaster over a lengthy period. Ann had come across parents whose children were in plaster but had not received proper guidance with respect to sores, smell, and daily care. Simple guidance and aids enabled us to protect the integrity of Sharon's plaster over three months, procedures that also ensured Sharon had comfortable progress along the way. After three months she was relieved of her weighty load of plaster and placed in a reasonably flexible Pavlic-Sling which would keep her legs bent and her hip stable for a further period of four months. Everyone's hope was that this period of intense daily care would lead to another attempt at walking. The Pavlic Sling was finally removed and Sharon began to master the art of walking. Sadly, all too soon, our hopes would be dashed.

At ninteen months, Ann noticed Sharon was limping. We returned to the Nuffield and a further consultation with Mr Goodfellow. X-rays confirmed that all the efforts had been futile and she would require surgery. We knew this might be the case but it was a tough blow. Sharon would undergo surgery very similar to Ann's back in 1947. The outcome would reveal a startling difference in surgical procedure. The hardest part for us was hearing that the procedure would require breaking Sharon's femur so that it could be aligned properly! We were told to expect an unusual angle for her left leg as she was wheeled out of theatre. However, God had other plans.

As we waited for the surgery date, one of Ashford's leaders, Ivor Houchen, visited us. He had been praying and read Psalm chapter 34 verse 20, 'For the Lord protects the bones of the righteous; not one of them is broken.' An Old Testament Scripture with a New Testament prophetic application to Jesus. The standard Roman practice, at crucifixion, was to break the legs of the victims to hasten death. When the soldiers approached Jesus, they discovered he had already died. None of his bones were broken. Ivor believed this word was for us and would be applicable to Sharon - not one of her bones would be broken. We asked our congregation to pray about this. When Sharon exited the theatre, her legs were encased in plaster and they were straight! Mr Goodfellow remarked, 'we didn't need to break her leg!' Six weeks later, we held our breathe as the plaster was cut away. The operation was deemed a complete success. Now the hard work of learning to walk began once again.

Every two years, apart from our time in the RAF, Ann had attended an appointment with an orthopaedic consultant simply to check out her hips. In 1973, she met with Mr Goodfellow at Nuffield. After examining Ann's hips, he was not unduly concerned over the emerging hip pain but encouraged us to return if the pain increased and affected her walking. Shades of visiting the surgeon who performed Ann's operations in 1947, when visiting him in 1963 to talk about our marriage, crossed my mind, 'Do you realise young man, that your future wife will require her first hip replacement in her mid-thirties!' Seven years after our first visit to Mr Goodfellow, in 1981 Ann was experiencing increasing pain in her left hip and we were back at the Nuffield. Mr Goodfellow's primary concern was Ann's age. She was still very young to have a replacement. He encouraged her to hang on, but, 'when you scream, I will operate!' Ann wasn't at the screaming stage but it was not too far away.

26

SPIRITUAL HUNGER AND A SURPRISING QUESTION

One of the immediate observations at church was the number of mature members who were experiencing a renewal of faith and a deepening work of the Holy Spirit in their lives. Across other nations there were increasing stories of similar encounters, with the Spirit of God filling lives and transforming churches in a fresh way. I too was on a journey of discovery. Every book on the work of the Holy Spirit was devoured with increasing hunger but also frustration. I followed the guidelines, prayed the prayers, fasted for days, and listened to the testimonies, but I grew weaker and spiritually dry. I also found myself irritated that people were visiting other churches during the week and coming back to ABC with stories of blessing. I listened through gritted teeth! Why was it that these things always appear to be happening somewhere else? As the remainder of 1977 flashed by, I became unsettled. The 'higher heights and deeper depths' that Cyril mentioned in 1974 were clearly being experienced by some, but in predominately private moments rather than affecting the whole church and, perhaps more importantly the community beyond church. The 'well of living water' was somewhere around the corner but, for me, just out of reach.

Once the pressure of dual commitments to college and church receded, I began to work out what pastoring a church full time looked like. At least my version - 'a la Spurgeon's College! Little did I know I was setting myself up for difficulties down the line. I was so determined to be the model pastor, visiting every home when required or not, being at the hospital at the slightest sign of problems, even getting to new births before the husband or partner - not to be recommended, although Ann loved to accompany me whenever possible - her love for babies knew no bounds! All the above, and more, was the image of the perfect pastor etched on my mind. We had great musicians, a superb youth team, fruitful work among toddler's and pensioners, burgeoning Girls' and Boys' Brigades with a wonderful team, and a great diaconate. The problem was an inexperienced Pastor eager to impress, seven days a week and twenty-five hours a day. Nobody stopped me, and I wasn't about to stop, but a stop would come that left a legacy for life.

On the family front the boys were settled together at home and Sharon was coping well with her frog plaster and skateboard! Ann was at her best, ensuring the plaster was dry and Sharon was comfortable. However, folks at church were not quite so confident or keen to take Sharon in their arms. Her very heavy plaster, and the possibility of dropping her, was sufficient deterrent! However, a few overcame the risks and took her to their heart and home. This was such a joy, and a blessing for both of us, as it allowed a measure of freedom to get on with everything else at home and church.

Andy was brilliant with Sharon. Perhaps a gradual healing time for him following the death of Elizabeth and the burying of emotions. Even into his early teens he loved babies and would readily volunteer for the creche rota at church! Tim was Tim, placid, simply getting on with things, nothing phased him! A trait that would no doubt fit him well for firefighting in the future. As the year progressed so the stories of spiritual renewal increased. I, on the other hand, became more frustrated. Prayer and fasting increased, but the more I hungered for the power of the Holy Spirit the weaker I became. Nothing I could do or pray changed the hunger within. Questions were inevitable. 'Why is your well of living water not here Lord?' 'Why must our church members travel for living water?' 'Why is fasting not producing a noticeable outcome?'

As I was searching for 'living water' a couple in the church were searching for a house. A knock on the door led to a surprising question, 'fancy buying a house?' Bob and Christine Jackson were Anglicans enjoying a Baptist Church! Bob was a deacon and Chris involved in the ladies' Bible study group. Following our induction at ABC they were preparing to move to Nottingham where Bob would begin his ministerial training at St John's Anglican College. They were also praying about investing in a home that would provide holidays for youth groups, families, bible college students, and anyone needing a break. Having already sold their house in Ashford, they could fund 50% of a house in an appropriate area. The budget would be £11,000! Following prayer, we agreed. Just one problem – we didn't have a penny! The journey of walking by faith was about to continue once again. After further conversation we narrowed the area down to North Wales. The plan was for Bob and I to spend three days visiting the perimeter of the Snowdonia National Park. We agreed the date and met early on a Thursday morning for the long drive to Bala, our first stop.

My Bible reading, prior to leaving Ashford, was interesting and would prove to be important. Habakkuk chapter 2 verse 3 'though it tarry, wait for it, for it will surely come.' We arrived in Bala in typical horizontal Welsh rain. Undaunted, our first stop looked hopeful, however as we exited the estate agency door to view a property, the agent said, with a Welsh lilt, 'you 'ave got a Land Rover 'avn't you?' It appears we needed to cross a stream! Though I tried to dissuade Bob, suggesting the girls might not want to ford a small river in the future, he ventured rapidly ahead. After several uphill stages, we arrived at the top of a hill to view a derelict cottage with no roof but a big lock on the door! As we returned, somewhat chastened, our prospective house was sighted in a copse, just in sight of our car – 'though it tarry' came to mind. For the next fifty-six hours we encircled much of Snowdonia without success.

Around 3pm on Saturday, our final day, we were tired and looking towards the last stop and the long journey back to Ashford. By now 'tarry' was not about hours or days but possibly months. We arrived in Caernarvon and what can only be described as a 'Dickensian' estate agent. A handful of black and white photos in the window, linked by cobwebs. One last scan of houses and there it was, a typical Welsh double storey house with a derelict shop attached. It was almost the last house in Goodman Street, Llanberis, at the heart of the Snowdon range. The price was instantly attractive, £10,950! Just £10 below our budget. We agreed to make it our last visit and then make our way home. We met the owner, Mr Parry, at Cambrian House. He then returned to his electrical business as we viewed the property. We were quiet throughout the tour, locked up the premises, and stood outside to pray. 'What do you think?' said Bob. 'I like it' I replied - he agreed. We settled on offering £10,500. If Mr Parry accepted, we would race back to Caernarvon and Bob would put down the £500 deposit. I, on the other hand, would reflect on where I might get my half! After a conversation Mr Parry had with his wife, in Welsh, he held out his hand and agreed the price. We just made Caernarvon before Mr 'Dickens' closed, paid the deposit, and began the long trek home. Tarrying had proved profitable. All I had to do was raise a deposit of £500, and £4,750 on a mortgage!

The first step was an offer from the church to buy our car for £500. My deposit sorted. The second step would reintroduce tarrying again! The Alliance & Leicester initially offered a £4,750 mortgage but after several weeks withdrew the offer. They were concerned about the house being used by youth groups. Two months went by and I became worried for Mr Parry and our agreement. Bob and I agreed a time limit for making contact. If we didn't have the mortgage by a specific date we would have to apologise to Mr Parry and withdraw. The date passed and I had to ring. I explained our dilemma. Mr Parry's response was amazing. 'Now then Mr Jones, we made an agreement, I'll get your mortgage!' I rang Bob, we rejoiced and kept tarrying. Six weeks later, 'ello, Mr Parry 'ere, got your mortgage!' I rang Bob and said 'I think God has just been on the phone.' We duly received the Abbey National cheque! I would need to write another book to tell the story of our twenty-two years of ownership, the hundreds of visitors from colleges, universities, youth groups, church leaders and families, not to mention the couples who fell in love and subsequently married, then returned with their children!

One of our own moments must suffice. It was our first visit to supply beds, get together as two families and start work on making Cambrian House a home for our guests. We had a big, old, Morris Oxford, piled almost to the roof with mattresses, bed linen and food - our £500 'deposit car' courtesy of ABC. Half way up the M1 the Morris died and was towed to a local garage. The head gasket was wrecked and would take two days to repair. We had no money to get home, no money to hire a car and no money to pay for an expensive repair. My first thought was to get in touch with Bob at St John's College and explain our predicament. The garage landline was offered and I got through to the college office secretary. After explaining our problem, I asked whether she could find Bob. She responded, 'I am afraid there are no students in as it is Friday afternoon, but I will go and check.' She opened the office door and almost knocked Bob over in the corridor! He had returned to college, before setting out for Llanberis, and was just popping in to check his post! When God is at work miracles take place. The next was even more wonderful, as Bob spoke, 'I wondered why I had an unexpected cheque in the post this morning. Go and hire a car.' The outcome was slightly comical as we moved the contents of the large Morris Oxford into a small Ford Escort! Andy and Tim spent the rest of the journey on top of the mattresses, almost pressed to the roof, whilst Sharon was on Ann's lap. To cap it all we arrived at Llanberis Pass around 9pm in thick fog, crawled up the edge of the pass, which didn't have the stone edge it has today, and finally arrived somewhat exhausted and hungry. Our tea was sausages prepared on a grill perched over two bricks!

27

DEEPER DEPTHS AND HIGHER HEIGHTS

As the New Year was just around the corner, my thoughts turned to the church tradition of 'looking back' in the morning and 'looking forward' in the evening. 'Back' was relatively easy to prepare as we reflected on what we already knew, allowing us to celebrate accordingly with thanksgiving and praise. However, my evening message was an increasing nightmare. At the beginning of the week, leading up to New Year, I had three words on my heart – 'the new thing.' Across the nation and in ABC the Spirit of God was stirring - now too obvious for me to miss. The problem was that this 'new thing' was not taking place in my study but clearly taking place in the spiritual travellers who returned to church with moving testimonies. I had been labouring all week in Jeremiah chapter 18 verses 1-11, desperately trying to put just one sentence down on paper about a clay pot! At that stage of ministry, if I didn't have the Sunday messages sorted by Thursday night I began to panic - it was now Saturday afternoon! I was tired, stressed, and spiritually as dry as a desert.

I left the study for tea, looked at Ann and said, 'I've got nothing for tomorrow night!' After tea I crawled back into the study and looked down at Jeremiah 18 in my open Bible - I was nearly in tears. As I stared at the page I heard a voice, as clear as a bell, 'you are in the wrong prophet!' 'Well Lord, that's a start, please show me the right prophet!' Contrary to all my training, that you should not select your sermon text by flicking through the Bible, I began to do that - I was desperate! Within seconds, my eyes alighted on Isaiah chapter 43 verses 18-21. 'Forget the former things; do not dwell on the past. See, I am doing

A NEW THING, now it springs up; do you not perceive it? I am making a way in the wilderness and streams in the wasteland. The wild animals honour me, the jackals and the owls, because I provide water in the wilderness and streams in the wasteland, to give drink to my people, my chosen, the people I formed for myself that they may proclaim my praise.' I picked up my Bible, threw it into the air and shouted 'God that's it!'

What happened next was beyond my received teaching, experience, or expectation - I lay prostrate on the floor. Every time I tried to get up and on to my chair I was pressed back to the floor. My message could wait, God's method could not. The weight of God's glory simply kept me in a place of surrender to the Holy Spirit. I had little idea of the time span but it was significant. When I eventually rose, the 'higher heights and deeper depths' that Cyril had mentioned back at Baker-Perkins seemed to express perfectly those awesome moments in the study. When I finally got pen to paper it was the simplest message I had ever written. My extreme dryness had been transformed into rivers of living water just as Jesus declared in John chapter 7 verse 38, 'He who believes in Me, as the Scripture has said, out of his heart will flow rivers of living water.'

The morning at ABC went well but without any apparent spiritual fireworks. I felt so sure about the evening that I encouraged everyone to try and make the service as I felt God had given me a very specific word for the church. We had grown significantly throughout 1978 and I am sure the prayers of those returning with fresh blessing from other churches were for God's new thing at ABC. When I arrived for the evening, the church was already filling and by the time the leaders had finished praying, and we exited our small prayer space, it was full. Well over one hundred had gathered, right across the age range. The atmosphere was electric. I was about to say things I had not planned and to witness things I had only read or heard about from others. I preached with power and authority on the Lord's new thing and the promised rivers of living water he wanted to pour out on us all. When I finished, I said, 'let's wait.' I had never done that before! According to one of my deacons we waited seven minutes!

The silence was broken when Ivor Houchen stood up, came to the front, and spoke. 'Terry has been talking about being dry. I am dry would you pray for me.' Another first was my response, 'would someone come and pray with Ivor.' Ivor was a prison officer. It was another prison officer's wife, Barbara McCulloch, who rose from her second row seat to pray. She promptly collapsed, taking her chair with her! Her husband Tom was sitting on another row, maybe it was the only seat left! As his face went white with concern, I ventured into yet another first, 'it's ok Tom, the Spirit of God has come upon Barbara.' From that moment on, God was in control not me. People asked their neighbour for prayer. Leaders prayed with those who were hungry for the fullness of the Holy Spirit. Heaven had come down on this small 'back street' Baptist Church.

One couple had come with their two young children; a couple we had been counselling and praying with for some time regarding their crumbling marriage. They were so still and appeared to be unmoved. When most of the congregation had left for home, they were still sitting in their seats, even the two young children! I went over, somewhat uncertain of the reception, and asked the husband what he thought was happening during the service. His answer blew me away. 'I saw a thin gossamer sheet over the congregation. Every now and then the sheet dropped on a person, lifted, then dropped on another.' It was the most perfect summary of the action of the Holy Spirit following the seven minutes of silence! One after another experienced 'living water.' The strong touch of the Holy Spirit fell appropriately as one after another responded to His presence. That glorious night would usher in several years of clarity and chaos, hope and healing, but also tragedy amidst triumph.

One beautiful moment of healing occurred the next day. The couple we were counselling were driving to Wales in their minivan. As they proceeded down the motorway the husband slipped his hand into his wife's hand and said, very simply, 'can we start again.' A timely reminder that God's grace gives us chances to respond to Him for the first time or begin over again.

28

SEASONS OF REFRESHING

One of the signs of God's blessing was the rapidly increasing numbers of people coming to Christian faith and being baptised. When I started at ABC, I had a baptismal preparation course lasting twelve weeks! During 1979 we had queues forming and I had to cut the course down from twelve to six weeks! It was exciting to see all ages coming to faith, including two ladies who were baptised in their 80s. What they had missed in 80 plus years they made up for in an amazingly short time. They shared their faith with enthusiasm and joy, bringing other members of their family to know Jesus. Wherever it was possible they served others practically and thoughtfully.

To add to the discipleship options, we also ran marriage courses and bible study groups. One of the most fruitful and exciting groups was 'Nurture-Church' – a basic beginner's course that worked through Mark's Gospel. Several attendees were those who were simply enquiring about Christian faith - a sort of 'not-yet' Alpha Course minus the trendy videos! A good number from that group accepted Jesus as their Saviour, were baptised as believers, and joined ABC.

The marriage course was the most emotional. Couples had a whole day without children, time to reflect in a group, but also together. Working through the teaching often resulted in tears, honesty, and some tough moments as previously hidden or unresolved issues were brought to the surface. The fruit of that course is not easily measured but neither Ann nor I could recall ever witnessing a divorce during the thirteen year pastorate, both as student then full-time pastor.

During the week there was a thriving youth work, both in Girls' and Boys' Brigade and Youth Club, as well as a dynamic Ladies Bible Study. It was especially precious to us when, after the Sunday evening service, young people would congregate at the manse. At times our lounge was overflowing and the youth would end up sitting up the stairs to Andy's room! Some of the rivers of living water would flow into our lounge and touch the lives of teenagers and young adults. Twenty-five years after leaving ABC we were invited to attend youth club reunions. Some of those teens in our lounge had married and now had children. What a joy and privilege, by God's grace, to see something of the fruitfulness of church members who had invested in the youth, as well as our small part in opening the manse at the end of a Sunday. A word of warning, it was all too easy to shut our boys out. To host the youth meant sending the boys to their rooms. While the youth ate the cakes and biscuits our boys sat in their rooms – no mobiles, video games or TV! Hindsight is wonderful, but I would be more careful, much more careful, to include our boys, given a second chance. Still, they did enjoy coming down after the youth had gone and devouring anything edible!

Our boys are fifty-eight and fifty-six as I write. Andy and Tim, I am proud of your journey of life despite my early failures and a few of yours! You have served others in a multitude of ways throughout your working life and continue to do so. Some of those early days were hard and long but you played your part in allowing us to serve others – thank you so much. Many of the youth who arrived on a Sunday evening had questions about what was happening within the church as the Holy Spirit moved among us. A good number became Christians and were baptised as believers in Jesus Christ. Your sacrifice was their gain. Thank you. Dad xx.

The Holy Spirit's work was not just confined to the church

building but at work in homes, community, and work places. These were not only heady days but, at times, totally chaotic. We were in new territory, seeking to understand and embrace all that God was doing - when we had an inkling and when we didn't have a clue! We had not been this way before and learning on the hoof meant mistakes were inevitable. However, I wanted our work to be authentic, genuine, and transparent. There are always charlatans lurking on the edge of blessing, seeking to build a ministry of their own and causing pain along the way. We had a few of our own.

One of the most exciting, chaotic, and unpredictable meetings was the midweek toddler's group. I would spend time mingling and enjoying the atmosphere while Ann and other leaders and helpers chatted to the parents, rounded up young escapees, and served drinks and food. Near the end I would offer a simple communion, sometimes with a short message. It was not unusual to witness the Spirit of God coming upon parents, visitors, and staff as they came forward for communion. At times some didn't make it forward but simply lay on the floor as the weight of God's presence filled the room and fell upon individuals. Taking communion became a mini obstacle course but it didn't appear to phase anyone, even with the chatter and noise. I can't recall any complaints!

When the Spirit of God is at work it is not always neat and tidy! It was also scary at times for me, simply because I was not in control or able to fully understand or explain what God was doing. To some extent, we were all in new territory as God fulfilled His new thing by releasing streams of blessing followed by rivers of life as we embraced the fresh breath of the Spirit of God. The fruit from such encounters, not just in midweek gatherings but in Sunday worship and ministry resulted in consistent increase in church attendance. It soon became obvious that we could not grow the church further without change.

29
NEW MOVES

It is common knowledge that you don't fill the seats you don't provide. Before a church building is full you see a revolving-door syndrome. People arrive and feel nervous about getting a seat. The outcome is that new people come in but don't return. Try as we may we could do nothing to provide a new building. The difficulty in Ashford was its proximity to Heathrow Airport and a forty-minute train journey to central London. Land for any type of building, with commensurate parking, was non-existent. After considerable prayer and discussion, we believed a church plant was the only sensible option. We had gifted preachers, worship leaders and musicians. We also had Christians itching to share their gifts and venture beyond the church building in evangelism and church planting. An area of Ashford, on the border of Sunbury, was earmarked as a district in need of a church and a place where we would not be planting close to other churches. The small Anglican Church, in Napier Road, was no longer is use and was offered to ABC as a venue for a new church – Napier Road Christian Fellowship.

The important principle for ABC was to let go, with our blessing, some of our best leaders and established members. NRCF would not be a satellite of ABC but an independent church forging its own ethos and work. Around twenty people came forward, including four of our church leaders, to begin this pioneering mission. On the 24th April 1983 Napier Road Christian Fellowship was constituted and opened its doors for the first time. It was a time of loss for ABC, that we truly felt, but it was the price we needed to pay to release vision, gifting and evangelism elsewhere. It was also a joy to see, down the line, two of those released leaders, Ron Goddard and David Priddy, becoming ordained Baptist Ministers following ministerial training at Spurgeon's College. Later, NRCF would move to another location and become Ashford Common Baptist Church. An amazing niche work among some of the most vulnerable and needy people, and ably led by David and Eileen Priddy. It continues to this day, forty years on!

30

TIMES OF TRIAL - TESTIMONIES OF CHANGE

It is important not to overstate the extent and impact of this time of renewal and refreshing. Spiritual blessing and deep tragedy are often intertwined; a phone call to the manse that led to the bedside of a dead baby. A last-minute dash to the hospital, urged on by Ann, that meant I made it to witness the sudden death of a Christian brother just minutes after my arrival. The peace of his wife as she thanked me for being with him as he died. A frantic call from a guy, at midnight, as a young mum roared like a lion and slid across her bed hissing like a snake. A spiritual battle in the bedroom accompanied by Caroline Houchen, my pastoral deaconess, before prayer broke the dark atmosphere and peace reigned throughout the family. The guy who hid his abuse of young lads whilst worshipping with us. Visting him in prison following his fleeing to Ireland and subsequent capture. A message, just before starting a Christmas Day service, that a young mum from church had been brutally murdered along with her mother, leaving two young children to escape the attack by their dad. A knock on the door of the manse as two sisters asked for help, one whose fiancé had been murdered by an ex-boyfriend, and she, left for dead with life-threatening injuries. The drama of the high profile Old Bailey trial and, on the last day of the trial the supportive sister telling me she had terminal cancer. Her baptism, weeks later, along with a young lady of fifteen from our Youth Club who had a lower leg amputated because of cancer. The Spring Harvest Christian Conference, just weeks later, when I received news that both had died within eleven days of the baptism. The anger and pain in all our hearts as we tried to make sense of tragedy. The walk around Butlins Camp, with Tom McCulloch, who had shared the baptismal service, as he and I felt the pain and tried to make sense of what had happened. How vital it is that pastors and people understand the importance of a theology of suffering alongside one of healing.

It was also a joy to witness a leadership team embracing the new thing God was doing and growing together in maturity and wisdom. We also needed wisdom and teaching from those who had been on this journey well before us. Douglas McBain, from Streatham Baptist Church, was especially helpful in leading services, training our leadership team, and praying for our church members and visitors. He also encouraged us to attend the John Wimber meetings in London. John had a style that was gracious, gentle, and anointed. As with any American evangelists, there would always be varied opinions for and against. I found him a blessing. His worship leading was sensitive, focused on Jesus and powerful. His teaching and practice were earthed in scripture and very effective. Never had I kneeled so willingly in response to his call for awe, adoration, and surrender in worship. It was as powerful within me as that evening, six years previously, when I lay on my study floor pressed down by the weight of God's revealed glory. Alongside the suffering we also witnessed steady growth in new Christians, believer's baptisms, and some powerful testimonies. A selection of which I have received, or recall, and gladly share to the glory of God.

Debbie Brydon

In 1985 I responded to an invitation, from my neighbour Tina, to attend a seekers group which was being run by Ashford Baptist Church. I had begun to question the purpose of life and felt that, despite having a wonderful husband and two lovely children, there was something missing. Having spent a few months listening to Christians teach me about God, and answer some of my questions, I made the decision to commit my life to Him. I remember thinking, reluctantly, that I ought to attend church now. Having come from a non-Christian background my only experience of church had been of large, cold, dark buildings with dreary music and songs I couldn't sing. The people seemed very serious, quite miserable, and I could never really understand what was being said by the men who wore robes and spoke in funny voices.

So it was, with some trepidation, that I went to church the following Sunday. Imagine my delight when I walked into a small, unassuming, single-storey building, in a residential road, which, although not amazing architecturally, was warm, bright and full of smiling, happy people who were so welcoming. The worship group had drums and guitars so the music was upbeat. Everyone seemed to really enjoy the songs they were singing - including me! This was not church as I knew it but SO much better. When the pastor, Terry, got up to preach, he was dressed in 'normal' clothes and spoke in a way I could understand and so relevant to life. I really enjoyed it.

I had experienced a traumatic childhood which had left me emotionally and spiritually damaged. Terry, along with Caroline Houchen, the pastoral worker, took time to support, teach, and pray with me as I stumbled my way into this new found faith. This was to be the start of a long, and at times arduous, healing journey as I gradually started to understand the father heart of God. Terry baptised me on Easter Sunday the following year.

Terry has such a deep love of people and has an amazing pastoral gift. He will always have a very special place in my heart as he was such an important figure at a defining point in my life. If my first experience of church had not been so positive and helpful, I have often wondered whether I would have managed to persevere in my spiritual life. I have remained with the Ashford Baptist Church family until this day and thank God for all that he has done for me through Terry and others along the way.

Gerry Matthewman

Gerry had been asked to stand for election as a deacon. I asked whether he had been baptised or considered baptism. In his own words, 'I decided to do this in obedience. I wanted to know the power of the Spirit in my life and prayed that I would feel this through being baptised in water.' Following his baptism, Gerry recalls two occasions when this power became evident.

'I was asked to pray with Maureen, one of our church members who had such pain in her back that she couldn't stand up from her chair. I was full of trepidation. Caroline Houchen, our pastoral deaconess, joined me and we laid hands on her asking the Holy Spirit to heal her. I remember the feeling of heat in my hands and then, in what seemed a truly miraculous moment, Maureen jumped up from her chair declaring her pain had gone!'

Gerry describes his second encouragement. 'During Communion on a Sunday morning the deacons decided to take 'stations' at the front and side that would enable the congregation to easily access personal prayer alongside taking bread and wine. One of the people who came to me was Bridget. I asked her if she would like me to pray with her and she said yes. I duly prayed and when I stopped and opened my eyes Bridget was in tears. I asked her if she was ok and she said, 'how did you know all those things about me?' I had no recollection of what I said but realised that the message in the prayer was so private for Bridget. God had spoken to her by his Spirit and I didn't really need to be included.'

Linda Matthewman

Gerry's wife Linda, whose teaching at the ladies Bible study was always inspiring and earthed, also recalls the blessings around ABC's period of refreshing and renewal. 'In the Summer of 1978 I had an encounter with the Holy Spirit. I was at home while my daughter Susie was having a nap and foster son David was at school or playing, (it might have been in the school holidays). I prayed that I would know a touch from the Holy Spirit and know his fullness. I began to praise the Lord tentatively in tongues and after some time I knew a sense of joy filling me. Later in the day our pastoral deaconess Caroline called round unexpectedly and, when I opened the door, she said straight away, 'what has happened to you?' Apparently, she could see from my face and demeanour that I had received a touch from God. That was quite an encouragement because I think we sometimes doubt ourselves and think that 'experiences' are our own imagination. Interestingly, I think Satan was wanting to rob me of this confirmation, because I was very impatient with David about something he did later in the day and I shouted at him, probably unfairly, and immediately felt that I had failed the Lord and that my earlier experience was a sham.' How often do we all feel this way?'

Roy Wharton

These are some of my encounters with the activities and movement of the Holy Spirit during the late 70's and the 80's. At that first meeting at Ashford Baptist Church, with Douglas McBain and his team, I received prayer after which I experienced an upwelling of joy, more an inward chuckle. That experience happily continues to occur on occasions. With the experience comes the sense of the Lord saying, 'It's me Roy, I'm here, and I'm with you!'

During an early visit of John Wimber, at a meeting partly

organised by Douglas McBain, my recurring slipped disc was beginning to play up. Later in the evening, during a time of ministry, a young member of John Wimber's team passed by praying in tongues. As he did so my neck began to ease. After passing by me a second time my neck eased further. Perhaps noticing signs of relief this man asked if his prayers were doing any good. I said yes and he prayed further. Praise the Lord my neck has not locked up since.

At the Wembley John Wimber conference I remember much laughter in the Spirit at one meeting and many people resting in the Spirit at another. It was his lectures and teaching tapes, however, that I found so helpful. Especially the idea that healing was an inbreaking of the Kingdom rather than a consequence of the atonement.

31

BREAKDOWN AND BROKEN!

When I began my ministry, I was a 'black and white' believer. No Catholic could be a Christian. The Authorised Version of the Bible was the only true translation of the original text. Speaking in tongues was demonic and so on. I also believed that Christians should not suffer stress or mental breakdown – until I got there! It was entirely my fault as I thought I was God's gift to the world. Days off- nah. Twenty-five hour days-yeah. Bearing everyone's pain, need and problems - of course. Preparing endless sermons, messages, studies, counselling - absolutely. Dismissing the signs of stress and refusing medication - you get the picture. Then it hit. A facial palsy that screwed up my mouth, displayed intense nervousness, and stopped me dead in my tracks. I could no longer preach or read the scriptures out loud. Eventually I was referred to a Christian doctor who specialised in counselling Ministers who suffered mental and physical breakdown. I was given some powerful drugs that knocked me out! At the same time, I took time out at a retreat home in Hertfordshire, adjacent to the emerging M25 motorway; my afternoon walks were accompanied by the laying of tarmac ready for the future opening - and eventual chaos!

The retreat home was quiet, reclusive, but with prayer from the hosts if sought. It also featured a tape collection on the book of Nehemiah, a template for building in a broken city, which inspired and informed me. I was not to know at the time how preparatory and prophetic those tapes would be. Eventually, I had to return home. As ever, Ann, despite ever-growing limitations and pain, held the family together whilst emotionally seeking to cope with my mental and physical battles. A battle that left a nervous facial legacy that remains, though not as intense, to this day. What an amazing wife God gave me over sixty years ago.

One of the ways I was able to relax, and enjoy time away from the pressures of ministry, was windsurfing. Ashford is surrounded by large reservoirs and lakes, so ideal for learning and improving as sailors and windsurfers. It was not a relaxed beginning! Every time I started out to learn, I was blown into a corner, with no idea how to sail into the wind! Poole Harbour however is perfect for beginners, generally calm and very shallow round the edges, so much easier to get back on the board when you fall in! Younger son, Tim, had been taking lessons with school so I bought a second hand windsurfer and looked forward to a few lessons. 90% of the time I am calm, cool, level-headed, and extremely patient - except when Tim tried to teach me! Tim, this is my unreserved apology! Eventually, I mastered a little bit of the art and began to enjoy my days off at the local lake.

One memory, that was not good for Ann, involved me disappearing into the English Channel, off Exmouth Beach, not intending to head for France! Going out was fine, with a stiff wind giving me an exhilarating and exciting speed. However, I was still a beginner and had not expected the wind direction to change so dramatically and push me well off-shore – I was struggling to return. After several falls, and increasingly difficult climbs back on to the board, I was exhausted. By now I had drifted along the beach front and out of Ann's sight. Eventually, I sat on the board and gave the SOS signal of waving my hands across my head. In time a surfer in a Royal Marines wetsuit circled me with one hand, probably posing, and asked whether I was in trouble! My humiliation knew no bounds as he dragged me back to the beach and a much-relieved wife who had been scouring the sea with binoculars! One further memory was not so humorous, though the newspaper report could easily have been interpreted that way, 'Baptist Minister in wetsuit and slippers in serious crash!' Occasionally, from my study window, I would see the garden trees blowing well in the wind. I could even estimate the force and envisage a good windsurf in store. As a Pastor's life is never 9-5, I would take a few hours off mid-afternoon.

On one occasion I could have easily lost my life. To avoid changing at the lake, I donned my wetsuit at home and put on my slippers. My route was along the Staines by-pass, a dual carriageway leading to the lake. I was doing around 40mph and glanced into my mirror to check the outside lane. I noticed a car coming at serious speed. As I watched in the mirror, almost in slow motion, the car clipped a raised edge adjacent to the barrier. My immediate thought was, that car is about to crash. I thought it was still some way from mine – it wasn't! The next ten seconds I had no idea what happened. I eventually coasted to a halt some distance down the road. When I exited the car, the driver's side was completely smashed, the back had been demolished and the passenger side was full of brick! The windsurfer had turned 90 degrees on the roof-rack and had swung over a railway bridge, and the passenger's side had slammed into the bridge wall!

It was the driver who stopped behind me, and had witnessed what happened, who explained the whole scenario. The woman who was speeding had clipped the central reservation, causing her car to flip right back on itself and begin to roll. He suggested that, inadvertently, I had probably saved her life, as her car began to roll, it slammed into my side – opposite way to mine. This effectively stopped her rolling and flipped the car the right way round. Had I not been there, she would have entered a sequence of rolls. The witness described it as 'two dancers in slow motion'. Unknown to me. my car had slammed into a brick railway bridge then coasted to a halt several metres further on. I went to check on the woman driver. She refused to say a single word! When the police arrived, she refused to speak to them also. Finally, I arranged for her to be picked up by a church member, Ivor Houchen, who took her home, round the M25 to Wembley. Apart from directions, she never said a word to Ivor throughout the journey, and, when arriving home, she was pulled through the front door with not so much as one word of thanks. I, on the other hand, was relieved to have survived without a scratch but felt like a right wally as I stood beside the road explaining to the police my side of the crash. A good Baptist in a wetsuit and slippers, with my board slewed at right angles to the car!

The woman was charged with dangerous driving in her husband's work car and docked points. If it's you, young lady, 'thanks' is still due!' The blue Triumph Acclaim was only fit for the breakers yard and the insurance would not fully cover a similar model. Not long after this disappointment, a church member pushed £800 in cash through our letterbox with a note inviting me to upgrade my replacement model to the CD version! A gold Triumph Acclaim CD was duly purchased and very much appreciated.

32

GLORY DEPARTED?

It was during this time that the intensity of the blessing we had enjoyed from 1978 lifted. One of our church members, Christine Anton, spoke to me about a picture and word she believed God had given her - a word of wisdom that so graphically summed up the lifting of spiritual intensity we had known. It was a picture of an empty canal with very steep sides. When looking at a canal it is impossible, given the dark water, to know quite how deep it is. Christine shared the picture and word she had received from the Spirit of God, 'You didn't realise how deep I had taken you until the water was gone.' For me it was a perfect picture and an important word. Most of the time we were playing in the shallows, unaware of the work God was doing in the depths. Yet God had revealed so much of His glory – His weight of awe and wonder – and, in some measure, we had let it flow out beyond church and into our local community. Whilst the intensity of the Holy Spirit's work had lifted, we were still growing in discipleship, faith, and numbers. Another 'new thing' was emerging.

The space we created when releasing a team to begin Napier Road Christian Fellowship was quickly filled. Once again, we were in danger of seeing the revolving-door experience by not providing space to grow further. It was time to consider another move – into a local school, Clarendon Road Juniors in the centre of Ashford. The Head was eager to help, and there was ample car parking. The downside, experienced by so many churches when moving into a school, was the amount of work shifting gear in and setting up early on a Sunday morning – but move we did!

33

THE OLD BAILEY

We never know, at any given time, what future events are shaped by past connections. Regarding the two sisters who knocked on our door seeking help, whom I mentioned earlier with respect to the trials that we faced in times of immense blessing, I felt it was important to accompany them through the trial. Given the press publicity surrounding the murder of a fiancé, the severity of the injuries inflicted upon the young lady, and the conflicting evidence over a hypo incident, the trial was extremely high profile. The highest judge in the land, Sir James Miskin, the Recorder of London, was the trial judge.

We travelled together to London and had to run the gauntlet of photographers each day. Against the odds, I was allowed to sit with the sisters in court. Given the array of Professors for the prosecution and defence, it was scary to think that the accused, found with knife in hand by a woman police officer, might walk out of court free! The case hinged on whether he had any idea what he was doing! On his first attempt to climb a ladder, in the dark, he had suffered a hypo fit and had to climb down, hide the ladder, and seek help. The outcome is almost unbelievable.

He swayed into the street. At the same time a police car was passing and stopped. The officers realised he was in trouble and took him to Ashford Hospital. Following treatment, the police took him back and dropped him round the corner from the house where they had previously found him. When the police car disappeared, he made his way back to the house, found the ladder he had hidden, propped it up against the wall and entered the home via a small bathroom window. From there he raced down stairs, triggering a panic alarm linked to the police. He found a knife in the kitchen before racing back up, entering the bedroom, and stabbing his rival to death, before turning his attention to the young lady. As he repeatedly stabbed her, a woman police officer entered the bedroom, shouted to the assailant to drop the knife. He did, and it landed point first into the wooden floor and stayed upright.

The trial hinged on whether the hypo fit had so affected the accused that he wasn't aware of what he was doing, despite finding the house again, lifting the ladder, climbing up to a bathroom window and, as a six-foot-four man, climbing through a very narrow opening. Then running down stairs, finding a knife, back up the stairs, accessing the right bedroom to murder one person and leave another near to death. The medical professor for the defence gave such compelling evidence, that I thought, at one point, the accused might walk free. However, at a critical moment in the trial, Sir James Miskin halted the medical Professor, who was in full flow, and asked him to repeat the key evidence he had just given. In a moment of pure drama, the judge addressed the court and the defence witness, 'Sir, I suggest you go home and get your facts straight.' The judge had spotted the flaws in the hypo argument and at that moment I breathed a sigh of relief. I knew for sure what the verdict would be. The jury found the accused guilty of murder and sentenced him to life.

The young lady recovered well and moved to a safe house well away from Ashford. However, the fear of the accused eventually being released, in under a decade, hung over her. Several years into his sentence, we heard he had died suddenly in prison. The relief, for all, was immense.

34

KNOWING ABOUT MURDER!

In a perverse sort of way, the drama of the trial would trace out the next 19 years of my ministry. The high profile of the murder case, and our support, was picked up by our denominational newspaper, the Baptist Times. That article was read by a retired Baptist Minister in Liverpool who was not a member of Toxteth Tabernacle Baptist Church but responsible for booking their preachers. His immediate thought was quite strange, 'if this man knows something about murder, we should invite him to preach at Toxteth Tabernacle!' That was the premise upon which I received a phone call from Harry Tootill, the church secretary, early in 1985, inviting me to preach.

I began to pray about, and ponder over, my response. Why would I travel two hundred miles, from a largely middle class suburban church, to the infamous inner city district of Liverpool? More importantly, what could I say to this small band of believers who remained in the once proud and significant Northern Baptist Cathedral? I politely declined. The week that followed my response troubled me so much that I rang Harry back, apologised, and asked if I could change my mind - a date was set.

On a cold March morning in 1985 we made our way North to Liverpool. The first thing I noticed was the huge, largely incongruous, notice boards outside the church - three names on each. Two would be known throughout the UK, and beyond, as greatly respected theologians, preachers, and authors. The other, sandwiched in between, was me. The boards shouted out to me of a church still trying to resurrect the past glories; the famous Northern Preaching

Centre with Dr Martin Lloyd Jones still invited to speak at the annual anniversary weekend. A church that for over eighty years, up to WWII, had birthed mission churches across Liverpool, sent missionaries across the globe, and packed its 1,800 seats each Sunday. Now an outwardly depressing building with graffiti ridden doors, 'keep out' palisade fences, and side ditches packed with six feet of community rubbish.

The church's last pastor, Alec Judd, moved to Northern Ireland in 1981. Sadly, as he was on his way to his leaving service, the 1981 Toxteth riots began and he was stopped by police from reaching the church due to the fires and dangers on the street. Four years later I turn up to a congregation of around forty in a vast sanctuary, so cold that most people were sat around their own cast iron radiator! Either side of the 'Tab' the buildings had been totally burnt out but, amazingly, the Tab had been spared.

At the beginning of the service, I was invited to stand at the front as Harry introduced me to the scattered saints. What happened next changed my life and that of our family. As I looked around at the remnants of a glorious building, and a proud history, I began to sob. I had always emphasised to Ann, when returning from preaching in similar buildings in London, 'I never, ever, want to accept a call to such Victorian monstrosities, especially those with 'this is the gate of heaven' outside – fortunately not on the Tab! Ann is sitting two rows back, with her hand raised to her mouth, wondering what on earth, or heaven, was happening to me. The same emotion welled up in the evening with a congregation around twenty-five. By the time we arrived home in Ashford we were convinced that we were being called to pray and consider what the Spirit of God was saying to us, and doing in us, with regards to Liverpool.

Following our time at the Tab the leadership contacted us,

asking if we would consider returning to preach again. There was no mention of settlement as their pastor, just another one-off visit. As I had a sabbatical booked, I mentioned it might be upwards of a year before returning. That was not a problem for the leadership. It turned out to be fifteen months with a date booked for June 1986. During those fifteen months we prayed, I read every book I could find on urban ministry and mission and visited a good number of urban churches, seeking wisdom, guidance, and reality. By the time of our next visit, we were in no doubt that God was calling us to the Tab. However, a big shock regarding timing was on the horizon.

If ever there was an opening statement, or a prophetic word, that was unlikely to endear you to settlement as their pastor, I had it. The Tab building was opened in 1871 and in 1986 it was in a parlous state. Rot was rampant, the ditches were choked with rubbish, no water flowed out. It was a picture of decay and neglect, a further derogatory statement to a community that expected the worst not the best. The 3,000 square feet basement was so dangerous, in parts, that you could easily fall through the floor. The multi-brown Willy Woods lounge was a wreck along with various rooms. The balcony windows were rotted and rigid. From a passers-by point of view the building and its palisade fencing shouted 'keep out.' It would have been easy for the dwindling congregation to take my opening word as a reference to the blight of the building – it was not.

I began, 'it is folly to bring a harvest into a rotting barn and it has nothing to do with the building.' Since WWII the church had been dying through division and the rot of self-righteousness. The glory had departed and the light was slowly going out. The remnant who remained received that word with grace and humility, as my reference was not about the building but the health of the Christian community. I sensed a determination, commitment, and will to seek a fresh vision.

At the close of the weekend, the leaders asked us into the Willy Woods lounge. It was a short meeting and to the point. 'We would like you to be our pastor.' One of the Christian friends I had visited, in the previous fifteen months, was my college principal Dr Raymond Brown. Ray knew the Tab and Toxteth well. His key guidance was a simple sentence, 'let Toxteth do the running.' Whilst we were convinced of the Lord's call, I knew the Tab leadership must make the decision. Before we left the meeting, we underlined this to the Tab leaders. 'Our minds are clear, we have been praying, seeking guidance, and preparing for fifteen months. We know this is God's call, it is now up to you.' We left expecting a swift confirmation.

Back in Ashford, the church leaders had been very gracious, knowing our hearts had been beating for Toxteth since 1985. I was so sure of the call that I mentioned, 'I think we will be in Toxteth in a matter of weeks' - God had other plans. As the weeks went by, without a phone call or letter, we began to wonder what was happening. I had to keep faithful to Ray's guidance, 'let Toxteth do the running,' so could not ring or write. The weeks turned into months and the months into years! Along the way I had quietly asked colleagues, who had preached at the Tab, whether they had heard anything - little came back. We had now reached December 1988. It was three years and eight months since we first visited and I wept, and two years six months since our brief meeting in the Willy Woods lounge. We had no idea what had happened. Once again, we realised just how gracious the friends at ABC had been. Keeping us on for almost four years, knowing we were desperate to fulfil God's call to the Tab.

As Christmas drew near, I shared my thoughts with Ann. We had been at ABC since my student pastorate year from September 1975 to September 1976, twelve years, apart from a short break. We had given everything we could and needed a fresh challenge. I suggested to Ann that we pray the Lord would give us something by Christmas. Christmas came and went and my response was to look up and say 'cheers!' However, this was swiftly followed by a revelation to Ann. 'You know what love, I think I can ring' – meaning Toxteth. I rang and the church treasurer, Bill Baker, nearly fell off his bar stool! 'We were only thinking about you a few months ago, whatever happened to Terry Jones?' I was dumbfounded but responded, 'Bill, I don't want an inquisition. Is God saying anything to you now?' 'We must meet' was Bill's reply. Mine, 'That might be a good idea Bill.' Several weeks later, contrary to the usual pattern of the Minister, and any family visiting the prospective church, the Tab leaders came to Ashford and spent the day with us. Signs of hope were now on the horizon. After so many years, when the call to Toxteth never left us, we were now eager to fulfil it.

Throughout the quiet years regarding our call, one of our primary concerns about moving to Liverpool was Ann's Dad's health. He had suffered terribly with his legs. A legacy of his years in the Fire Service when he had so many falls. As we were contemplating the Lord's timing, Jim had suffered a nasty fall and broken his femur, which put immense pressure on Ann's mum Margaret. They had moved back to Leigh-on-Sea from Wokingham, but with Dad immobile, caring for Jim was taking its toll on mum. Six weeks before our meeting with the Tab leaders, Jim was taken into hospital with lung cancer and would not come home. He fought for another five weeks. Literally hours after we said goodbye to the Tab leaders after our meeting in Ashford, Ann received a phone call to say that Jim was unlikely to survive the night. He soldiered on for two more days. Given the enormity of mum's care for Jim, and the toll it had taken, Jim's death was a timely relief for mum. In time she had a new lease of life, energy, and freedom to attend church, join craft meetings, and finally get her choice of décor in the new bungalow - Jim had always called the shots! She was also sensitive to our long journey of waiting to fulfil the Lord's call to Toxteth - she would send us on our way, in due time, with her blessing.

As certain as we were regarding the call, it was clear that it would be, for both parties, a huge step of faith. The Tab was down to around twenty members, and with just three wage earners, no easy way to pay my stipend. There was no manse and little dedicated money to buy one, though there was money in a building fund. However, the call was crystal clear and our pattern of faith-moves was the model we would obediently and willingly follow. We would make the move and look forward to the many ways God would provide, both for us and the Tab.

Finally, after a last-minute request from their leaders to go and pray at our church, the agreement for us to proceed was finally sealed. I subsequently learnt that the Tab leaders returned to Liverpool with a degree of concern about where we would live and how we would be paid! Yet, more concerning issues arose when I informed the North West Baptist Superintendent of our plans!

35

OPPOSITION, PROVISION AND COMPLETION

Just when we least expected it, and after years of uncertainty, another twist in the story emerged. The Baptist Superintendent for the North West wrote a sharp letter forbidding us to proceed. 'Under no circumstances whatsoever are you to go to Toxteth' – wow! I wrote back, 'after four years of waiting do you not think there might be room for grace?' The reply was underlined in double red (in my day the colour of offence), 'there is absolutely no room for grace, you are not to go!' I was relieved, some years later, to receive a letter from the new Superintendent which stated, 'I want you to know that I do not concur with my predecessor's remarks.' The letter, demanding we do not go, caused a lot of pain, tears, and frustration, but we prayed and proceeded. We set the date for moving – August 1989. An initial house provision, that we knew nothing about, was being prepared via our eldest son Andy!

We owe a great debt of gratitude to Ashford BC for the patient and prayerful support they had given us over four years. They knew, on our return from Toxteth in March 1985, that our hearts had been moved and were set on responding to God's call, yet there was never a moment when we felt we were under pressure to leave. We had travelled together, in the best of times and the worst, and finally God's timing prevailed. Our leaving was not just from ABC but the Thames Valley Baptist Churches, of which I had been secretary for over a decade. I had forged close relationships with some of the Ministers and counted them friends. Two of those Ministers, David Ollerton and Paddy Beresford, and their churches – Esher BC and Walton-on-Thames BC, would have a profound influence on our, and Toxteth's ability, to sustain our work over the long haul – an amazing story to come!

ABC also had strong connections with a small group of churches in our locality. We had joined with King's Church Staines Congregational in opening 'Canaan', a Christian Bookshop in the centre of Staines, on Saturday 3rd November 1979. Roy Castle agreed to officially open the shop, staying around for two hours to sign copies of his book. We have a great picture of our two boys standing next to Roy and his trumpet touching the tip of Sharon's nose! Under the long-term guidance of the manager, Andrew Gilmour, Canaan continues to serve the local community forty-four years later, not simply as a Christian bookshop, but a place of welcome, counselling and administration of small and large Christian events.

It was clear that we would be saying our good-byes in more than one venue! The final meeting, based at King's Church, was so powerful, prophetic, and inspiring. Many individuals gave us scriptures, pictures, prophecies, and blessings that were crucial at our leaving, but also in the years to come. Time and again, in the future, those accurate words would sustain us in the hard times and inspire us to keep going. Though not exhaustive the list that follows gives something of a flavour of God's directing and encouragement at that final meeting.

2 Timothy 2:15 - God has tested you and approved you.
Jeremiah 29:11 - He knows the plans.
Deuteronomy 28 - The blessings of obedience.
Isaiah 1:19 – A promise we have received many times.
Jeremiah 1:17-19 - Courage and protection.
Isaiah 58:11-12 - Rebuilding, restoring, refreshment - given many times over the years.
A prophetic word given - 'Be careful how you build ... my heart delights at the building we shall do together.'
Acts 15:12 - 18 - Rebuilding in the kingdom.

A prophetic word given - 'We shall sail together. Look for the wind. Catch the breath of God. Take care how you build.'

A picture given - 'Human dereliction; someone picking up stones and putting them together. A builder-repairer.'

Exodus 25:9 'Make sure you build according to the pattern I show you'. This was the text on the front of a booklet I produced after twelve years in Toxteth.

I had based a lot of our vision and work on the book of Nehemiah. Jerusalem in 445BC and Liverpool in 1989 were alike. Cities under siege, full of human dereliction, fear, physical destruction, pain, loss of pride and identity. After twelve years seeking to rebuild, restore faith and overcome constant opposition, Nehemiah reported back to King Artaxerxes who had made possible his work in Jerusalem. We too would replicate Nehemiah's 'report-back' – an amazing story just about to fully emerge!

Finally, it was time to say goodbye to ABC after thirteen amazing years of association as student pastor, visiting speaker and full-time minister. We could not have asked for a more loving, gracious, patient, generous and spiritually blessed company of Christian friends. We had navigated immense pain, rejoiced over deep spiritual growth, outgrown the church building, moved into a local school, started a new church, baptised over a 100 new Christians, married a host of couples, and witnessed three colleagues heading for training to become Pastors. Some of my friends from college had experienced very difficult first pastorates. We were deeply grateful to have had such an amazing apprenticeship into Christian Ministry. Almost thirty-five years later, and in a new church building, we always enjoy renewing friendships, hearing of those who have moved on, remembering those who had died, and being introduced to new faces. What a joy to be inspired by their new Pastor, Danny, and observe a church of different nations clearly growing in discipleship and numbers.

36

DÉJÀ VU AND DIFFICULTIES

As we prepared to move, Andy, now twenty-three, had moved jobs from Datasolve in Ashford, working as a Network Analyst, to Nabisco in Reading in the same role but gaining a huge increase in pay. Sue Gollaglee, the young lady he was dating, was moving to Liverpool from Manchester to train as a teacher at St Katherine's College. Andy suggested she look for a property - he would buy it, and she could rent it. A suitable home in Wavertree was duly purchased and rented out to Sue. However, long-distance relationships are never easy, romance didn't blossom, and the relationship petered-out.

After eighteen months with Nabisco, Andy was made redundant again and decided to move North to Liverpool and into his Wavertree home, just a stone's throw from Penny Lane. Very quickly, he obtained work as a Systems Analyst with the Royal Life Insurance Company, working out of the 'Sandcastle' – Scousers typically give nicknames to all sorts of city establishments. The building is castle like and sand coloured hence the nickname!

His next romance was in a kid's pool in Gran Canaria where Andy and his best mate Rob had booked a holiday. Rob spotted a stunning young lady, cooling off in the kid's pool. She attracted Rob's attention. He suggested Andy make her acquaintance! Evidently, she was so tanned that his first question was, 'are you English?' Not a usual chat-up line but it worked. Their first date was arranged on holiday and, on return to the UK, Andy paid a visit to Sue's home town of Sunderland - romance blossomed.

As this point, we stepped in and asked Andy about a rental of his house at 22 Hillingdon Road, near Penny Lane. We were praying about renting a halfway house, prior to finding a home in Toxteth. As ever, in God's economy, the timing was perfect for us and not simply a coincidence. Henley had forged a journey of faith, with regards to house provision, and given us a spiritual template that we would follow for the next thirty-five years! The Tab leaders worked out a rental agreement with Andy, we moved in, and the search for a suitable home in the Dingle area of Toxteth began.

Andy sold Hillingdon Road and bought another home not far away, where he stayed for a year. When redundancy arrived again at Royal Life, he sold up and moved to Sunderland to be with Sue. Two years after meeting, on 25th July 1992, Andy & Sue were married at Sunderland Registry Office, followed by an exchange of vows at Lumley Castle in County Durham. It was my joy to lead the ceremony and Rob's to deliver the best-man's speech. It remains the most honest, sincere, and risqué best-man's speech we have ever heard. Thirteen months later, on 11th August 1993, their first and only child, and our first grandchild, Ben, was born.

One of the things we love about Andy is his perseverance and determination to overcome challenges, especially with respect to redundancy. Since he was fifteen, and on a Youth Training Scheme, right up to the present day, he has never failed to find a job. With his passion for football, his dream job opened up in Sunderland. Staff were being sought for Sunderland FC at the new Stadium of Light. He was duly recruited and so began a twenty-two year period of work in the ticket office. As in every port-city, not least those which have suffered mass dock closures and unemployment, football is often the lifeline of a close community - allegiance runs historically deep through generations. Andy found his extended family at Sunderland FC and soon adapted to the 'Mackem' dialect, though calling mum 'mam' took Ann some time to accept! Sadly, redundancy beckoned again when Sunderland plummeted two leagues and were forced to cut back drastically on staff. Battles with mental health followed, and were not helped by Covid and a spate of relatively short-term jobs. On the plus side, several of his close friends in the 'Mackem' family gave him superb support and encouragement. As parents we were, and still are, deeply grateful for the love, guidance and friendship shown to Andy at a very difficult time in his life.

Back to Liverpool, as we were discovering a temporary home, via one son, we were depriving the other of a home in Ashford where he had lived for the past 11 years! Usually children leave their parents, we were leaving Tim with a mattress on the floor of the manse and not much else! Such moments are written into family folklore but were not easy for either of us. Suffice to note, Tim was taken in by a friend, who also had a frame for his mattress! I think we have been forgiven!

Tim had begun an apprenticeship in printing at seventeen but found the shop floor equipment dangerous and the work unfulfilling. He was at home one evening and shared his frustration and despondency. At the same time Ann had been reading the local free newspaper and spotted an advert for the Fire Service. She mentioned this to Tim and showed him the advert. He said he had always thought about becoming a firefighter but didn't think he was tall enough. We stuck him up against the kitchen door, got the measure out and discovered he was just the minimum height required to apply. He was quick to fill in the application and, to all our joy, duly accepted for training at the Surrey Fire Service in Reigate on July 4th 1988.

Following the completion of the sixteen week course, he was assigned to Staines Fire Station, just a couple of miles from Ashford, so an ideal posting. During his first couple of years, he completed the Fire Service Physical Training Instructors course, during which he broke the Surrey Fire Brigade 'dirty dozen' circuit record. His prowess reverberated around the Fire Service community! One of his scariest moments was high up on a ladder which was resting against the Round Tower on the night of the Windsor Castle fire. Tim was at the top, with a hose, spraying into the raging abyss. He could feel the wall moving!

On the romance front, Tim met Sheila at a friend's work night out in August 1988 and a courtship began, eventually leading to their marriage at Ashford Baptist Church on 26th June 1992. Tim had been baptised at ABC, but like so many teens, had drifted away following our move to Liverpool. Their first child, Tierney, was born on 10th January 1995 followed by Aaron on 13th July 2000.

Aaron developed major eye complications near his right eye, just weeks after birth. Blood vessels began to swell and move across his face towards the nose. He was diagnosed with 'Infantile-Haemangioma,' a benign non-cancerous growth that can diminish over time. Sadly, the growth continued and he was admitted to Moorfields Eye Hospital in London. During an operation his eye membrane was split and he lost sight in the eye. Almost overnight aged five, Tierney became the most efficient and caring nurse! I am pleased to report that Aaron's left eye is so perfect he drives a car and plays darts like Luke Littler, well, not quite that good! It was a heartache for all of us when both Andy and Tim's marriages broke down with all of the complications that follow divorce. We remain friends with Sue and Sheila. Both Tim and Andy would move on to new relationships but no further children.

Sharon was just twelve so would be moving with us to Toxteth. This was our greatest concern and battle. There was never any doubt in our minds that we needed to do what no Pastor at Toxteth Tab had done in one hundred and eighteen years – live in the inner city right at the heart of the community we would serve. Not just any urban inner city community, but one devastated by riots in 1981. The butt of national jokes, riddled with drug gangs, noted by the tabloids as lawless and, with the rest of the city, stigmatised by people, press and politicians. According to Margaret Thatcher, and certain members of her Cabinet, the right course of action was to starve the city of finance and pilot it through a 'managed decline.' Mercifully, one Minister of her cabinet, Secretary of State for the Environment, Michael Heseltine, thought otherwise. Dubbed 'Minister for Merseyside,' he visited Liverpool, walked the streets, talked with locals and reflected on the city's proud maritime history, grand buildings and future prospects. When viewing the derelict wasteland of the Albert Dock - the largest collection of Grade One listed buildings in the UK - he declared, 'this is where we need to start.' Thirty-eight years later, he said of the city's renaissance, 'it was the pinnacle of my career.'

As we began our move in 1989, parts of Toxteth were still considered 'no go' zones. The renaissance had begun, but the jokes still lingered; 'if you fly over, you will lose your watch, if you drive through you will lose your wheels.' This was the destination for our daughter, along with inner city schooling and a southern accent. The journey would not be easy for us or for her, but the outcome would be an amazing story!

It was a strange experience for me, as I had grown up a stone's throw from the now famous Penny Lane and just around the corner from Andy's first home. I was returning to my formative roots but also many painful memories.

For Ann and Sharon, it was a move into the unknown and unfamiliar.

Once the invitation to the pastorate had been sealed, early in 1989, we travelled to Liverpool to search for schools. St Hilda's and Archbishop Blanche were the two Anglican schools nearest to Toxteth and top of the search list. Our first appointment, at Archbishop Blanche, was less than helpful. After an initial conversation, whilst Sharon was shown round by a pupil, the Head announced, 'well, we don't have places anyway.' On the other hand, St Hilda's Headmaster went out of his way to accommodate Sharon. This school was Sharon's much preferred choice, which was sealed by the Head's final comment. 'If I can't find a place for a Minister's daughter, that would be a great pity.' It was a relief to know Sharon would enter a school with a fine reputation and one which would train her so well for university, teaching in London, and long-term mission in Peru.

At the end of August 1989, we moved into Andy's home and began our orientation and preparation for induction at the Tab, or as locals would say 'the Tabby'.

37

PREPARATION, PARTNERSHIP AND PROBLEMS

As I prepared for my first year in Toxteth, the fruit of patient waiting would now be realised. During our four year wait, knowing God had clearly called us to Toxteth, I had been busy preparing. I read many urban mission and ministry books, visited urban churches, and learned much from long-term urban ministers whose wisdom, guidance, warnings, and encouragement, were especially pertinent. 'Go and bury your head and don't let me hear of you for ten years,' was Dr Colin Marchant's wisdom after decades in the inner city of London. In other words, prepare for the long haul. Do your work without fanfare. Don't parade your vision ahead of time, because urban life and ministry is costly and ought to be lengthy. My 'breakdown' studies, several years before, in the Old Testament book of Nehemiah, would prove priceless; a route map for navigating a long ministry in a tough environment.

The first applied value from Nehemiah was a degree of 'hiddenness'. When Nehemiah arrived in the burnt, broken, and battered city of Jerusalem, he announced, 'I told no one what my God had put into my heart to do for Jerusalem.' Nehemiah chapter 2 verse 12. My four years of waiting had given me time to pray, read, and reflect on the nature of my ministry once I arrived in Liverpool. I had read a good number of books about the history, culture, and demise of the city, also Christian books written prior to, and following, the 1981 riots. To complete my preparation, I read W.P. Lockhart's autobiography and history of Toxteth Tabernacle. He was the founder and first pastor of the Tab. Much of the vision he had in 1871, would be put into practice in my own ministry.

I was clear in my own mind that pastoring in Toxteth would look vastly different to that in Ashford. ABC was ready for growth, the Tab had suffered decades of decline, division, and physical decay. I was part of building an expanding, young church in Ashford. At the Tab I was called to turn the building inside out, respond to community need, as opposed to church priorities, and work on a vision that would enable the church to grow and not die.

My initial message to the small, but faithful leaders and congregation, was one of hiddenness and patience. My first year would be one of visiting throughout the community, listening carefully, and preaching strategically from the book of Nehemiah - the exciting spiritual blueprint for urban service, mission, and ministry. Nehemiah, the city builder, assumed nothing until he had surveyed the challenge, heard the cry of the people, felt their need, and assessed the plan of action. He would also become realistic about the opposition and obstacles on the journey of rebuilding.

In the meantime, we continued our search for a home in the heart of the community and trusted that God's provision for both home and stipend would be revealed at the right time. The issue of finance turned up within a month! David Ollerton, pastor of Esher BC back in Surrey, rang to ask how things were going. My answer included four issues:

- We are not sure we can be regularly paid.
- We presently have no home in Toxteth, and unsure where money will come from to buy one.
- The Baptist Superintendent told me, 'Under no circumstances whatsoever are you to go to Toxteth.'
- The Baptist Home Mission Fund, that might have supported me, could not. With just three wage earners, they believed there was no viable future. Otherwise, David, everything is fine!

His response was precise, straightforward, affirming, and encouraging. 'Here's the deal, £300 a month in the first year, £200 in the second and £100 in the third, after that you are on your own.' Once again, faith in what could not be seen resulted in that which could. It was a wonderful reassurance to us but also to the Tab leadership. They had stepped out in faith, like us, and this provision blessed them and our small congregation.

Just weeks later, I had a phone call from Paddy Beresford, pastor of Walton on Thames BC, the church that had planted Esher. 'I hear David Ollerton is supporting you, might we?' I always joke, 'well definitely not Paddy!' The deal would be identical to that from Esher. Once again, I would report to the leaders that we now had another £300 a month towards our stipend. £600 a month from two churches 200 miles away. Amazingly, Walton BC were still sending us £300 per month ten years later! On paper, as the treasurer would occasionally tell me, 'We are not sure we have your stipend this month.' 'Par for the course', was my stock reply. The miracle was, ten years later we were paying up to eighteen full and part-time staff! That story is waiting in the wings, so please keep reading!

38

EARLY MISTAKES 1990-1991

What do you do with a building that makes so many negative statements? 'Please keep out' states the menacing palisade fence. 'Come in'... if you dare climb the forbidding and cracked steps. The Tab was known locally as the posh Church, where the majority of the congregation commuted from the more affluent suburbs. For many it was the epitome of a past age, an irrelevance to a post docklands community; a social, financial, and even spiritual liability.

The answer was clear, bring it down - now! We had commissioned a report on the building, the last line of which stated - 'close down now!' Dreams were dreamt. Plans were made. Architects were employed. Vast new premises were proudly unveiled to a small congregation via the architect's plans. Large sums of money passed lightly across our lips, but try as we may it would not come down! We were too hasty, perhaps too big for our boots, too presumptuous, too proud. Instead of small steps of faith that build strong spiritual muscle, we assumed we could take a giant leap of our own, way ahead of time.

Two visitors to our Sunday services, one in the morning and one in the evening, put us back on track. The morning word was a picture. A huge crane with a ball on the end, the sort that demolishes buildings in a few crushing swipes, heading for the Tab. The visiting prophet sat down. Two people, in unison, urged a vocal reply, 'what happened?' A two word reply came back, 'it missed!' The evening word was equally straightforward, 'God says, take your hands off the building and I will show you in due time what I will do.'

At our Monday leader's meeting we reflected on what we had heard. How could we miss or dismiss such clear prophetic guidance. We folded up the plans, paid off the architects, and said sorry to the bemused church. Proverbs chapter 16 verse 1 is very simple and very clear. 'We may make our plans but God has the last word.' A new church building was not the obedient step that God had outlined for us in Exodus chapter 25 verse 40, 'Make sure you build according to the pattern I show you,' but a timely lesson in taking things slowly, building step by step, and waiting for God's perfect timing. A 'new build' will come, but not under my watch.

The lesson outlined, soon bore fruit with respect to grant funding. I had previously, and proudly, announced to the Barings Bank Trust Manager, Mike Butterfield, that we were looking at a £1.5 million new church building project. I was so sure that he would be mightily impressed but he dismissed it out of hand with a blow that crushed my spirit but quickly informed my mind! When humility returned, I approached him again about a much more sensible and manageable second step in our response to a community survey – a coffee shop. He visited within a week and, after a brief conversation about our plans, granted us £15,000 on the spot! Presumption and pride are subtle enemies for a visionary! I had learned a vital lesson.

39

STRATEGY, SURVEY AND SIGNS

It was interesting to note that our arrival in Toxteth coincided with two other Pastors accompanied by church planting teams. Both were beginning a new work from scratch. One would survive, flourish, and become a blessing to the city and its churches. The other, arriving with fanfares, big plans, and massive initial growth, would eventually implode and disappear. I had the unfortunate experience of receiving leaders from that church, who announced they would be planting a new church in the Dingle ward of Toxteth. At that time money was pouring into Toxteth in response to the needs highlighted in the 1981 riots. I encouraged them to discern where might be a suitable area to reach, also, to respect the churches in that locality. They could not have been more arrogant or disrespectful. Within months, they began their work right next door to a local, evangelical church. Within six months, they came back to visit me and announced, with a degree of venom, 'these people are animals, we can do nothing here!' They assumed they could waltz into a community without the hard miles of listening, learning, and an overdose of humility - love and respect didn't feature. Such soulless strategy never bears good fruit. The collapse of that church was no surprise to me, especially when grant money muddies the water.

I began my mission by listening and learning from the perspective of the street not the church. Very early after arriving at the Tab, one of the leaders, Joyce Ritchie, shared her frustrations regarding the setting up of a Mums and Dads Tot's group. It just wasn't working. I asked her if she had taken a picture from the street. It is easy for churches to assume they know what the community needs without asking the community! Mums, Dads and Tot's is a middle class model. The expectation is that parents will accompany their children, then read or play with them before going home together. We vowed not only to visit our community but ask, via a survey, what the needs were from their viewpoint. We had a few surprises regarding training requirements. 'I would like to be a ballerina, solicitor, accountant,' and a few more outrageous responses, but, overall, the results from the survey were conclusive. Some of those results would, with reflections from my personal visits across Toxteth and input from leaders, set the vision of the Tab over the next fifteen years.

Two of the top responses were a playgroup and a café. A playgroup where children could be left, giving mum or dad an opportunity to find full or part-time work or training or, perhaps, simply go home and care for the rest of the family. For some parents it might mean a break from the rigours and challenges of living in a tough urban environment. The picture from the community, as opposed to the church, simply revealed a small shift in understanding from, doing something *for* them to doing something **with** them, and most difficult for churches, doing something *of* them – embracing their vision of what was needed, not ours. We had listened carefully, prayed strategically, and responded willingly. Huge faith steps would be set in motion to provide a playgroup, then a café, and as I love to declare - in time, a restaurant!

To begin a playgroup, we needed around £35,000 to transform a large hall into a multi-purpose space. We would need paid and trained staff as well as volunteers. All legal and statutory requirements, which were many, needed to be in place and a stack of new equipment bought. For a church wondering about paying their pastor and financing a manse, it was a huge leap of faith but one we knew was the right move at the right time. However, it was not just a playgroup we were seeking, but an opportunity to employ local people and offer NVQ training in childcare. Planning and resourcing, of course, takes time but the dye was cast. For Joyce Ritchie, as a retired trained nurse and midwife, it was a natural step to move from trying to run a struggling tot's group to taking a lead in a future playgroup.

To facilitate this, and future projects, the Tab set up 'Toxteth Vine Project,' an umbrella organisation for the vision the Lord was gradually unveiling. Around the same time, Richard Steele, one of the Tab leaders, had a picture for the whole church that would encapsulate God's new thing among us and out to our community.

Richard's story:

(Notes for a display on the 150th anniversary of Toxteth Tabernacle August 2022 with minor adjustments and additions from Terry.)

This picture stems from a time when the Tab had gone through a major restructuring and redirection in the mid to late 80s and early 90s. A lot of people had left the church in the mid 80s, following a discussion about whether we should close completely. The remaining small group recognised a call from God to remain, but focus much more on the local community rather than the preaching centre/commuter and student church that the Tab had become.

The building was a major concern, with rainwater pouring in, a lot of dry rot, and very outdated and dangerous plumbing and wiring. The remaining group had managed to raise funds to refurbish what is now referred to as the pre-school hall, together with the rooms above. The remnant members of the Tab were meeting there, considering the long-term view that the hall should remain and the rest of the building demolished.

Into all this, the church had appointed a Pastor, Terry Jones, together with his wife Ann and daughter Sharon. Funds were not available to support them, so we were reliant on the generosity of two Thames Valley churches, Esher and Walton Baptist, who had stepped in when they heard Terry's story. It is therefore easy to appreciate, that at that time, there was a lot of concern amongst the church members about what the future would hold, and indeed whether we really had a future! Had we bitten off a lot more that we could chew?

One Saturday I was driving in North Wales, with some time to spare in the afternoon, and I decided to walk up to Aber Falls. I was thinking a lot about the church, when at the side of the path a tree caught my eye. The tree had been huge, but all that was left was a stump. From the middle of the stump there was tender new growth – a small but very vulnerable sapling. As I looked at it, God started to speak to me about our future together. The salient points were:

1. Here was new life coming from an old root stock. The tree had fallen but was still able to provide a firm and secure foundation for the new sapling.

2. The new tree shared the DNA of the old. The founding vision of the first Pastor, William Peddie Lockhart, together with that of the first elders and deacons, continues to flow through the church and it is remarkable in reading Lockhart's story to discover that he founded the church to meet the needs of the local community as the streets around were still evolving.

3. The new sapling was extremely weak and vulnerable, needing the shelter and protection of the other trees around, speaking to us about the importance of having other more mature churches

around who could support us, and not feeling any guilt in accepting that partnership. Over time Esher and Walton churches went on to provide significant financial support over many years. They also provided, prayer and music teams, working parties and skilled professionals to help renovate the building. It is worth mentioning Mike Denham who worked on transforming the basement into the space we needed to run Level 3 Skills School, and Richard Toms who rewired the building. Following that, other groups have helped us from time to time. Norman Hamilton from Belfast associated with Jesus in the city, Bloomfield Presbyterian Church and Queens University Christian Union all come to mind. Later, First Baptist Church, Zephyr Hills, Florida, sent teams, finance, and hosted a return visit for Terry and Ann, when on sabbatical. YWAM (Youth with a Mission) teams from the US and UK would come to support the Tab with mission on the streets - First Steps Mission.

4. Whilst the DNA was shared with the former tree, the new sapling would grow to reflect the environment of today. It would be shaped by the prevailing winds; its growth rings would point to the lean times and the times of growth and plenty in which it had matured. In the same way the new church growing from the old foundation would reflect today's physical and spiritual environment and should be ready to understand and adapt to what is going on around it. It needs to remain flexible and avoid becoming a rigid and dying structure which would ultimately lead to its demise.

As I had, for many years, been interested in photography, I had my camera and tripod with me so took a picture of the tree, which, on sharing with the congregation of the time, helped us to appreciate that we did have a future within God's plan and that we should continue to value the past history and ethos of the church, whilst it was ok to move on and adapt as we mature into being salt and light in the world of today.

Richard also brought to the church a challenging and prophetic word about 'sharing nothing' at a time when our resources were consistently on the debit side! He directed us to I Kings chapter 17. Here Elijah asks a widow for the 'nothing' she has - a meagre last meal before death. As that 'nothing' was shared, so together, Elijah and the widow discovered God's abundant supply. Our task was to identify a church with nothing and give them our nothing! Not a very hard task at all!

Following this word, we heard about and contacted a church in Bristol which had just lost their building through vandalism, had their pastoral monetary support stopped, but whose Minister, Ian, felt they should stay with the handful of people God had given them. Though we had no idea what 1 Kings 17 would mean we gave them the text and little else! Within weeks we received a gift of £3,500 and God prompted us - 'remember Ian.' So began a few years of sharing low key support, mutual visits, times for prayer and encouragement. Nobody was acting as big-brother telling the other how to do it - we didn't know anyway! We simply shared our hearts, divided our resources when God prompted, and generally did all we could to bless one another. Like many other partnerships, it was for a season.

Primarily such partnerships have been about people who have shared their lives, prayers, and gifts with us. Students who have sacrificed their lives away from the trendy, large student churches, leaving something of value in the heart of the inner city. Many have endeared themselves to local families and individuals by their simple love, persevering service, and genuine concern for people - class and culture have been invisible in such a climate. Others, such as our Careforce workers - Iesah, Peter, Jo, Kate and Amy, who invested a year serving the church and community. Some have experienced the Jeremiah call; 'build houses, settle down, plant gardens, marry, have sons and daughters, seek the peace and prosperity of the city to which I have carried you. Pray to the Lord for it, because if it prospers, you too will prosper.' Jeremiah chapter 29 verses 5-7.

40

PROBLEMS, POLICE, AND 'PASTY'

Houses feature throughout our life story, but none are as dramatic as 19 Glendale Close. A couple of months after arriving in Liverpool, we began the search for a home. Estate agents were combed carefully but it was a free newspaper through our door that gave us the breakthrough. The advert we focused on, featured a semi-detached, three bed house in the Dingle Ward of Toxteth, around a mile from the Tab and Sharon's school. All the information in the advert fitted our requirements, just one thing would help – a tree! Being an avid gardener, wanting to bring colour to the urban environment was important, but it was a copse of trees that would signal the right place.

As we journeyed for a viewing I said to Ann, 'if you see a tree opposite the house that may be a good sign we are in the right place.' As we turned into Glendale Close, right opposite number nineteen was a small copse! I asked for one tree, but God gave us a mini wood! We also spotted a small garden front and back. Entry to the house was somewhat confusing. It was like something out of Vogue; lavish drapes, huge TV, plush sofa, beautifully and stylishly furnished throughout. A single mum with a toddler, duly showed us around.

We had peace that this home would be ideal for us and reported back to the leaders. Whilst the church did not have a fund for a house, it did have a building fund, believing that a new building would be required in the future. After consideration, the leaders agreed to apply the building fund to the purchase.

None of us knew anything about the history of the home. The site of the estate had once been that of an Oil Terminal with a service jetty on the river. The Southern Fever Hospital was a few yards up the road. When both were closed, the land was cleared and an estate planned. Most would be council or housing association property, but the eighteen houses in Glendale Close were privately built and owned. Number thirteen was missing and would cause us problems when seeking to complete the deal! Number nineteen could not possibly exist in a Close with only eighteen houses!

As we visited the home again, to agree terms, we were greeted by three guys along with their sister - the young mum who had showed us around. They were very civil and courteous. The presence of a Rolls Royce and Porsche outside certainly made us think! We duly completed the purchase, and moved in mid-1990.

The first hint of problems was a conversation with neighbours regarding the history of the property. They informed us that the house had been raided several times by the police. It was owned by a band of brothers involved in massive drug dealing, three of whom I had met! Further insight was gained when the house surveyor visited and related the tale of surveying the loft timbers prior to the sale. His colleague had opened the loft and immediately called to the boss to come and look. The surveyor described it as, 'the size of a Corn Flakes box which would take 48 packets of the largest flakes – brick-size wads of money wrapped in cellophane.' and according to the surveyor, 'in excess of £1,000,000!' He ended the conversation, 'we closed the loft and took advice!'

A couple of months later, we were suddenly awakened by noises at the front of the house. I jumped out of bed, opened the curtains, and saw two armed police on our drive and two further armed police next door. I ran downstairs, in my pyjamas, just in time to stop the door being kicked in, and exclaimed, 'they are not here!' Clearly, the police had not done their surveillance homework. I expressed my fear that they would burst in and discover that we had a thirteen year old daughter in the house. I was told that they had no forwarding address for the gang so had to presume they were still at number nineteen! It took us a year, and a good friendship with a Community Police Officer, to finally convince the Police HQ that the gang had moved on and a 'Pasty' was in residence! (Pasty being an affectionate scouse name for Pastor!)

Suffice to note, the stash of cash was not in the loft when we moved in! However, Sharon did find £30 under the kitchen cupboards when searching for her lost hamster! In time, the gang were charged with bringing £150,000,000 worth of cocaine into the country in zinc containers. The trial was at Newcastle Crown Court and they were cleared on a technicality! It was an interesting introduction into urban ministry and a life in the heart of Toxteth.

Over the next seven years we would have our car stolen twice, our shed raided, numerous items, from stones to eggs, thrown at the windows, two brand new bikes stolen, Ann's car trampled on, the trees opposite vandalised, and, in a moment of madness, me driving on the pavement to attack a group of lads who had hurled stones at the house windows just after I had settled after a particularly tough day. At church, we had constant vandalism, broken windows, graffiti, thefts, and my office ransacked, with church and personal effects scattered across the floor.

One immediate shock occurred when some of the leaders visited the office to survey the damage. It taught me a lesson about the ease of inculturation. How, over time, it is possible to close our eyes and minds to the effect of much inner city culture; the graffiti, mindless vandalism, rubbish, petty theft, drug dealing, and violence etc. After a cursory look at the chaos spread around, including my personal affects, and the 3" thick Victorian door ripped off its hinges, one of the leaders responded, 'It's not as bad as that one we had a few years ago!' Because it was not as messy or severe, it was an 8/10 not a 10/10. I was really hurt. It may not have been as bad as '70 or '81, but it was my office, my belongings, and my work, and it left a wound, but also a determination not to diminish the effect of anyone's vandalism. Year's later, on a visit to Peru, I detected the same issue of long-term missionary inculturation with respect to local driving habits. How easy it is to join the crowd rather than respect your passengers!

With respect to a church building, it is my belief that the outside is as important as the inside. A neglected, rubbish and graffiti ridden outside sends a powerful message to a community who tend to expect the worst rather than the best of facilities. We can easily become insulated and immune from it all and accept that nothing can change. That was never, even after 15 years, a mindset I would accept, which is why, a few months after arrival, I spent a lot of time six feet down in the church ditches, cleaning out, with others, years of rubbish. I also discovered, being in the ditch, where locals looked down, was a parable of humility, identity, and a servant heart. It was also a parable of the cross, a place where Jesus removes the rubbish of sin and a new beginning initiated. Many new connections were made as local people stopped to ask about our presence amidst the community's rubbish. As a Baptist Minister, water also featured! By clearing years of rubbish, water finally flowed out of the ditch and away from soaking the basement walls and causing endless rot; a powerful reminder that the work of the Holy Spirit, inside the building, must flow out to the community surrounding it.

41

UNFOLDING VISION:
PLAYGROUP 1990 - PRE-SCHOOL 1999

Some thirteen months after arrival, and in response to the primary need identified in the community survey, we took the first step in transforming a side hall into the new 'Tab Playgroup.' Stepping out in faith to call, pay and house us, had already built a solid foundation for church members, which would always be, 'make the move then trust for the resource' – faith followed by sight. This had always been God's way for us and he had never failed us along the way, though we had often been tested to the limit with respect to patience and timing!

Our 'Bezalels', (Exodus chapter 31), Mike Denham and Richard Toms, the skill gifted partners from Walton BC, would make the first of many journeys North to transform the hall with new storage, kitchen changes and brighter décor. Five paid and volunteer staff would need to be prayed-in and meld together as a team. Up to twenty-five children (2-4 years old) needed equipment - lots of it! By the grace of God, the faithfulness of many volunteers led by Joyce Richie, and our first paid staff member Tracey Caulfield, the playgroup began in September 1990. Within weeks we had a full complement of children and a waiting list that would be active for the next decade! Two years on, Brenda Taylor arrived, along with local volunteers, Margie, Adele, and Brenda Ford. When Tracey left for a teaching post, Anne Bass took over the leadership followed by Brenda Taylor.

There are also some memorable testimonies of God's grace and mercy in those early years. The parent who brought her son James, dying of an inoperable brain tumour, who had a life expectancy of months. No other group could take him, but Joyce, as a trained nurse, welcomed him in. His mum asked me to think about taking his funeral. I asked if she would welcome a home visit and prayer for James – she gladly agreed. Along with a couple of the leaders, I visited the home to pray and anoint James with oil. Very simple prayer was offered and no great claims were made. Several years later, I met his mum in town. James was still inoperable, not clinically healed but his months of expected life had stretched to years!

After eight years, the playgroup became a pre-school with all the massive changes that brings. More staff, teaching upgrades, curricula, Ofsted inspections! As in times past, the reputation for care, love and excellence continued to draw more families than could be accommodated. We were unashamedly Christian in ethos, practice, and teaching. This occasionally brought us into conflict with the authorities. We fought each battle with prayer and faith, and rejoiced in a consistently positive outcome. Different faiths were represented, as well as none, but all knew we were a Christian pre-school. After eleven years we saw the fruit of that early investment as past play-groupers and pre-schoolers came to the Tab Kid's Club.

Changes were always important. As a response to need, the school added afternoon sessions for the 2+'s, with the hard miles of grant funding bringing in a further £30,000 to upgrade the upper hall and the school office. As well as the school we offered training in Childcare NVQs 1-3, time in the school for parents, and access to job information. Trainees came from the locality as well as local agencies. Students fourteen-sixteen years old from our Level 3 skills-school had an opportunity to spend time relating to children and staff. (Level 3 story to come.) Occasionally, staff became confidants, with the opportunity to listen, identify with struggles, and offer practical help and prayer. God was at work, often in ways we could not quantify or naturally discern.

Another inspiring testimony is that of a local resident Brenda Ford. She lived a few houses away from the Tab and would stay in the playgroup with her daughter, Francesca, who suffered from a serious lung condition and feeding disorder. We prayed for Francesca and occasionally rushed her to Alder Hey Children's Hospital. Over time she improved – seven years to come off oxygen and thirteen to come off a special diet! Some prayers take years not months!

It was interesting to note that Brenda was often the first port of call for mums who needed to talk. Being a local it was natural for other local mums to make a bee-line for someone they knew well, especially if it was a crisis or a difficult issue. Brenda was a great listener. Noting that connection, we asked her if she would consider taking an NVQ in Childcare. Her initial response was, 'I couldn't do that!' Such a response is typical of many people who have been told in their youth, 'you'll never do anything.' We knew she could! She gained Level 1 and we encouraged her to continue. The same response would come each time, 'I couldn't do that.' After gaining all three qualifications we took her on as a staff member.

Another local issue was the need for 'alley-gates' - locked metal gates at each end of a back alley to prevent criminal activity and escape routes. The locals asked if I would chair the group. I said no, believing they should appoint a resident affected by the open alley issue. When I approached Brenda, and despite her amazing achievements so far, she was her usual reticent self. Nevertheless, the residents knew better and voted her as Chair. It took a fight, and some time, but the alley-gates were eventually installed, along with a community celebration. My final word to Brenda, along with congratulations, was, 'what are you going to do next?' 'Next' was never quite on Brenda's radar. Imagine my joy, twenty-five years later, when I visited her to fill in the gaps and she brought out her awards file. Level 4 Special Educational Needs provision - University equivalent 5 credits. A stack of niche certificates from Supporting Individuals with Learning Disabilities to Liverpool Early Years SENCO - Training Programme. No surprise she ended up as Deputy Manager. A triumph for a Toxteth lass who was told she would never amount to anything.

The glorious sequel to the story is that Francesca survived her many physical challenges and went on to complete NVQs 1-3 in childcare. She became a staff member in the pre-school for four years before moving on to Honeypots Pre-school, run by a previous leader at the Tab, Julie Hurst. What we gave to Brenda and Francesca was prayer-support, belief, hope, and confidence to achieve more than they ever imagined.

42

STEPPING STONES COFFEE-SHOP 1992

Two years after playgroup, and following a visit to Belfast by Richard Steele, where he visited such a facility, we began our second community response – a community Coffee Shop. I was now devoting a lot of time nurturing the art of grant funding applications. Like any skill, practice is essential, learning vital and failure inevitable. My nightly reading involved trawling through the very large Charities Aid Foundation book. I even had my own 1-5 stars penned beside each trust. 5 star was a trust most likely to entertain an application in line with their grant funding criteria. 1 star - probably best not to waste my time! We raised £35,000 in just three months and the date was set to begin the work of transforming the old, multicoloured brown 'Willy Woods' church lounge, into a bright, welcoming, and community centred coffee shop.

A couple, Brian and Angela Benford, who had worked for Heinz in Wigan, but retired back South, were asked to return on a short-term secondment. During the secondment, they enthusiastically anchored their lives at the Tab on a Sunday. They were members of Walton on Thames BC and had joined the teams who ventured North to support us in our early years. They came to us at just the right time. Their expertise in food production and café installations, insight, and enthusiasm, was infectious. Once again, Joyce Ritchie was at the heart of pulling together a volunteer team to start in the Coffee Shop once the transformation work was complete. Brian and Angela would attend advisory meetings, inspire the prospective volunteer staff, and, in an act of typical generosity, took them all down to London to attend the Olympia Food Exhibition. The aim was clear; enable and inspire the team to 'fall in love' with food! I sensed the Coffee Shop would quickly become a restaurant!

As well as our partnership with Esher and Walton BC's we now added a team from East Sheen BC, another of the links I had made with the Thames Valley Churches. Our skilled-partners Mike and Richard made another pilgrimage North, joining with our own church members to demolish, rebuild and install everything needed for a coffee shop to flourish. It was interesting, and very encouraging, to see a congregation increasing their commitment to another stage of our 'fresh vision.' The faith that had stirred the leaders to run with the initial vision had clearly been a model that the small congregation were fully embracing. With a united, skilled, and willing team, the lounge was rapidly transformed into a modern, welcoming, colourful, and inviting coffee shop equipped to the highest standards. The philosophy, which undergirded all our vision was simple; in the worst of areas, where the worst is expected, we aim to bring the best. With respect to décor, food and service, everything was about quality, good customer service, and respect.

Following our opening of Stepping Stones Café, the first customers were a mix of church folks and a few locals. A few months later, at a time when taxi-drivers were not too busy after 9.30am, we had a line of black cabs outside and a full complement of men inside. The freshly cooked all-day breakfast was so good and the word got round fast! Some of the local drug dealers had brothers who were taxi drivers. The dealers would camp opposite the church in the Farmer's Arms - a notorious pub for dealing. It didn't take long for the dealers, who noticed their brothers going into the church building, to ask a question, 'dat's a church, wat's r kid doin' in dare?' If you are not familiar with the scouse guttural accent: 'That is a church, what is my brother doing in there?'

194

The first drug dealer I witnessed entering Stepping Stones was a revelation. He waltzed up to the counter and announced his order - almost a loud command rather than a request, 'giz an all-day brekkie will yer.' The waitress replied, 'if you'd like to be seated, I'll serve you.' I swear I could see unseen cogs switching on in his brain as he took his seat – 'nobody treats me like that.' While we didn't like what they did, when they crossed the threshold, we treated them with respect and courtesy. As I loitered in Stepping Stones, for my morning coffee, I got the opportunity to introduce myself as the 'Pasty' and heard some of their stories.

James McCartney (Jimbo)

My journey to work and back, whether walking or motoring, was interesting. The occasional bunch of lads, already outside the pubs or still loitering from an all-nighter, as most Toxteth pubs had no closing times. The police informed me that it's better to have 'likely-lads' inside than on the street! Midday the gangs were forming, each connected to one or two local streets and families. Yet, it was one guy who always stood out for me. He was almost always alone. Maybe it was the stick that hindered his ability to fit in. Maybe the reputation as a heroin addict. Maybe the scrounging for money. Maybe it wasn't trendy or helpful to have a disabled lad in the gang. Whatever it was, this lad touched something inside of me. I began to pray regularly for him over a period of two years and heard from others that everyone on the street knew 'Jimbo' and the McCartney family.

Entering the café one morning for my coffee, I noticed Jimbo sitting by the door. Most likely unsure whether someone would bash him over the head with a Bible. Near the door offered easy escape. A few weeks later, I saw him sitting in the middle, clearly more at home. Then, a few

195

weeks later, he was right up by the counter being cheeky to the staff. He had found a safe home. I began to sit with him and hear his story, especially the reason for his limp, paralysis down one side, and stick. His mum died suddenly when he was fifteen. The delayed shock brought on the paralysis and he began taking drugs. By the time I was getting to know Jimbo he was addicted to heroin, alienated from his family and very much alone. Just one brother, Terry, cared and cared enough to pin me to the café wall and say, 'Youse gotta do somethin' for 'im. I'm gonna find 'im dead one day.' Terry was a taxi driver who came to Stepping Stones for his all-day breakfast and loved his brother enough to plead for help. Jimbo takes the story on.

'I first met you in the Tab café and slowly got to know you better. We got talking, but a few weeks later I was in hospital and bumped into you coming out of a lift. You gave me some money and I thought, 'e's ok 'im'. From there I started going to the café a bit more. One day I was struggling with my addiction, had no money, so passed over a forged £20 note to get something to eat. As you knew my brother, Terry, you told him it was ok, but he took me back to see yer and all yer said was 'it's ok Jimbo'. We had a chat and you said you could get help for my addiction and you had been praying for me for years. You gave me a form for a 'Teen Challenge' rehab centre in Bradford. 22 years down the line, I am still free from my addiction, all because you introduced me to our Lord and Saviour Jesus. God bless yer for your kindness towards me all those years ago. Love ya Pastor and Ann. God bless ya x.'

It's important to add, that it was while Jimbo was in Bradford that he was counselled well and committed his life to Jesus. He went on to Teen Challenge in Llanelli and was taught to read and write. One lovely incident occurred when Ann and I went down to meet him. We called at the Teen Challenge house which appeared to be empty. As we walked through the corridors nobody appeared! Making our way out, we heard a noise and followed the sound. Just one old lady in the kitchen cooking dinner. I said, 'I'm looking for Jimbo.' 'Oh' she said, in that lovely South Wales lilt, 'e's at the gym.' We duly arrived at the Camarthen Sports Centre and asked for Jimbo. We heard him, holding court, before we saw him! He was surrounded by a crowd of lads and in his strong guttural scouse most likely sharing his faith. As we walked towards the crowd, he spotted us and, in a very casual way, announced, 'that's my Pastor!' He had no idea we were coming and simply continued addressing the crowd.

Two things always choke me up and release tears. Whenever we have met up, he repeats, 'thank you for invading my darkness!' I don't think there is a sentence spoken to me that impacts me, and moves me, more than this one. The other is the 'preaching certificate' he sent me after a lot of training and care at Llanelli Teen Challenge. He was reconciled to all his family, many of whom travelled to Llanelli to witness him being presented with his certificate. For a guy who could hardly read and write this was a triumph. As was his later marriage to Louise. Twenty-two years on he still shares what Jesus has done, touching the lives of many across the South Wales chapels and churches. Sometimes, I see his brother Terry working out of the taxi rank at the Toxteth Tesco Store on Park Road. He always thanks me for saving Jimbo's life and I always remind him, 'it's not me Terry, it's all about Jesus.'

We sometimes quote, 'Stepping Stones is often more church than church.' It is a model that deserves both observation and consideration. Where prayer is sought it is offered. Where a chat is on, it is shared. Where truth is needed there are tracts, bibles, and videos. Banter is frequent. Laughter is ever present. Service is key. The crockery matters! The Holy Spirit is doing His work in all manner of ways - recognised and not! Where once we joked that £9 in takings reflected a good day, later on there was disappointment if we were under £150. That is not the big issue, but it's important that professional and caring staff know that their service, in Jesus name, is rewarded in the outcomes. After five years, Stepping Stones employed two, local, full-time staff, Barbara Davies and Brenda Roberts, plus a part-time paid helper. Priceless volunteers made up a great team to cater, shop, clean, serve and manage. Without their selfless volunteering we could not possibly function. It was also a great venue for facilitating a host of different gatherings; Church meetings, Minister's fraternals, Christmas meals, Leader's prayers, Community hub, not to mention the staff canteen – not just a café but a restaurant now!

43

LAND REDEMPTION AND THREATS 1993

One of the crazy words God gave us at the beginning was this, 'you shall look to the right and the left'. This is not simply an injunction to survey land, but to scan the human situation and respond where God directs. A car park is not an exciting faith project, but it was helpful to redeem land in one place so we could use it to serve in another. The plot for sale was across the road from the playgroup hall. A small church building had been burnt down in the 1981 Toxteth riots and the site cleared. Putting a small car park there would release land on our church site for an accessible and safe toddler's play area adjacent to the playgroup.

Just over £20,000 was raised, both to purchase the land, lay tarmac and build a surrounding brick and steel wall. Yet again, our partnership links with Walton brought Mike Denham and Richard Toms back to build and further enhance the playgroup facility. It's impossible to overstate the immense debt we owe to such people, and those such as Mike and Janet Hall, who shared our needs and joys with their home church in Walton as well as making trips North to pray with us, engage the community and, often, bring a gift of money to support our vision. This on top of the £300 a month Walton had been sending from the beginning of our pastorate. Keeping the communication channels open between our link churches was the key. They were spiritual ambassadors and vibrant supporters, willing to visit then inspire and involve their home church in generous and prayerful partnership. Their consistent visits and encouragements, combined with prayer, were our lifeline and spur, especially in times of spiritual and physical attack. Attack was clearly a possibility once we began the car park wall.

One Friday a local guy paid a visit to the Tab and met the playgroup leader, Anne Bass. He wanted to see the Pastor and talk about the price we needed to pay for his protection of our embryonic wall. £200 to put his sign up but no protection! I had learned in my first year, when visiting businesses, that protection rackets were rife in Toxteth. Anne mentioned it was my day off, but I would be around on Monday! He put his hand firmly on Anne's arm and said, 'Monday will be too late, get him to ring me now!' When he left, Anne rang me immediately. I might have said, 'cheers Anne.' This guy had a string of violent convictions and jail time – someone not to be messed with! My immediate action was to ring our leaders, link churches, friends, and allies, seeking urgent prayer support.

Every Saturday the Tab Leaders would meet for prayer and set out the church for Sunday. Following prayer, I went up to the church store to help bring down the PA equipment. Scattered across the floor were several 1" square steel cubes and a significant amount of glass. I rang the police, who replied, 'you were lucky, it was his warning call, he could have easily torched the building!' My heart missed a few beats over the weekend as I awaited the outcome of this guy's threats - he never appeared! On Wednesday, I saw the police on another matter, regarding the theft of our bikes. The detective asked about the steel cube/window situation. I replied, 'our spiritual resources were greater than his physical threats.' The detective remarked, 'that's profound', I replied, 'It's also true!'

Another threat was linked to our youth work. We had a visiting team of young people from Northern Ireland who were meeting our youth on a Friday night. In the middle of the evening there was a loud thump on the hall door. When it was opened, a man stormed in demanding we close the club immediately. He was accusing the visiting team of damaging his car on their way to the church. As he made his way out, he told us he would be back with a group of other men within the hour. We prayed together and prepared for the expected return of local men. In the meantime, I decided to put together some drinks and choc bars from Stepping Stones Restaurant. The men duly arrived and sat down. I introduced the drinks and choc bars and, in a light hearted moment, apologised that I had not been able, yet, to turn the cans of coke into wine! That simple sentence brought laughter, diffused the anger immediately, and allowed us to talk together. The outcome was apologies for kicking off, carry on with the mission to the youth, and the weekly youth club. Many an argument was diffused by humour.

One of my steep learning curves, both at home and church, was the strategy required to disarm attack, threat, and vandalism. Basically, it requires an alternative to the expected verbal response. When kids started throwing stones at our windows, I threw back toffees. They responded. 'He's throwing stones at us!' 'No, sweets!' I shouted. The toffees or stones exchange lasted for a few seconds before they exclaimed, 'it's toffees!' They stopped throwing stones and gathered at our door!

Occasionally, bringing a camera out and pretending to take pictures avoided conflict. Our trees opposite the house were especially poignant and precious as they symbolised guidance to our home. When lads discovered some metal 'S' bars they would hook a branch with one curve and pull down on the other to break the branch. Instead of the normal, local, practice of f*** off, I chose to engage them with a proposition. 'I'll give you 50p for the bar.' It was an instant deal. The lads handed over the bar and I the 50p. However, urban lads are canny and entrepreneurial and an hour later they were back with another bar re-enacting the scenario!

No strategy lasted forever so it was a constant battle to invent a new one that would disarm their antisocial behaviour.

One of my most effective and long-lasting strategies was to get the lads to plant seeds in small pots, put their name on a sticker and ask them to return weeks later to collect their plant. Another winner was to pot up cactus plants and tell the lads to take it home to their mum. One of the fun comments I had from a lad, when I left Toxteth after 15 years, was, 'me ma's still got that cactus yer giv' 'er.'

44

FIRST-STEPS MISSIONS 1993-95

Our church mission statement held two aims in tension, 'Making Jesus Known - Serving the City,' an evangelistic passion with a social servant heart. Since 1871 the Tab had an awesome history of passionate evangelistic preaching and service to the community, church-planting across the city and worldwide missionary endeavour. Two World Wars had taken their toll on that fruitful endeavour. Divisive splits, among leaders and members, had almost emptied the church of people and passion. Our task now was to restore faith, unity, service to the community, and evangelistic zeal.

We began three years of 'First-Steps Missions' with no illusions. It would be a highly visual 'Street-Mission' with one primary aim; taking one step, in Jesus' name, towards our community and inviting the community to take one step towards Jesus. There is a scale, helping to measure belief in the nation, called the Engel Scale. Most people in our nation are now edging -9/10 which is labelled, 'awareness of the supernatural/no effective knowledge of Christianity.' Our aim was -8, 'initial awareness of Christianity,' with -6 as a real bonus, 'awareness of the basic facts of the Gospel.' -2, which is 'the challenge and decision to act' would clearly be a 'Second-Steps Mission!'

Many might consider such statements as lacking in faith, yet we have received teams who gave scant attention to where people were on the scale of Christian understanding. They assumed a few spiritual laws scattered on the doorstep, followed by a prayer, results in new birth! It may, by the sovereign action of the Holy Spirit, but there is rarely any lasting fruit from such presentations. What fruit we saw from our first three years of First-Steps was quantifiable and internal. In the first year we had almost sixty YWAM (Youth with a Mission) team members and four from the Tab! In the second year we had thirty visiting team members and nine from the Tab. In the third year we had fifteen visiting team members and twenty-eight from the Tab! Not the fruit, yet, of salvation, but certainly discipleship.

The format for these missions was clear - colourful, dramatic, highly visual, dance, drama, testimony, and food! We covered streets, pubs, open spaces, and church car park BBQ's. The area was saturated with prayer and targeted to reach specific places over a three year period. At times we simply asked the Holy Spirit to guide us concerning 'stopping' places. Often no one was in sight but we began anyway and gradually people came. Some of the most dramatic encounters occurred on very dodgy corners, such as the occasion when a car drew up as the team were enacting the crucifixion. The driver got out, placed a brick-size packet of drugs on a wall and made a deal with a local guy. Some of the young members of the YWAM team were transfixed but it gave them a clear visual reminder of what we might witness daily! It also fuelled prayer. Divine appointments did take place. People received prayer; tracts and bibles were left. Stories of local living conditions and heartaches of family pain were listened to with concern and compassion - classic sowing that one day we, or others, may reap. Some 'decisions' were registered in these times but there was little assimilation into church life as growing disciples. This is primarily our fault as we wrestle with the problem of being a largely middle class church in a working class area. The comfort is that it's not new, and few people, over 200 years, have easy answers to the problem of integrating working class believers into middle class churches.

We also began to consider how we might encourage Christian young people, whether at university in the city, taking a gap year, or completing education, to consider investing their lives in a tough urban environment. The kind of environment from which so many churches and Christians have fled – the so-called 'white-flight' syndrome. We also gained information about Careforce, an organisation that places young people, for a year, in varied church assignments across the UK. It would prove to be a very precious connection, as five young people, Iesah, Jo, Peter, Amy and Kate, would not only invest a year at the Tab, but for Jo, Amy and Kate it would cement their future lives, marriages and children! They stayed in the city, married, and had children! All three families settled in the stigmatised L8 postcode of Toxteth. In 1989, when we arrived, just one young family, Richard and Alison Steele, and their two children Helen and Elaine, lived in L8. They pioneered where others would follow, in line with Jeremiah chapter 29 verses 5-7 noted earlier.

Alongside our mission in community, there was also a mission within the church. We were custodians of a huge building; a potential resource for serving our church and community. The Playgroup and Restaurant were thriving and giving us contact with many new families. Our prayers and planning now turned to the three thousand square feet of unused space in the basement. The echo of my meeting with Reg Quirk, back in 1989, now resounded clearly. Four years on it was God's time for us to act.

45

LEVEL 3 SKILLS-SCHOOL

Patience and timing are key in any long-term vision. It would have been easy, following my meeting with Reg in 1989, to rush into a massive and costly project, making the same mistake as that of a new church building. Tackling the playgroup and restaurant first, enabled us to build trust, faith, and good practice. We were now about to enter our most costly, long-term, and challenging build, a 'Skills-School' for excluded students aged 14-16 years.

Some of the fruit of visiting in my first year now became visible. Patience is not just a virtue, in city work it is vital! My talk with Reg revealed a small, but soon to explode, level of school exclusions. One story from Reg remained vivid in my mind. Gary was eleven and likely to remain out of mainstream education for his expected school life. He visited Reg and asked for help. 'Eh Reg, I wanna make sum arma'. (I want to make some armour)! Reg replied, 'Gary, I've got a coffee pot and a pool table, but no metal work equipment.' 'No' said Gary, 'I want sum cardboard, can yer get me sum cardboard?' Reg got him cardboard. Six weeks later, Gary appeared at the office with, in Reg's words, 'an immaculate suit of armour.' My immediate response would prove life-changing for the Educational Welfare Office and their teachers, volunteers, and partners. It would also bring hope for some of the students written off as unteachable, untrainable, and unwanted in local Toxteth schools.

My response to Reg was inspired by Gary's story. 'Reg, one day I would love to complement your work in our three-thousand square feet of semi-derelict basement.' The vision was born in that moment, but awaited a fulfilment time in the plans God had for us, plus an expected £500,000 to transform the basement into a hi-tec skills-school; a school built to the best standards possible, where the worst might be expected.

Work to gut the interior began in 1993. Our faithful partners Mike and Richard, plus unemployed local men, began a process that would last over three years, with additions five years later. Another huge leap of faith with no initial resource. As we prayed, worked hard on trust funding, and did what we could, so small and significantly sized amounts of money came in. Grant managers who had trusted us with relatively small amounts of money for Playgroup and Stepping Stones, and who subsequently saw the quality of our work, now invested much larger sums. We too learned to stop asking for crumbs and went for loaves instead! We still got many crumbs but some large helpings of bread also. The faith that trusted God for such was infectious and, from time to time, really impacted the lives of our casual workers. God became real in meeting daily need. We had treated them with dignity by investing the best in terms of wages, now they could see how God was being generous to his people as we relied on Him for miracles of provision. I recall one occasion when I told these local guys that we needed £10,000 by the end of the week! They moved to one of the corners and laughed together. It was priceless to see their faces, at the end of the week, as I waved a cheque for £10,000.

There were many such miracles in the early days of building, as there were through the ten years of operating the school. As local men took stories back to a tight-knit community, so the perception of who we are, and what God is like, began to slowly change. We were beginning to win hearts through our patient and largely unparaded work of serving the community.

Over three years, our friends Richard and Mike, camped with us, and along with countless other individuals and professionals, built with zeal, skill, and endless late nights! The vision was born of God but the hard work belonged to those who shared the dream and offered themselves, wholeheartedly, to be part of its fulfilment. As the physical rot and dereliction gave way to new beams and floors, so we recognised, in symbol and sign, that the rot of sin could one day be removed from human lives and structural powers in our city and community.

Over those preparatory years, I visited Reg on a regular basis to keep him informed of progress. His words were so encouraging, 'we cannot wait to see the school open.' This was not the case with the Local Education Authority, who were opposed to our work from the beginning. Fortunately, this would not always be the case.

46

SACRIFICIAL MOVES

One of the biggest issues facing any, largely white, urban church is the retention of Christians committed to serve in tough environments. It is reasonably natural, and understandable, to want to live in a nice house and a safe neighbourhood, relatively free from endless vandalism, graffiti, and rubbish. A place where crime, poverty, and fear do not dominate local culture. Yet it was those who chose, often amidst great personal sacrifice and loss, to make that move into the inner city, who modelled real 'incarnation.' John chapter 1 verse 14 says of Jesus, 'The Word (Jesus) became flesh and blood, and moved into the neighbourhood.' Another paraphrase says, '… and moved into our street.' That was what Toxteth needed. Christians who would move into the stigmatised L8 postcode and become salt and light on local streets and in local workplaces. There were a few who had stayed around, following the exodus from church in the 1970-80's, but it was also the example of new Christians who moved in, and locals who became Christians, who would inspire and model a love for the inner city that gave the church hope for the future; Richard and Alison Steele, and their two girls Helen and Elaine; Anne and Bill Bass, returning from mission work in Indonesia with their four girls, Judith, Rachel, Sarah and Ruth, made a decision to move into Toxteth. Anne's story is one of faith, perseverance, pain, loss, triumph, passion, and incredible hospitality.

About a year after settling in their home in the suburbs, Anne came to me with a startling word, 'I believe God has told me to move into Toxteth.' I responded, 'have you told Bill?' She answered, 'no.' I said, 'it might be a good idea Anne!' When she told Bill, he agreed. They began the search and found a four storey Victorian house in one of the toughest areas of Liverpool 8. Prior to moving, the family paid a visit to missionary friends in Holland. Sadly, I received a phone call from Anne, in the early hours of one morning, to say that Bill had died. They were due to move into their new home the following week. I flew to Holland to help with the funeral. A week later, with other church members, we moved Anne and the girls into their new, urban, home. A lot of vandalism and theft came quickly, but Anne said to me, 'they can take everything, I am here to stay.' And stay she and the family did.

The cost for many was theft, break-ins, car loss, broken windows, stones, eggs, and sometimes personal attack, not to mention serious damage to the church building and theft from it. Daily stress can be greatly intensified, and all this with children as well! Some made every effort to stay away but God changed their hearts. Others camped on the edge and finally made the journey in. Their modelling of incarnation paved the way for others to follow, so that today, a good proportion of the church live in Liverpool 8. Their stories are ones of faith and struggle, pain and joy, triumph and defeat, but without such moves the church in the city could not survive as a credible and effective witness to its local people.

One important caveat, that eases any guilt Christians may feel for not moving into the centre of the city, is found in Nehemiah chapter 11 verses 1 and 2. 'Now the leaders of the people settled in Jerusalem. The rest of the people cast lots to bring one out of every ten of them to live in Jerusalem, the holy city, while the remaining nine were to stay in their own towns. The people commended all who volunteered to live in Jerusalem.' (I bet they did). It was the leaders who set the pattern and the example, then just 10% of the people who would also move into the urban centre, and be clapped enthusiastically as they entered the city - possibly out of relief they could stay in the suburbs! Support structures for the tough places are essential. We could never have survived without the generosity, prayer and practical support given over fifteen years by Esher, Walton, East Sheen BCs, and a host of others both near and far. Here were strong churches outside of the urban, supporting a small inner city church with a big vision.

Level 3 was a prime cause of such battles to move into the inner city! As we began to plan the interior so God brought the first of many staff members. Along with her husband, Nick, Donna Bold really wanted to return to the lush pastures of the South of England. God, however had his way, her heart was changed, and their lives surrendered to the present and perfect will of God. Donna became our first staff member with many hours spent planning rooms and considering the curriculum.

As work progressed so others were called to join the staff team. Elaine Rees, the Northern Regional Coordinator for Careforce - an organisation that places students and others into churches for yearly placements - joined with us for two weeks in a First-Steps Mission. As she experienced urban culture on the street, and felt the need of local people, God broke her heart and spoke clearly about coming to the city and the Tab. A week after the mission, she wrote to me and shared what God had put on her heart. Within a year Elaine arrived. At first, we had no idea where she would serve, or how she would be paid, but the Holy Spirit opened the way into Level 3. Her wage followed! We now had an Administrator, and later, a Head Teacher. I had really enjoyed working with Donna on the initial décor, equipment, and layout, but Elaine made it clear it was time for me to let go of the vision I had nurtured from Reg's office in 1989 to the start of building in 1993. Elaine was right, but it was still a form of bereavement!

As the opening date drew near, Level 3 now had a pottery, large woodwork space, textile room, computer suite, staff office, games room and the poshest toilets in Toxteth, with tiles from floor to ceiling! Every facility was built and equipped to the highest standard, with the latest technology. Reg kept telling me that all the Educational Welfare Officers could not wait to see it opened. Neither could we! We had also increased our staff, with some further sacrificial moves. Charles McGregor, a CDT teacher, came on board, commuting daily from Crewe, a classic example of someone who supported from the outside. His first day was memorable. I had applied to Children in Need for three year's salary and expectantly awaited the outcome. The letter from CIN arrived that morning – it turned out to be a rejection! Grant funding is a tough environment, full of hard work and lots of rejections. Charles reply was typical of the faith and trust of all who have come as staff members, 'there are no problems, only fresh challenges.' My wife Ann took on admin with Alison Steele overseeing accounts. Anne Bass moved from the pre-school to teach English, Steve Bodman Maths and Mark Higginbotham Geography. It is vital to underline, that in a Pupil Referral Unit, the team also fulfilled many other roles, including dog minding, caring for siblings, rescuing pupils from derelict buildings and, sadly, convincing reticent parents that keeping their children in Level 3 was vital for their future! Supplementing staff on a regular basis were our wonderful Careforce volunteers.

Jo's story is just one of many that I could share.

'The first night I arrived in Liverpool, in the late 1990s, Cheryl, the Children and Family Worker, took me to the 'Kwikkie' (Kwik-Save) to buy some food. They had a large selection of meat pies but nothing for a veggie like me. I had a little cry to God thinking, 'is this really the place for me?' But within days I was sitting in the coffee shop where

Brenda, Barbara and Joyce served with kindness and love. I was listening to Terry Jones tell me of God's vision for the community, seeing all that had already been achieved in the coffee shop, the pre-school, a growing church and now Level 3 - a PRU in the basement. He was so passionate about how God was at work. I heard how God had brought Elaine to take over Level 3, where I was working. God had perfectly prepared her and I was inspired by how Elaine was so willing to trust him in her role. She was such a wise, honest, and caring boss. I loved how Charles was willing to drive every day from Crewe, because he wanted to be obedient to God's call and he loved the kids we worked with. (We taught some amazing kids). Donna, Ann, Anne & Alison in Level 3, all responded in obedience, served with humility, and showed God's love in every day-to-day task. They set such an amazing example of living as God's people here in Toxteth that it made it so easy to say yes to God and settle here myself - I just wanted to be like them.'

After three years of planning, demolition, rebuilding, endless grant funding applications, overcoming set-backs, and navigating pauses in the work, we were almost ready to open. Staff had been recruited, rooms fitted out, equipment installed to the highest standards. It was time to open. Nobody could remember the exact date in September 1996! However, the Level 3 basement was filled with representatives from the Educational Welfare Office, LEA, Baptist Union of Great Britain, staff, church members, and local people who had worked on the building. It was an honour to be presented with a medal, from Reg Quirk (Chief EWO), commemorating the opening and our commitment to work with excluded pupils. The words on the medal are very simple, 'Liverpool Education Committee to Terry Jones from Liverpool Education Welfare Service.' Whilst a personal gift, it belongs to every single person who believed in the vision, stood by it, and brought it to fruition.

I could fill another book with the story of Level 3 over the next ten years. The students whose lives were transformed in an atmosphere of love, patience, personal training, and hope for the future. The endless fight, from highly committed teachers, to persuade parents of the importance of education for their children. The disappointments over the students who walked away, but the pride staff felt over those who gained certificates, produced stunning work, and went into apprenticeships and work places. The massive change of heart, and eventually policy, in the LEA when they finally accepted the quality of work being done with our students. The pride we all felt when out staff were invited to other schools and units to inform, inspire, and encourage their work. The staff who worked tirelessly to raise huge amounts of money, and the immense satisfaction of gaining European grants to fund Level 3 work. Not many, if any other churches, can say they have helped to change LEA policy and gain European funding!

In the end we did ourselves out of jobs. As our model was increasingly embraced by local schools, instead of sending students to Level 3, the LEA and EWO's were able to place them in local PRU's. It was a bittersweet decision to close, yet a time to give thanks and rejoice over all that Level 3 had achieved in a decade. It was also inspiring and heartening to know that six of our teachers moved to important educational roles. Elaine Rees became Deputy Director of Education Action Zone, later Head of Kingsley School in Toxteth. Anne Bass taught in two PRU's. Steve Bodman began teaching Maths at a local Toxteth academy, later becoming Head of Maths. Mark Higginbotham, had a few other jobs before moving to teach Geography in St Helens and Jo Sims, our Careforce worker, began teaching in Gateacre Comprehensive School. Alison Steele moved to Liverpool John Moore's University as a librarian and, prior to closure, my wife reignited her shorthand and typing skills as secretary to the chief chemist at a pharmaceutical company located in Knowsley, a timely move that laid the foundation for work with that company over the next ten years, both down South and on our return to Liverpool five years later. The investment in Level 3 shaped all their future careers - a priceless legacy.

One of the important considerations that churches need to review regularly is when to close ministries, when to re-evaluate vision and when to start something new. Far too often we hang on to things when the life has gone and the season has passed. 'Behold I am doing a new thing' is a vital theme throughout the Bible and expresses God's heart for change when change is needed. During my fifteen years in Toxteth, dozens of local churches closed - a stubborn inability to change was a primary cause. However, it is important to note that, in their place, several new churches have been started in old church buildings, schools, shops, warehouses, homes and even hotels! The church is alive and well, but it may not be the same as it has been because God is always eager to do 'a new thing'!

Another inspiring and remarkable testimony is that of Cheryl Kidd who became our first Children's and Family Worker.

'I started attending the Tab during my teacher training year and was baptised soon after, around November 1995. I knew Primary school teaching was a step to something else in terms of ministry, possibly overseas, and so I was never very settled in teaching. One Sunday evening at the Tab prayer meeting, I asked Terry to pray that I would know whether to hand in my notice at school the following day. I then had total peace that was the Lord's will for me, so I did just that. I had been training for a promotion to deliver the Numeracy Hour in schools so my resignation was a shock to the Senior Management Team but I knew it was of the Lord. At some point before this, when I had been asking the Lord where I would be working, He had given me a picture of the Colemans Fire Depository near the Tab, so I assumed I would again be volunteering locally and would need to give up my rented house. The Tuesday after handing in my resignation, was a day full of doubt and fear - what had I done? How could I have so quickly thrown all my education and training away? What would I do now?

Unbeknown to me, the manager of a local firm, Spillers' Mill, visited Terry on the Wednesday to see the work that was being done at the Tab to bless the community and bring life in Jesus' name. Terry explained that Stan, the Community Outreach Worker, was leaving for home in the USA a few weeks later. The manager immediately offered to pay two thirds of another worker's salary for three years. Terry and the Tab leadership team saw this release of finances, resulting from my step of faith, and offered me the Children's and Family Worker's post at the Tab, with a start after the summer holidays. I was bowled over at God's goodness, that within three days of resigning the Lord had provided so miraculously for me!

During my three years working at the Tab, I served in the nursery, helped run the Sparklers Carers and Tots group, ran summer kids clubs, and began the weekly Kids Club, which included visiting each family every week! I will always remember that the summer kids club, prior to starting the weekly club, miraculously had double the number of children attending, so that the weekly club began full, with thirty children attending. Only God could have done that! We also took children to Nefyn camps, had weekends away as a group and started a Kids House Group for those who were hungry for more of God. Obviously, all this was only possible with an amazing team of volunteers. It was an incredible time of seeing the Lord's hand at work in the details, big and small!'

47

CHANGING THE ATMOSPHERE

Two events at home hurt us more than others. Although bullied at school, Sharon was tough, and received excellent grades in her GCSE's and A levels. She was set to read Geography at Sheffield University. When children leave home, whether for education, work, or other reasons, they never quite return the same. I bought two new bikes, the first Sharon had, so I could ride with her through the summer before she left for Sheffield. Around 11.30pm one evening, a gang of lads removed the barbed wire covering our side wall, jumped on to Ann's car, putting dent marks on the roof and across the bonnet, then broke into the greenhouse where the bikes were stored and locked. Within a matter of minutes, they had broken the locks, heaved the bikes back across the car and scrambled over the wall.

As this was happening, I was in the loo, which was the nearest room to the action! I recognised the sounds as being inside our garden not outside! As I raced to dress, I could hear the lads making their way back over the car and on to the wall. By this time, Sharon had arrived from her bedroom wondering what was going on. We got out of the house just in time to see the lads disappearing up the road with the bikes. It was futile, and potentially dangerous, to give chase. As I held Sharon on the street, we cried together - a tough moment, but the atmosphere was about to change.

The second painful experience has become a legendary story! Around six years in, my aim to bring vibrant colour to the inner city had been achieved. Both front and back gardens were alive with a range of shrubs and flowers. Either side of the porch, stunning hanging baskets flowed down with trailing plants. Neighbours, and residents from other roads, would regularly stop, or make a detour, to check out our garden. As if we were paving the way, gardens down the road steadily improved. Urban culture is alive with a mentality of jealousy or a desire to go one better. Two things tend to happen - one is destruction, the other is determination to improve. We experienced plenty of both! On the side wall of our small drive, I had cultivated two sizeable and stunning hanging baskets. The passing ladies, and occasionally men, would stop and ask, 'can yer teach me 'ow to do dem hangin' basket tings?' 'I can', was my reply.

On a beautiful June morning, I left home for work and immediately saw the destruction. One basket had been ripped off the wall completely and the trail of begonias spread up the road as the culprits carried it off. The other had been smashed repeatedly on the wall leaving a crushed lump of soil, mangled plants, and twisted metal. My immediate response was not typical – 'you bastards,' followed by an internal reflection - 'Baptist Minister!' Forgiveness for my outburst was not on my agenda, revenge was! I left for the office with a lump inside. All day long I was hurting as if a cancer had invaded my heart. No other loss or pain, destruction, theft, or attack, had affected me as much as two destroyed hanging baskets. I wrestled with my thoughts, 'Why would anyone destroy something so simple yet stunningly beautiful?' 'Why is vandalism so mindless, pointless and destructive?' 'Who gains?'

I arrived home, around 5pm, with a restless heart and mind, and began to potter in the greenhouse. Within a few minutes two responses became clear. The first was the sense of a voice within – 'put a cross outside.' The second was an Old Testament passage that sprang to mind. The Ark of the Covenant, the most precious spiritual icon for the Israelites, had been captured by the Philistines and was in foreign territory. Sadly, the Philistines underestimated God's power and anger, and were struck with tumours. However, their response was wise - 'let's push the Ark back into Israelite territory!' I prayed immediately, 'Lord, make that hanging basket as obnoxious as the Ark of the Covenant was to the Philistines.' 1 Samuel chapters 4-8.

I set to work immediately on a simple wooden cross. Adjacent to our mini-drive was a small patch of soil that successive gangs of lads boots had rendered unplantable. I knocked the cross in that rugged patch and retreated to the greenhouse. Within ten minutes my first gang of 8-11's appeared, and in the very best guttural scouse, one of them declared, 'Wat's dat cross doin' dare?' He yelled at another lad, 'kick it out da' ground.' The response was quick-fire. 'No, you kick it out da' ground, I'm a Cath-lic!' All of which echoed into the greenhouse, followed by a knock on the door. 'Ey Pasty, wat's dat cross doin dare, your budgie's buried dare isn't de?' I swiftly pointed to the budgie running up and down the windowsill. 'Well, who's buried dare?' In a moment of divine inspiration, I replied, 'nobody is buried there, I am angry and I am giving my anger to Jesus!' The look on the lad's face was priceless. I closed the door and he reported to the gang, 'eh, the Pasty's angry and e's givin' it to Jesus!' I smiled and rejoiced!

Around 8pm, the 12-15's arrived. Same scenario, with an argument about who would kick it out of the ground and who was 'Cath-lic.' No knock on the door. At 11pm, with our windows open on a hot June night, the heavy mob arrived to view the cross! As they kicked off, I turned to Ann and, slightly faithless, mentioned that, 'I wasn't sure the cross would be there in the morning.' As I opened the door in the morning, the cross was in place and beside the cross - the hanging basket, minus begonias! It was a supreme moment of triumph as I let out a long and loud 'YEEESSS...' followed by a fist-pump and a moment of sheer divine ecstasy! Prayer on earth had been reciprocated in heaven. I felt that the atmosphere had been changed and the effect would flow out to church, community, and city! I had prayed, with many others, the prayer Jeremiah encouraged the Jewish exiles to pray, around 597BC, when they were in Babylon. 'Seek the peace of the city where I have exiled you. Pray to the Lord for that city, because when it has peace and prosperity, you will have peace and prosperity'. Jeremiah chapter 29 verse 7.

Over time, theft, vandalism, opposition, and intimidation significantly lessened, both at home and church. Teams that had visited in our early years, to pray and walk the local area, and had given us pictures of 'low, dark, menacing clouds over Toxteth,' now responded seven years later, 'the clouds have lifted.' Practically, it was evidenced in a new spirit of cooperation and help from the local community. Three events, over several months, spoke clearly to me that the atmosphere was changing:

A stolen handbag

One of our Level 3 staff had her handbag stolen from the church office. A few weeks later, one of our regulars for an all-day breakfast in Stepping Stones, an old guy with a wooden leg, told us he had approached lads in the street who knew those who had stolen the bag, (local people know these things). He went up to them, pointing a finger, 'don't youse be nickin' anything from the Tab, cos' sum of us believe in what they are doing in there!' Those lads could have easily kicked his leg away. He chose to confront the lads and defend our work. After seven years we were now being defended by the locals.

A Police question

I received a phone call, around 8pm one evening, from the

local police Sergeant on duty. 'Was I the key holder and how long before you can be at the Tab?' I was and it took me five minutes. When I arrived at the Playgroup entrance there were eight police cars, a large Alsatian with handler, and the Sergeant. Before we entered, he said two things to me, 'always stay behind the dog' and 'what is happening? We have had five consecutive phone calls!' 'Grassing' is not a regular part of inner city urban culture. Informing the police via one phone call, would have been unusual, but five? I logged both statements, about dog and phones, away in my mind. Local people heard alarms ringing, glass breaking and had seen shadows moving through the windows of the church. Hence the large police presence.

There was a moment of humour as I tried to stay behind the dog as it tore around the massive upper-level balcony. It was our very own greyhound track and the dog was determined to break the track record! I turned to the Sergeant and said, 'a bit difficult to stay behind the dog.' News filtered back, via police radios, that three lads had been found in various areas of the church, with one left on an outside window ledge of Stepping Stones Café. He was holding a microwave and shouting at a considerable crowd of locals, 'get rid of the bizzies' (police). As I watched the crowd, my impression grew that they were on our side and eager to see the lads taken down and charged with breaking and entering along with theft. The reaction of the crowd was further tangible evidence that the atmosphere was changing.

A new respect

The third affirmation of a change in the atmosphere occurred with respect to the security of cars and building. I had spent seven years watching windows break with bricks, stones, and squares of steel. Damage to, or theft of cars, was not an epidemic, but it was real and expected over time. It was rare to have a knock on the door or a phone call warning us about threats. On occasions, residents would simply stand at their doors and watch without intervention. Now, the doorbell was rung and locals explained what was happening - lads on the roof or in the car park. 'It's ok Pasty, leave it to us, we'll sort it!'

The irony for me was the theft of cars from home, all of which were returned, some with damage others requiring shrewd adaptations. I had a VW Golf stolen and returned by police. The ignition barrel had been badly smashed and the wires rigged to bypass the lock and start the engine. On return, I arranged for a new barrel to be inserted under the dashboard. Several weeks later, the car went missing again from our drive. At 3am the next day I was woken up by a police officer, who said, 'we have found your car. If you just look over the road and down a side street, you will see your bonnet peeking out of an alleyway.' The lads had been stumped by the absence of any ignition barrel so had pushed the car just out of sight. I said to the officer, 'thanks, I think I can drive it back from there.' So, in pyjamas at 3am in the morning, I retrieved the VW! This was not so much a change of atmosphere but a change of tactic!

After seven-plus years of trial, pain, attacks, and a lot more, we were entering a seven year period of respect, support, and openness to the impact we were making in the local community, the church building, and in our home estate. The future was brighter than it had been since we arrived.

⟨48⟩

LIKE ANTS IN A SUGAR FACTORY!

An enquiry from our Baptist Union Superintendent, Keith Hobbs back in 1994/5, as to whether we could use a missionary couple, eventually led us to contact Stan & Jan McFall and their three children, Anna, Graham, and John-Ben. They could not have been based in a more diverse location than Toxteth. In Jan's words 'my kitchen looked out on the azure blue sea of the Indian Ocean surrounding Reunion Island.' Ill health for Jan, brought about by extreme heat, forced them into leaving the island where they were French speaking missionaries with the International Mission Board of the US Southern Baptist Convention. They obviously knew of the cooler weather in the UK and wrote to the UK Baptist Union asking whether they had any churches that could use a missionary family. On receiving the list of vacancies, they spotted Toxteth, and in their own words, 'we were like ants in a sugar factory!' They believed this was God's call and, after we exchanged numerous emails and letters, they finally arrived in 1996. Their outlook from the kitchen of their new home was on to a back street alley rather than an azure blue ocean!

Stan's evangelistic zeal and Jan's pastoral heart soon endeared them to many. They developed mission, preached with passion, encouraged individuals, took bible studies, shared in the life of the church, and made dozens of local contacts over three years. Sadly, what had started as a realistic five year placement was terminated by a change of mission strategy in the International Mission Board of the Southern Baptist Convention. Just as the real work was developing, and showing signs of fruitfulness, we had to say goodbye and entrust them to God's further work in the pastorate of a Baptist Church in Southtown, Minnesota.

As Urban work is a long-term call, we were sad to see them leave but recognised that whilst they had arrived in the UK as missionaries, they returned to the US as pastors. No difference whatsoever as to their passion as Christians, but we trust it owed something to the way God worked in them as well as through them, during their time among us. They are still fondly remembered and still in touch twenty-eight years on.

49

A SURPRISING SABBATICAL

After seven tough but exciting years, it was a joy and relief to have an extended break. With a fresh input of leaders, a charity overseeing the community ministries, and every aspect of the church mission in good heart and growing, it was time to be renewed spiritually and physically.

We had prayed about connecting with urban churches in the States but had no idea how we might afford the trip or where we might travel. Just prior to beginning the sabbatical we had our first Christmas off for many years. We were about to close our door and head off to spend Christmas with our son Tim and family. If I had left home just ten seconds earlier, I would have missed a call from Baptist HQ. A colleague, Graham Sparkes, had received a phone call from Derek Tidball, the Principal of London Bible College. Derek's Chair of Governors, Denis Cole, had received a request from Steve Odom, Pastor of First Baptist Church, Zephyr Hills in Florida. Denis passed it to Derek and Derek to Graham and Graham was on the phone to me - trust you grasped the handovers!

Denis and his wife Linda travelled regularly to Florida, staying in their condo and attending First Baptist Church, Zephyr Hills on a Sunday. Steve asked Denis if he knew of an urban church in the UK that needed support - one that was evangelistic but also concerned with social action. Both Denis and Derek were busy men so the request was passed to Graham and he thought of us in Toxteth! As we were off to Ashford, near Heathrow Airport, I promised Graham I would ring Denis as soon as we returned. On the journey down to London we discussed the timing and

225

content of the call. Here we were starting a sabbatical, having a goal in mind, but no idea how it would work out. Was that God on the phone?

We returned home after Christmas with a degree of nervous anticipation. I duly rang Denis and was about to be blown away, not simply with the news of a generous gift from First Baptist, but the outcome of my conversation with Denis. I mentioned our sabbatical and desire to visit an urban church in the States. Denis responded, 'what are your plans?' I said, rather meekly, 'we don't have any.' He then explained a little of the passionate social action at First Baptist along with their evangelistic ministry. Denis then mentioned that he had two condo's at Saddlebrook Golf and Tennis Resort at Wesley Chapel, just a few miles from Zephyr Hills. An invitation followed, 'would you like to stay at Saddlebrook?'

My mind immediately went slightly askew with thoughts of 'how much?' 'Just leave it with me, and I'll check the vacancy slots and get back to you.' As we both sat in tingling expectation, Denis had already mailed a brochure of Saddlebrook Resort. Two golf courses, a large American Tennis school, the biggest pool in Florida with smaller pools servicing blocks of low-level condo's and, to add the cream, an over abundance of wildlife! Oh, my goodness, this was way, way out of our league, but not God's generosity! Within a short time, Denis was back with available dates. Now the crunch. When I asked about cost, Denis replied, 'no cost at all!' Yes, God was on the phone! We now had just over a week to book flights, get our luggage sorted and do as much research as possible about Florida. This was not how we, and especially Ann, worked. Like any organised woman, Ann needed to know plans way ahead of the game – not this time!

A week later we were on a Virgin flight into Orlando. We

put down in Montreal to offload a very sick passenger and were informed it was -30 on the runway! Please don't ask us to get off as we only have warm weather gear! After a short delay of forty-five minutes, we were on route down the East coast. It was noticeable how far down the snow stretched, even into the warmer climes of South Carolina and Georgia. When we landed in Orlando the situation became clear. Almost every airport on the Eastern Seaboard was closed. Orlando was packed with thousands of passengers who had nowhere to go, plus thousands more who had flown in and were stuck.

Now, late in the evening, we needed a bed for the night. We joined a long enquiry queue. When we made the desk, with two receptionists, and asked about a hotel they looked incredulous and told us there were over 10,000 passengers stranded in the airport. We had no hope of securing a room. However, as we turned away, one of the ladies gave us a card and suggested we drive beyond the city boundary and hope for the best. We prayed. By the time we collected our hire car and found the hotel it was around midnight. Wonderfully, for two very tired travellers, they had a basic room available. It was just as well we arrived in the dark as it shielded us from the surrounding area. We were in a motel on the other side of the tracks! The door on the room had a significant number of 'jemmy' marks indicating multiple break-ins! It was at breakfast, in the bar, that we got the full picture. Lots of cowboy hats and interesting ladies! Not a million miles from Toxteth at its worst, so we were really at home; though perhaps not the cowboy hats!

We had deliberately booked our flight four days before we were due at Saddlebrook. Our goal was to reach the Gulf of Mexico and, with a limited budget, find a suitable motel near the coast. We hit the coast, South of Tampa at Fort Myers Beach, and began our search just as the sun was sinking with all the dramatic splendour of colour in a warm climate. Finding a hotel was more difficult than we imagined given our strict budget of $70 a night. As the light began to fade, we were aware our options were disappearing fast. Our last hope lay the far side of a high and long bridge spanning 'Big Carlos Pass,' a massive inlet into Estero Bay Aquatic Preserve - some eleven thousand three hundred and eighty-one acres! As we drove across the bridge, one high apartment block caught our eye. I parked up and noticed the sign, 'Lover's Key.' My first impression was, 'It's out of our league again.' The surroundings were utterly spectacular. A State Park to one side, a pure white beach, azure blue sea with dozens of yachts and other craft returning for the evening. The reception was immaculate. I enquired about the cost and, as expected, it was way beyond our budget but not God's. As I turned towards the exit an unexpected angel appeared from behind a pillar. A middle-aged lady gripped my arm and pulled me to the side of the lobby - not your everyday occurrence! She informed me that the building was half hotel and half apartments. As it was low-season in January she had an apartment at a discount and could show me straight away. I jumped at the offer. Eight floors up she ushered me into the apartment and I let out a 'wow.' The view was breathtaking as the sun set over the Gulf. The beach below and the sea beyond shimmered with a riot of colour and the apartment was elegant quality throughout. 'Oh Lord, please give me your peace and guidance' echoed in my mind. Price was everything now. She wanted $100 per night. In an act of bold faith I said, 'If you could drop to $75, we will take it for three nights' - she agreed! As I exited the apartment, I noticed a plaque at the entrance with a text from the Bible. To this day I cannot recall the text, but in that moment, it spoke so clearly to me that I had made the right decision to stay.

As Ann had remained in the car during this time, perhaps expecting another 'no', I wanted to get her up to the apartment as quickly as possible. As we entered, she expressed a 'wow' of ecstatic delight as the sunset blazed deep red over the Gulf. She then saw the plaque and together we shared how perfect it was. When we wait upon the Lord, He often has the very best in mind because He knows how to give good gifts to His children. We had navigated seven years of significant trials and tests, but this was a moment of abundant blessing. Suffice to note we had the most awesome three days ticking off all manner of wildlife from our laminated guide to Lover's Key State Park, and yes, the sofa was also awesome! (you might recall a previous remark!) Lover's Key it certainly was.

It was now time to leave our lover's paradise and experience even more unexpected blessings and surprises. We retraced our route up towards Tampa and, twenty miles further North, arrived at the entrance to Saddlebrook. The guard at the gate, no doubt used to lavish limousines as opposed to a small automatic, gave us a thorough grilling before directing us to reception. We soon realised we were in an exclusive setting with stunning villas, houses, apartments, swimming pools and manicured lawns, some owned by celebrities, tennis stars and notable golfers.

We were ushered into the reception and our car duly parked up by the attendant. I pondered what it might cost to get it back! Reception was a five star affair with all the amenities leading off multiple corridors and the largest pool in Florida at the rear! It was the most fabulous place we had ever witnessed and almost intimidating given the opulence. We booked in and were directed to our condo about a mile across one of many lakes on site - some with their resident alligators. A tip sufficed to retrieve our car! We arrived at our condo and noticed a couple moving across the car park, laden with food and a large bottle of champagne! We had never met Denis and Linda Cole, who were overlapping our holiday, but we knew instinctively it was them. 'Just wanted to welcome you and show you around' were Denis's first words of greeting as they passed over the brown bags.

Our condo was on the upper floor and, as we stepped inside, I think we sank inches into the carpet. Everything was just perfect and the welcome such a blessing. Just before leaving, Denis invited us to a 'meat evening' later in the week, at the resort restaurant. A few days after that special evening we also had a first when they invited us to a Japanese restaurant in Tampa - so posh we had our own chef to cook the meal at our table! As very ordinary folks, these extraordinary and generous hospitality invites were very precious indeed and remain as truly special memories in a wonderful holiday. Little did we know then, that we would be blessed three more times in the future, venturing across the ocean to Saddlebrook, courtesy of such generous hospitality from Denis and Linda.

As if we had not already been royally gifted, our goodbye capped it off. We were saying goodbye to Denis and Linda as they were leaving for the UK ahead of us. Denis asked if I had taken Ann to Busch Gardens. With a couple of days to go, and few precious dollars left, we had looked at the price - way beyond our budget. With one more act of generosity, Denis placed $200 into my hand and told me, kindly, 'take Ann to Busch Gardens!' Wow, did we enjoy that day! It was a revelation to discover the incredible attention given to disabled visitors. Ushered to the front of every queue. The best seats at the shows. Courtesy and assistance in spades.

50

HOOTERS, HOLINESS, HUMANITY - FIRST BAPTIST CHURCH ZEPHYR HILLS

Whilst it was such a blessing to relax and renew body, mind, and spirit, we were also in Florida to meet the pastor, Steve Odom, and see the work at the church buildings. We met in his palatial office in the church and very quickly established a good rapport. Our journeys into ministry followed similar paths, and our vision models - to share the gospel and care for those outside of the church building - almost identical. As I had been invited to preach on the first Sunday after arrival, I was eager to discover as much as possible about the people as well as the place. As in a lot of Florida churches, 'snowbirds' were in abundance – folks who move South from Canada and North America for the winter months. A nice option, but not always helpful in building a local church and engaging in community ministries. It was this aspect of church life we were now about to explore with Steve.

We were ushered into a very large warehouse and introduced to a team of warm and welcoming volunteer retirees. This space catered for just about every need in the community. Food, toys, clothing, financial aid, household furniture and everything for a newborn baby. Hand knitted clothes, prams, bedding, cots, food, as well as practical advice and English classes. Everything was colour-coded, labelled and presented professionally with a massive helping of love. Many Puerto Ricans, Mexicans and Cubans lived locally and were the main clients. Another ministry was for women, of any age, who had been abused. An old motel had been converted into a refuge for around twenty residents. This was compassionate humanity at its best.

One of the most innovative responses to need was the Postal Service annual collection of non-perishables from post-boxes in Zephyr Hills. Families or individuals left the packets and tins in the home post-box. Those donations were then collected by the posties and delivered to a sizeable facility in the warehouse. Here they were catalogued and made available to needy people in the area. Locals, refugees, and immigrants could literally visit the warehouse facility and be provided with everything they would need to set up home, feed and clothe their family, and enrol in a wide range of classes to help them settle well. In time a Spanish speaking service, with a paid pastor, would draw many Spanish speaking residents into the life of the church. It was inspiring and humbling to see a beautiful balance of passionate evangelism and social action.

During our conversation, Steve mentioned the possibility of bringing a small team over to Liverpool. I agreed and promised to discuss this with the Tab leadership on return to the UK. I had bittersweet memories of both individual guests and church teams from abroad, so approached the offer with a degree of caution. Knowing the culture of any locality, not least in a different country, is vital to sharing the gospel. In due time Steve brought a willing team over to Toxteth but the culture issue was never quite overcome. However, seeds of any sort are always welcome. Who can truly judge what the Holy Spirit can ignite given time. One thing was clear, Americans and Scousers tend to get on well, which makes for open relationships and open doors!

On the Saturday night before my preach, we were looking for a restaurant and saw a sign for Hooters. Nobody had warned, or informed us, about its reputation - short skirted and skimpy topped waitresses! Very interesting, but not when you begin your message on 'Holiness,' with the opening line, 'last night we went to Hooters!' The whispers rapidly shot along the pews of conservative Southern

Baptists like Exocet missiles! It was not only disconcerting but disastrous! From that moment on I was on a losing wicket! No wonder the congregation had disappeared before I had finished the benediction! Clearly Ann and I were not very holy! We returned to the UK suitably chastened, but with a twinkle in our eyes!

51

FACILITATING

As our ministries developed so they attracted more and more interest; visitors from Baptist HQ in Didcot, ministers and members from urban pastorates, students considering urban mission, teams from Youth With a Mission, church elders from Northern Ireland, a massive school party from Denmark, numerous individuals, and our faithful friends from the South of England who kept coming, praying, and giving to every element of the work.

Richard Steele's prophetic words in the past, about an increase in 'facilitating,' were about to take a huge leap forward. Many saw our vision as breaking something of the historic divide between evangelism and social action. Uniting conservative evangelicals and, apparently, liberal Christians – a passion to see lives transformed by faith in Jesus and needs met by appropriate and compassionate action. Some saw us as pioneers who were bridging gaps between church, community, and city. That had always been my heart and call from the outset and, interestingly, that of William Peddie Lockhart, the church founder. We were returning to our roots.

One of our visitors was Rev Graham Sparkes from Baptist House, who featured significantly in our US sabbatical. Following his interest in our work, the Baptist Times followed up with a full-page article. It was a massive healing moment. I may well have been labelled as a renegade or a rebel on denominational files, having entered two pastorates in unconventional ways, but I had simply prayed and obeyed the guidance of the Holy Spirit. In God's eternal irony my integrity was being remodelled and somewhat restored. Such irony, in a few years, would lead me right into the heart of Baptist HQ!

The format for facilitating was an invite to 'Urban Eyes-Urban Mind' – a weekend of looking, learning, worshipping, prayer and engaging with urban culture. My good, biblical friend, 'Nehemiah', offered the basis of biblical foundations for urban mission and ministry along with a renewed perspective on God's view of cities. Guests arrived on Friday afternoon and left after lunch on Sunday. Staff from the restaurant provided our meals. A tour of the local area, praying on street corners, fending questions, observing specific landmarks, all facilitated discussion.

One of the interesting cameos was a black and white sketch, from the 1600's, of an upstream mill leading down to the site where the Tab would be built in 1871. The sketch featured a pathway running alongside a stream with a chilling one line description underneath, 'known as the "black-pad" for its frequent night-time robberies.' Three hundred years later it was the Windsor Street area. No church had survived by the early 1980's. Some of our most difficult encounters took place at the heart of the inaptly named 'Sussex Gardens'. Tenement blocks where drug dealing, prostitution and robbery was rife, three hundred years on from the 'black-pad' stigma. It was a reminder that successive generations often copy the one before. Knowing such history fuels prayer and action. It also avoids many stupid mistakes! Places and people can change and be changed!

Those weekends were very special. There were rarely more than a dozen attendees but the interaction was personal, and for some, priceless preparation for future urban mission and ministry. One group of elders who came across from Northern Ireland were especially humble at the end of the weekend. They knew first hand what urban mission was like, not least through the 'troubles' of sectarian warfare in Northern Ireland. Prior to coming they had this mindset. 'We thought we were coming to tell you how to do it, but we are leaving having learnt so much more.' It was a very gracious and kind word and one that helped us to appreciate all we could bring to the table. As a leadership we also made our own forays to Northern Ireland and brought back inspiration, ideas and hopes.

As we encouraged attendees to catch a 'scouse' culture, so we needed to understand the culture our friends were facing. Not least the importance of 'locality-culture' – not just our city but our adjacent streets. Urban culture can often be reduced to a small segment of a large city! Bishop Derek Worlock, who served the Roman Catholic Diocese of Liverpool alongside Bishop David Shepherd in the Anglican Diocese, defined Liverpool culture as 'the way we do things round 'ere' – ar street!' Several times, when I engaged the community with varied issues, the reply was 'wat youse gunna do for ar' street?'

A very humorous moment occurred when I hosted a meeting between local residents and a spokesman for an agency putting computers into local homes. The spokesman told the group of residents they could get training at the local school, just a half mile down the road or two stops on the bus. A loud voice echoed from the back row, 'Dat's too far, youse can do it Terry in your basement!' It was a command not a question! As for agreement in cross-border community meetings, especially where money is available, you are in serious waters. I, only once, attended such a meeting in which they argued for two hours as to who was going to chair the meeting. Who gets the chair is likely to get the cash. Near midnight I slipped out quietly and a little wiser!

52

CARPE DIEM - 'SEIZE THE DAY'

From the moment Ann had her first of three hip replacements, in February 1982, aged 38, we increasingly pondered what future challenges might look like. A complicated new hip replacement would eventually wear and require an even more complex revision. Our surgeon Mr Goodfellow, at Nuffield Orthopaedic Hospital in Oxford, was very honest about a future operation, stressing carefully, 'I hope this never needs a revision'! He had delayed the surgery for over three years, stating to Ann, 'you are very young for a hip replacement, but when you scream, I will do it.' It was tough to see the pain and limitations she endured, but when bone started to grind on bone she eventually screamed.

Given the many dangers Mr Goodfellow had pointed out, he performed an amazing operation. We were also deeply grateful for the many church friends, family and colleagues whose prayers backed up the surgeon's skills and brought Ann through a very long procedure. Practically, the support was immense; keeping an eye on Andy (15) and Tim (13), as well as school trips for Sharon (4). Endless meals over the three weeks Ann spent in hospital and beyond, plus the constant stream of people who called in, following Ann's return home. What a joy to have such an extended family at Ashford BC.

Mr Goodfellow had warned Ann that she would be in hospital much longer than most other patients, such were her complications and long recovery time. Other, hip replacement patients, were up the day after surgery, Ann would stay in bed for a week before starting her recovery regime with the physiotherapists. Mr Goodfellow also advised her to always use a walking stick if she wanted to protect her new hip joint beyond the expected fifteen years longevity. His wisdom and experience proved correct. Thirty years later – twice the expected longevity – Ann would be on the list for a very risky revision! Prior to that, her right hip would deteriorate, and be replaced at Wrightington Hospital, near Wigan in December 1999. She managed to escape on Christmas Eve! As we reflect on our NHS history, over a lifetime, we owe a great debt of gratitude to a long line of GP's and Surgeon's, with their teams, who have given us guidance, wisdom, and their awesome skills, as well as sharing our grief in the death of one of our two babies, Elizabeth. As already mentioned, Germany was awful, and, largely, the NHS had been awesome!

Knowing our future re travel might be greatly affected, we made up our mind to do as much as we could afford way ahead of retirement. For the first twenty-five years of our marriage, we had little spare cash. We relied on my sister Phyllis's hospitality, plus another friend in Jersey who offered her home in the centre of town. We also discovered that Mr Billy Butlin provided free holidays for Ministers at his holiday camps, which went down well with the boys. However, Butlin's rooms, at that time, were not exactly user friendly. I took a bath one day and, as I slid down in the water, I came eye to eye with a rotund stomach next door! The gap between the flimsy wall and our bath offered full access to the bath next door! Being a good Baptist with a passion for full immersion I slid out of sight! I have it on good authority that Butlin's rooms have improved since the 1980's!

1988 was wonderfully different. It was our 25th Wedding Anniversary in June, and we were planning our first package holiday in Alcudia, Majorca, at Playa de Muro Hotel, a rather swish establishment. We would only have Sharon with us. We had saved hard, but with very little spending money. God had other plans. We began to receive gifts, both small and large, from church friends, family and well-wishers. As more gifts arrived, I felt the need to keep passing money on. It was if I felt guilty about receiving so much! Mid-stream in my overflow of giving, God spoke clearly to me about His generous heart and passion for abundance - 'can you not receive my grace?' It's as if God simply wanted to bless us without my need to feel guilty about the amount. We left for Majorca with a thousand pounds and had a memorable holiday with no money concerns, and especially for Ann, no cooking for two weeks!

From that time on we were so greatly blessed with respect to stunning holidays. Connections with friends at Walton Baptist Church led to our whole family being offered an amazing detached villa with pool in Javea, Spain. Javea features high on the list of the 'most healthy places to live in the world.' We made the most of the superb amenities at the villa as well as the stunning beaches, coves, and promenade restaurants. More family folklore was also added on the first of our visits to Javea. I managed to get lost several times, deep into the night, on the way from the airport to the villa. Tim, Sheila and two tired grandchildren were in the car behind! 'Never follow dad' is now a recurring mantra when on holiday or just out with our kids!

53

40TH WEDDING ANNIVERSARY

June 29th 2003 was our 40th Wedding Anniversary. We asked each other for the No. 1 place we would like to visit. Ann chose the Canadian Rockies and the Rocky Mountaineer rail journey from Vancouver to Banff. I chose a destination over one thousand miles away by air – Grand Canyon! By now, given Ann's physical limitations, I was used to thorough preparation of our holidays with regard to access. The surprise element of our trip of a lifetime was a US website, www.affordabletours.com. It popped up unexpectedly as I was searching for hotels in Vancouver. One of the adverts featured a week-long cruise from Vancouver to Alaska for $600pp! As the exchange rate was almost $2 to the pound, we were looking at £600 total for a week's cruise to Glacier Bay, on board Holland America Veendam, calling at Ketchikan, Juneau and Skagway! We simply could not turn it down. Well, it's not every week you have a milestone anniversary!

We landed in Vancouver a day ahead of the cruise and immediately fell in love with the city. Stunning vistas, snow-topped mountains, endless logs floating together - an iconic Canadian scene, with float planes as numerous as taxis! This was our first cruise and we were like kids with an overdose of candy. It was the first of the season to venture up the Inside Passage - think massive canal - and a journey of eight hundred and fifty-three miles.

I would love to present a detailed travel guide but Ann tells me I am already beyond a book trilogy! Suffice to say it was breathtaking, relaxing, exciting, and not to be missed. We saw endless American Eagles, whales, dolphins, bears, salmon and so much more. The crowning glory was a four hour slow rotation of the ship at Glacier Bay. Small icebergs dotted a glacial melt sea; a breathtaking vista of snow covered mountains ranging from six thousand feet to Mt Fairweather's fifteen thousand three hundred and twenty feet enveloped the bay. The Hubbard and Margerie glaciers were thrown in to overdose the senses. It was a double spiritual moment as six hundred passengers strolled to the front of the ship in a degree of awe, wonder and quiet contemplation. The 'stillness' was palpable.

One couple, returning from the front of the ship, caught my eye. They were a very opinionated Australian couple, in their 70's, who were on our dinner table in the evenings. They would vigorously oppose any form of spiritual conversation. As we passed by, they stopped, looked us in the eye, and the man spoke a simple, but telling, sentence, 'I am going to have to think about this.' I didn't need to hear anything more. One glimpse of awe-inspiring raw creation had triggered something deep within his soul. Perhaps the beginning of something new within – the missing piece of the jigsaw of life. As we strolled to the bow, to gaze ourselves at the awesome beauty, I whispered a 'yes' and a 'thank you Lord!'

On return we stayed two days in Vancouver before boarding the Rocky Mountaineer and beginning a breathtaking journey through the Rockies. Ann was a partially stranded snow-widow as I made endless trips to the viewing platform just outside our carriage. The ever-changing mountain and raging river scenes were addictive. Just when you think you have viewed the best panorama, and returned to your seat, the next bend would open another even more breathtaking vista, and up I would jump, declaring a vocal 'wow' and resuming my outside vigil with camera at the ready!

As Banff beckoned, we had been sated with beauty. Ann

had chosen well and I looked forward to my quite different awe-inspiring choice at the Grand Canyon. Just one more trip was planned, from Banff to Athabasca Falls on the Icefields Pathway, then on to Calgary Airport and another stupendous and dramatic of change of scenery. Because we had just one day to explore the drive along one hundred and twenty km of the IP to the Falls, I said to Ann that we could only stop a few times each way – we stopped about five times in the first twenty km! The road skirts alongside the folds of the Rockies, ranging from three thousand to twelve thousand feet, winds dramatically along the Athabasca River and, for us, ended with truly breathtaking views of the Athabasca Falls. Jasper, further on, was out of reach given our time restraints. Every twist and turn in the road, was greeted enthusiastically with yet another louder 'wow.' A magical day, with grateful tears and emotions, as we overdosed on the drama, beauty, and majestic vistas of the Icefields Pathway.

You could hardly visualise such a contrast as we flew from Calgary to Las Vegas! However, we are urban people, so not phased, just excited at what lay ahead. We checked into the Venetian Hotel and opened the door to our room. 'Room' is not appropriate! I immediately went back to reception and said, 'I think we have the wrong size accommodation,' to which the receptionist replied, 'no sir, all our standard rooms are that size!' I could have lost Ann for half a day, but with two gigantic TV's, on two levels, we would have been entertained! The following morning, we were up early for a helicopter flight over the West Rim of the Canyon. Ann had always wanted a flight in a helicopter, but it was a major effort for her to navigate the skids without getting hurt – her endless grit got her on board! The pilot fitted two couples in the back seats and invited us to sit beside him on the front row, with Ann right next to the pilot – clearly as a vivacious co-pilot! All headphones were turned on. The pilot was an absolute hoot. 'Your first flight?' 'Yes.' 'Mine too!' 'Anyone want vodka?!' We travelled low across the desert. Pilot to Ann, 'do you know the route?' 'No...' 'Well, keep your eyes open as I'm relying on you to guide us back to Vegas!'

We were clearly near to something special when the pilot announced, 'you all ready for this?' We could see a dark line ahead in the sand. We thought it might be the edge of the rim. I primed my video camera. Nobody, apart from the pilot, was ready. We hit the rim around thirty feet off the ground and immediately dived vertically into the canyon! I yelped 'wow' and dropped my camera, the back passengers screamed, and Ann just took it all in her stride.

The West Rim is nowhere near as spectacular as the South Rim, but it was still awesome, breathtaking, and scary as we skirted close to the canyon wall. Finally, we landed on a patch of Indian territory on the canyon floor beside the Colorado River. The crazy pilot was also very sensitive, allowing Ann to stay in the helicopter and avoid the scramble over the landing skids. Ten minutes after exploring the canyon floor, and with light gradually fading, we clambered aboard. After skirting the Hoover Dam, we travelled along the Vegas 'strip' with its hotel skyscrapers, neon lights, and the famous Bellagio Hotel Fountains. The experience was worth every penny, or should I say dollar, and fired us up for a return visit one day to the South Rim. That 'one day' would come quicker than we expected. Meanwhile, back in the real world, I was about to lead prayer at the Baptist Assembly. An occasion that would change the course of our lives and ministry once again.

54

AN UNEXPECTED SUGGESTION

David Coffey was General Secretary of the Baptist Union of Great Britain and was never late for anything! I was going to be late for breakfast, following my leading of prayers at the Baptist Assembly in 2003. By the time I had cleared up the tech-gear, breakfast had begun. As I walked in late, so did David! As no spaces were immediately evident, we joined together on a spare table. During our conversation, David suggested, very casually, that I might like to look at a job application that would be released soon with respect to a post in the Mission Department at Baptist House in Didcot. They were seeking the first ever Urban Mission Advisor. I had been at the Tab for fourteen years and about to turn sixty. The post would give me five years until retirement. As many urban pastors have discovered, it is easy to burn out amidst the excessive pressures of a tough pastorate and local environment. In many ways, I was beginning to consider, both for myself and Ann's sake, whether I could invest my final ministerial post elsewhere.

I logged the suggestion from David away and worked my way through the Assembly. My batch leader at college, back in 1974, Derek Allan, now Head of the Mission Department, was also at the Assembly. As we packed up to leave the hall, after the final meeting, I bumped into him at the door. As I recall, it was a swift goodbye and another suggestion, 'would you consider sitting on the panel assessing applicants for the upcoming Urban Mission Advisor post?' I was happy to oblige. My journey home was an interesting mix of prayer and consideration. On one hand, the suggestion from David was to look at the post myself and from Derek an invitation to join the panel and assess the applicant's suitability! I certainly could not do both! Should I assess or apply?

Once home I shared the conversations with Ann. Her initial reaction was, 'I thought it was both ironic and hilarious.' God clearly has a wonderful sense of humour. Quite innocently, but prayerfully, I had entered two lengthy pastorates in circumstances that were not entirely in line with Baptist protocol. I may have ruffled the feathers of Area Superintendents and General Secretaries and incurred dubious insertions into my denominational records! Now I was being invited to consider a post working out of Baptist House!

After prayerful consideration, I applied, but too late to make the initial assessment. The panel duly sat but were not able to appoint a candidate. I subsequently received an invitation to attend the next panel in October 2003. Each candidate gave a fifteen minute PowerPoint presentation on urban mission followed by questions. It came down to two applicants, me and a very experienced and capable colleague, but not with extensive urban ministry experience. The defining question, among the panel, was shared by Juliet Kilpin, a respected, long-term urban Pastor. She asked the panel, 'Do you want an advisor with considerable urban experience over fifteen years, or one who is capable but without that experience?' The issue was now clear and the panel decision went my way - I duly accepted. I would now be in unfamiliar territory, working in Baptist Headquarters Mission Department and not a church office. It was not to be merely a desk job. My heart was always at the coal-face.

One consideration we didn't expect was the offer to pick our own home. Ann has always been a wonderful homemaker so it was a special joy for her to think about priorities. Following a small number of viewings, we opted for a detached property on Ladygrove Estate, a short walk from the town centre and railway station, and near enough to Baptist House to walk to work. We were very grateful for this provision, especially as it was slightly over the budget guidelines! Just one more of the amazing house provisions that feature in our life story.

In March 2004, fifteen years after arriving in Toxteth and around our 60th birthdays, we moved from a small semi-detached in Toxteth, to a somewhat palatial home in Didcot. At the time, Didcot was labelled as a 'one-horse' town and the 'horse had died!' We understood a little of the problems, when moving from a city to a rural town, when we tried to buy hardware for our new home and groceries – one grocery shop and a very overpriced Focus hardware store!

One very special blessing, that you could never envisage without divine preparation, was Ann's work. Wallace Pharmaceuticals had just two sites, Knowsley in Liverpool, Ann's workplace when she left Level 3 at the Tab, and Abingdon near Didcot! She would leave her work in Knowsley and start again at Wallace Headquarters in Abingdon as Administrator with responsibility for stock-control and regulatory issues. Five years later, on retirement, she would be invited to move back, and stay with Wallace again. This time in their new city centre offices in Liverpool and a reunion with her former boss! A tribute to the respect she had earned and the skills she possessed.

55

URBAN MISSION ADVISOR

Following my arrival, I was invited to submit an article for the April 2004 edition of 'Transform' magazine which was sent out to every church. My thanks to Mary Parker for unearthing the text as well as timely reminders of past detail regarding my call to the Mission Department.

Transform article

Jimmy popped by today. 'Everybody is really upset you are going. You will really be missed. You are liked all over the estate. We had this done for you.' Inside the large brown envelope was the most detailed pencil drawing of Toxteth Tabernacle, so fine and perfect it brought immediate tears and the first hug in fifteen years for one of my 'tough' mates. In cosmic terms all we had done was sow, in Mark Gornik's phrase, 'a thousand small kindnesses.' A card and minor present to every neighbour on Christmas Eve, years of planting seeds with local youngsters who would shout across the street, 'me grans still got that cactus yer give us!' Signing passports, sorting union pensions, listening to addicts and gang leaders, trying to care when the problem appears overwhelming. Wrestling with urban culture and context that defies Christianising and Church, but has a depth of spirituality and wisdom that, at times, deserves more than casual consideration.

Then, there's the Tab. Fiercely independent, needing nobody for a hundred years, and then, on the brink of spiritual death, needing to humbly seek partnership and provision. Fifteen roller-coaster years of hell and heaven. An inch-by-inch renewal of place and people that has transformed so much life within, but also the attitude and perception of a close-knit neighbourhood towards church, and we pray, towards Christ. Now we leave, with no less tears than when we first knew God had called us in March 1985 - a call finally sealed at our induction in September 1989 and completed in February 2004. Thank you, Lord, for all the pain and suffering, joy and grace, partnerships and facilitating, friends and colleagues that have accompanied quite an amazing, yet humanly ordinary 'scouse' pilgrimage.

'If you can smile when things go wrong, you have someone in mind to blame' - maybe those who suggested I think about a vacant post and insisted I, 'look at the job advert on Thursday!' In the end, of course, it is the peace that the Holy Spirit gives that finally guides our decisions and illuminates the right path at the right time. As I approach the final period of mission and ministry, I'm smiling at the one-liner that says, 'I don't have a solution but I admire the problem.' My heart is 'urban.' My passion is the city, yet I am also aware of a team to serve, a diversity of tasks to embrace and a kingdom-people to represent. Patience will be a virtue, peripatetic incarnation vital, listening key. In all this there is a note of glorious God-planned irony. Thirty years of being a bit of a rebel in the 'Union's' side now I'm inside the 'Union'! So be it, Lord!

Terry Jones (Mission Adviser for Urban Mission/Social Inclusion). One gorgeous wife, Ann. Three children, Andy (37), Tim (35) and Sharon (26). Three lovely grandchildren Ben (10), Tierney (9) and Aaron (3), and one budgie - 'Lunatic!'

****

Like any new workplace, it took time to settle in. It was thanks to a brilliant department team that I survived the early months! 'Mary, can you sort my grammar please and where am I supposed to be today.' 'Fiona, am I spending too much money?' 'Nick, my PowerPoint is not working!'

'Derek, am I on the right track with this file?' For my moments of vocal frustration, repeat visits to your desk, or any other transgression, I offer my unreserved apologies to all.

From the outset, my goal was to visit as many urban pastors and churches as possible. It is never wise to assume you can be of help until you have walked their streets, observed their challenges, and understood the local culture. As is often the case, I came away with more blessing than I assumed I had left. It was humbling to hear one Pastor say, when I rang to suggest a visit, 'you would come to me?' How easy it is to send missives from a desk or via a file. It was the personal connection that I valued most. It also enabled Ann to accompany me, occasionally, and to share her own experiences of urban life with the Minister's wife and other ladies who might be around during our visit.

Alongside visits, I shared with the team the possibility of day visits to Baptist House by individuals or teams, for specific issues such as 'Coffee Shop Facilitation Days' for those churches wanting to start or expand an existing work. 'Money Advice Days' - especially grant funding from me as well as input from other staff. I had previously been on the Mission Executive so was familiar with 'Church, Community and Change' a Tear Fund initiative helping churches to understand and respond to need in the local community. It was interesting and inspiring to sit on the 'Against the Stream' and 'Green Shoots' committees, allocating funds for varied church initiatives. The most disappointing meetings, for me, were the management meetings. It was interesting to receive broad news from across the diverse range of Baptist churches, but it was very frustrating to consistently find the 'urban' report last on the agenda. Often, I was asked to speak at the fag-end of the meeting, sometimes given five minutes before lunch! It spoke to me of just how unimportant urban ministry was in the grand scheme of things. Baptists love to do the middle-ground well, though I suspect it may not be the case today, twenty years on, when we live in a vastly different, diverse, multi-ethnic, and increasingly 'urban' world.

56

HOLIDAYS, HEARTBREAKS AND PAINFUL DRAMA

In 2007 Sharon had been in Peru for a year. Because of a special 'holiday' legacy Ann's mum left to us, we looked forward to an amazing trip to Peru, via half-way stays in Las Vegas and Cancun. Our second Las Vegas stay would be the fulfilment of a promise to visit the South Rim of the Grand Canyon, following our 40th anniversary helicopter flight to the West Rim in 2003. It would not be without heartbreak and trauma! Sharon would join us in Cancun, for a week's holiday, before flying on to Lima together in time for Christmas.

One of the highlights for us, when travelling to the US in the winter, was standing at the back door windows of the plane and surveying the vast tracts of snow and ice covering Greenland, Canada, and many of the East Coast States of America. Creation is awesome and we just took it all in with a sense of wonder.

We duly arrived back in Las Vegas and booked into the 'pyramidical' Luxor Hotel. As there were no helicopter flights to the South Rim, we booked a flight to Flagstaff Airport and a ninety-minute coach journey to the Canyon. As our flight was early the next morning, we stayed for a salad buffet at the Luxor. Later in the evening Ann started to feel unwell. Over several hours, food poisoning was setting in and it was obvious Ann was not well enough to fly. Despite my protestations, she insisted I go and not lose money on both tickets. It was hard to leave her in the room but, unknown to me at the time, I would never have got her to the rim! On arrival at Grand Canyon village, the temperature was below freezing and a thick coat of snow and ice covered the entire reception area and cinema complex. The route to the rim was slippery, dangerous, and hopeless for pushing a wheelchair! At least Ann was comfortable, warm, and hopefully recovering!

First stop, before the walk to the rim, was the Imax Cinema and the epic production of the first discovery of the canyon by Europeans. In 1540 Don Lopez de Cardenas, of Coronado's expedition, discovered the Grand Canyon. Stories told by the Hopi Indians to Don Pedro de Tovar, a Spanish soldier and Colonial Administrator, led to a search by a detachment of soldiers led by Cardenas. A very emotional scene in the film shows Cardenas arrival at the rim and his response – he kneels in awe, wonder and worship. I don't know how many in the cinema had tears, but I certainly soaked my hankie! I still have tears today as I write. I wonder what emotions you have had in life, prompted by the awesome wonder of creation? A glorious legacy God gave us as a means of experiencing his presence and amazing love.

The second, and equally dramatic, section of the film, features the incredible exploits of American naturalist John Wesley Powell and his team - the first white people to navigate the Colorado River to the Grand Canyon. If you want to see what they faced, check out Dan Snow, 'Operation Grand Canyon', as he and his team replicate Powell's journey. The cinematography of the white-water rapids is breathtaking and very scary! The difference for Powell was he had no back-up in an emergency. Six of Powell's team of ten, in three boats, made it to the canyon, one left and survived, three left together but were never seen again.

As if one cinematic overdose of emotion wasn't enough, the South Rim was stratospheric. As I approached the edge, with a coachload of visitors, there was an eerie and expectant silence. Nothing can prepare you sufficiently for that first moment. The sheer grandeur, majesty, and extent of the canyon at this point. The West Rim is simply the trailer for the South. As it was so cold at the rim, and my clothing was not suitable, all I could do was rush around and take as many pictures as possible before making a hasty retreat for the next coach back to Flagstaff and the flight to Vegas. I was greatly relieved to find Ann recovering well, but part of me didn't want to say too much and add to her disappointment. However, I made a promise to return again, so she could stand in awe as I had done. I didn't expect to return twice! We were not to know the drama waiting in the wings.

We were arriving for a week's holiday in Cancun just a few hours behind Sharon, who was flying in from Miami. She booked into the Hilton and decided to get a taxi to the airport and surprise us. She had told me and not Ann, so it would be a surprise for her! On our arrival at the terminal there was no sign of Sharon, and after waiting an hour to see if she would turn up, we left the airport and picked up our hire car. When we arrived at the hotel, we checked to see if Sharon had arrived. The receptionist confirmed her arrival but told us she had gone to the airport! Somehow, we had missed her so we just sat outside waiting. After three hours we began to grow increasingly concerned. It was now 11pm and my mind was racing with possible scenarios. A single female in a Mexican taxi conjured up some scary options.

I decided to return to the airport. The fear inside overwhelmed me on the journey. I scanned every taxi for a glimpse of our miracle daughter. Sobbing and prayer were intertwined. On arrival at the airport my fear was compounded. The airport was ghostly. The arrival boards were blank. If she had arrived to greet us, and missed us, she would have made her way back to the hotel an hour or more before my arrival to search for her. My journey back to the hotel was a living nightmare. I could find no other explanation for her absence than abduction and began to experience severe nausea as I walked from the car park towards the hotel. Ann had been sitting on a seat, scanning every shuttle bus, accompanied by a compassionate receptionist. It was now past midnight. As I approached the seat, I saw two figures but believed it was the receptionist - I was distraught. Then my mind shifted gear and I realised it was Sharon. I burst into tears and sobbed uncontrollably as I held her. The tension left me being very sick all night.

Eventually we unravelled the mystery. Sharon thought we were coming in from one airport, Dallas, but we were arriving from Las Vegas! It turned out the Dallas flight was delayed, and as she was so tired from her own overnight flight, she found a spot to rest at some nearby tables, just out of view of the terminal exit, and waited. Once the Dallas flight finally arrived, she was so excited and expectant to see us but that quickly turned to despair as one by one everyone left the airport. It was the last flight in that night. Through tears and in a panic (she didn't have enough money for a taxi back to the hotel) she managed to blag her way onto a hotel transfer shuttle bus with her last $12. She sat squished between the driver and a tourist, both of whom were very concerned about her constant crying. Meanwhile Ann was despairing of any more buses or taxis back, after scanning every arrival! Finally, when Sharon's bus arrived, she saw her emerging and burst into tears. Sharon couldn't believe her mum was already at the hotel, her own confusion mixed with relief. Now, together, they began to wonder where I was until I turned up a total wreck!

To compound matters, the hotel had booked us into one room when we paid for two. As there were no other rooms available for that night, we made the best of a truly dramatic day! We were suitably recompensed in the morning when the receptionist moved us to a suite with a large jacuzzi on the veranda. To the West we looked inland over a lake, and to the East the Caribbean Sea. From that moment on we had a wonderful holiday, making the most of the swimming pool, sea, jacuzzi, and various sightseeing trips to Aztec ruins. Xel-Ha was an amazing place where we snorkelled with an array of tropical and ocean fish, including barracuda! Ann was not exactly in her element, with large fish circling her, but she was determined not to miss such an experience. More drama was awaiting us on the final leg to Lima.

57

LIMA

Our flight to Miami was delayed and we missed our connection to Lima. The airline that managed our delayed flight from Cancun to Miami did nothing to help us with our missed connection. Instead, we queued at a busy American Airlines counter, with Sharon in tears as they said they would put us on a LAN flight the next day. They sent us off to a hotel, some distance from the airport, but we asked to be moved to the main airport hotel that was connected to the terminal so access would be easier with Ann and the wheelchair. We spent a restless night and returned to the terminal early in the morning. After some hours waiting, Sharon, quite randomly, went to an empty LAN counter, with one worker attending, to see if we could leave our luggage early. She said no, and Sharon turned away, but on an impulse, turned back and asked if she could check we were on the flight American Airlines had said we were on. Much to her surprise, it turned out we were not on it! However, this lady may well have been an angel, as seeing Sharon's distress, she just took our details and put us on the flight, no questions asked! We were extremely grateful for that 'angel' and our arrival in Lima on Christmas Eve.

Despite the trauma and tears of the previous twenty-four hours, at midnight on Christmas Eve we watched fireworks from Sharon's roof. All of Lima was celebrating. We were now ready for sleep! On Christmas morning we swopped presents in stockings, before a Christmas meal with missionaries from Latin Link, courtesy of Andy and Brenda Parkins. It was a joy to meet them and hear something of their work. Lots of laughter, mayhem and games followed, with a few crazy pipes stuck out of mouths! (Wooden Peruvian holders for making nice little compacted rice shapes.)

Returning for a moment to Sharon's orientation with Latin Link before leaving in September, 2006. She was in a prayer session, contemplating her future in Peru, when she had a vision of a barren hilltop with shanty town homes up the hillside to the very top. As she stood on the top of the hill she had a 360 degree panoramic view over Lima. Shanty towns in each direction for as far as the eye could see. As dusk descended, lights began to appear across the streets. She saw doors open but only in some cases did light shine out into the street. Then she saw Jesus walking along, inviting those around to come with him. Suddenly Sharon was there, in his place, extending the same invitation to walk with Jesus. She didn't know where it was until after her language studies, when she began to investigate options working alongside another missionary. The day she stood at the top of La Roca and saw the same scene from her vision, she knew God was calling her to this place.

Now, on our second day, we were heading for that very place. A couple, Richar and Mari, and their two young daughters Angie and Anita, were struggling to develop a church plant which was one of a number started by a long-term Latin Link missionary Margaret Saunderson. The challenge was to get Ann to the top of La Roca - around eighty steps! I and two other men began to lift Ann in her wheelchair. I think we managed eight steps! If you want an example of heroic grit, the next seventy-two steps will suffice. Little by little Ann ascended the remainder of the steps by herself, but with guards on each side! She was determined to reach the top and present one of the three banners she had made to Richar and Mari.

Neither of us were aware of Sharon's earlier vision, but as we settled at the top, Sharon told us about it. As we lingered near the summit, we took in the panoramic view and shared a divine moment. The lights began to flicker across the endless shanty towns and Sharon's vision was realised in our own sight. Tears emerged freely. Richar took me a little higher and I began to weep as I embraced the poverty. Finally, when we pulled ourselves together, Ann was reminded of Hannah's story in 1 Samuel chapter 1 verse 1 – chapter 2 verse 21. The story of the mother of Samuel the prophet. Hannah had been infertile but the Lord intervened, heard her cry and, in time, her son was born. She named him Samuel, saying, because I asked the Lord for him.' 1 Samuel chapter 1 verse 20. Following the loss of our two children and the advice 'not to have any more,' we prayed about another child. God gave us Sharon.

Any loving parent will know how hard it is to surrender a child to adult life, university, or other ways and times of letting go. Samuel was so precious to Hannah, but she promised Elkanah her husband she would 'present him to the Lord and he will live there (at the Temple) always.' La Roca was Ann's 'Hannah moment' of letting go and it gave her peace and confirmation of Sharon's call to Peru. Sharon was our daughter, but also God's child. We knew this was an important moment of surrender to God's will for her life.

Two further shanty towns followed. The inaptly named 'California' stretching for miles on the sandy desert, and Lurin, with its fruit orchards, pottery, and green surroundings, where Ann presented another beautiful banner to the Luz en las Tineblas church, leaving just a little of our heart in each church. Ann had previously provided a cooker for the family in Lurin. Just one problem; the family could not afford the gas cylinder! When we arrived at Rosa's home the cooker was pristine! It taught us the importance of the ongoing support and deeper understanding that we had completely missed.

In the following days we attended a cell group in Cristo Vive church in California. Ann's physical limitations were being stretched as she had to walk across a narrow plank, over a drainage ditch, to reach the door into the house! She was also in her element, as young children sat on her lap on two occasions. One little 'Dickensian' child, with oversized and lace-less shoes, promptly fell asleep on her lap – for over half an hour! Such moments always moved us to tears as we wrestled with life in such poor conditions. Nevertheless, almost universally, these children were clean, well dressed and rarely without a huge smile lighting up beautiful white teeth! They were also immune to danger. The pottery run by Rosa's family in Lurin, involved youngsters stuffing wood and chaff into a small but flaming-hot hole in the family brick kiln! Selling pots was their means of income and the whole family played a part. On another visit to Santa Anita, children hung off the unfinished side of a house – twenty feet above ground with no wall for protection!

It was a beautiful sight, at one location, to watch over fifty children arriving across fields, from every direction, to attend kid's work run by Sharon. They sat together in a large circle, quiet, well-behaved, and attentive as Sharon shared the stories of Jesus. They may have been extra-good, given the presence of Dad and Mum, but so precious for us to see the impact just one faithful servant can have on so many children. One of the highlights was the opportunity to present Ann's final banner to Cristo Vive church in California shanty town, then preach with Margaret Saunderson interpreting. What a joy to share a retreat day with this church and participate in baptising six people in an outdoor pool as they confessed their faith in Jesus as their Lord and Saviour. Food, footie, fellowship, and lots of fun in the pool, featured well throughout the day.

In between visits to the shanty towns, we visited the Inca ruins at Pachacamac, twenty-five miles southeast of Lima in the Lurin River Valley. The site was first settled around A.D. 200 and named after the 'Earth Maker' creator god Pacha Kamaq. It survived for 1,300 years until the Spanish invaded. Sharon also led us on a tour of Lima, taking in the exaggerated slow-motion, pause mid-step goose march, of the 'toy-soldier' guards at the Palacio de Gobierno Palace - home to the President of Peru. How on earth they manage the pause on one leg I don't know. One of those 'don't try this at home' health warning movements! They were however, extremely smart and capable at the midday parade.

Miraflores, one of the more upmarket areas of Lima, was a revelation with its world class restaurants, swish hotels, and Pacific Ocean vistas. Ideal for people watching, pushing a wheel chair and romantic hideaways in the Parque Del Amor. It is also perfect for launching off the cliffs with a parachute! Motoring, on the other hand, is not to be recommended in Lima. It can be reasonable at times, but is mostly chaotic. Traffic jams are common, horns always blaring and accidents frequent! Small, brightly coloured red, blue and yellow 'moto-taxis' rule! Buses tend to stop anywhere, given a casual wave from the side of the road. However, fear not traveller, the long-distance coaches are luxurious!

Lima is not short on colour. Everywhere you go there are small and large, and occasionally huge, murals. Artistic talent knows no boundaries, whether across buildings, walls, houses, city squares or transport. The markets are a riot of colour, whether clothes, paintings, bags, hats, souvenirs, banners, even the food shouts 'rainbow-offerings'! There may be extreme poverty everywhere but there is also joy and celebration.

As New Year beckoned, our days were numbered but we were grateful for all we had seen, heard, shared, and enjoyed. We had shared laughter and tears, joy and pain. The key tourist sites, such as the breathtaking Inca city of Machu Picchu, the amazing rock formations in Cusco, the awesome vista from Huaraz towards Mount Huascaran - the highest in the Andes - or the mystical and mysterious Nazca Lines in the Southern Nazca Desert, were beyond our reach. Our goal was not so much to be tourists but partners in Sharon's missionary endeavours. It was information, insight, and identity with the locations, struggles, needs, and joys, among some of the poorest people in Lima, that we wanted to experience. Seeing the poverty, listening to the struggles, and embracing the people, enabled us to understand just a little bit more of the culture and challenge Sharon, and other missionary friends, faced daily. We learned about perseverance, living on little, facing a daily battle for food or income, and hope for a better future. We discovered sacrificial, prayerful, and grateful communities of believers who were making a difference where God had placed them. As parents, our special joy was to walk 'Sharon's streets', share her mission and pray for her ministry, not just in Lima but wherever God has taken her across Latin America.

As we hugged, cried, and released her once again to God's plan for her life, we were grateful for this precious opportunity to be together, through the trauma of Cancun and Miami to the joys of finally making it to Peru. New challenges in the Mission Department were awaiting me on return.

58

FRESH HORIZONS

There are days when a fresh breath of inspiration and opportunity is stimulating, interesting and somewhat exciting. My boss, Derek, was an encourager and prepared to consider new initiatives. He popped by my desk on such a day and dropped a couple of books and a proposal into my lap. 'Could you read these and consider tackling the issue of ageing.' At this point I was probably around 62 - maybe he was thinking of me!

Following my reading, which helped me to differentiate clearly between Third and Fourth Agers, I responded with enthusiasm, but commented, 'only the Third Age.' I was not yet, and still not at 80, thinking 'old'. Derek agreed and I worked on a proposal embracing three key responses:

> ➤ Production of an online Third-Age mission file
> ➤ Six CD testimonies from Third Agers
> ➤ Fresh Horizons Day Conference across the UK

Mission File

BUGB had a selection of online files covering a wide range of subjects. Mine would cater for a new group of retirees who don't do 'old.' Though a generalisation, you can spot them generally kitted out in trainers, jeans, sweat-shirts, and the occasional gold medallion! World experience, good health, time-rich, often with good pensions, radical and rebellious, suspicious of authority, not accepting of the status-quo and desperate to be valued and used according to their experience, values, and skills. As one quoted to me 'we will do anything in church, but please give us significance and opportunities in line with our gifting.' With respect to church, they were looking for challenges, both at home and abroad, but would baulk at being devalued, side-lined, or ignored. They were sure of their relationship with Jesus, often great prayer warriors, theologically astute, spiritually aware, and eager to serve. Many found that church offered no challenge at all which matched their deep desire to make a difference in Jesus' name.

CD Testimonies

The joy of visiting churches, and a timely meeting at a Prague Conference, led me to candidates for Fresh Horizons testimonies. Three would share their story of finding a challenge in their home church and three would share their experience of serving abroad following retirement. The range was just right. Dear 'Dave' from Romford whose infectious love for adults and children led him to serve in the toddler's group, simply putting out the kit, letting the children come to him, and cleaning up afterwards. On Saturday's he would be present at a divorced-dad's group who needed somewhere to go with their children. Dave spoke of his joy on seeing couples in Romford High Street who had been working at reconciliation.

On the opposite spectrum, but no more or less precious, were Bill and Nancy from the US, with whom I shared breakfast at the Baptist Seminary in Prague. They were librarians who had retired at fifty-five and were praying about how God might use them. If Dave was one end of the service spectrum, Bill and Nancy were at the breathless end! They started out in China, helping to prepare rooms for students. Following that they moved to learning mandarin - as you do - and volunteering in a playgroup. Bill progressed to teaching English from the Bible!

University Professors, Army Officers, and anyone else interested, were his students. Nancy spoke about Jesus to the playgroup staff. Following on they were both invited to handle international conferences for the university! When that calling ceased, they moved to Russia and returned to the ordinary work of preparing students accommodation – nothing too menial! When I found them in Prague, they were screwing mirrors to walls!

Within a week of returning home to the US they were getting bored. Nancy popped into the local surgery and asked, 'Is there anything so obnoxious that no one wants to work at it?' The staff pondered for a week then contacted her. 'Our files are in an awful state, could you sort them out?' Nancy sorted the files. 'Could you oversee our medicines?' Nancy obliged. 'Would you consider doing small medical tasks such as blood tests?' Nancy responded with joy. Together they moved out again across the world in obedience to God's directing. The common denominator in all six testimonies was humility, obedience, service, and willingness. Nothing was too menial or challenging.

Fresh Horizons Conference/Workshop Day

By the time I had completed the Mission File, and arranged for testimonies to be filmed at Baptist House, we were approaching our final two years prior to retirement. With a new Head of Mission, Ian Bunce, several changes of mission staff, and the spectre of financial constraints, which would especially curtail visits to urban churches, I was glad of a fresh initiative that would connect me with the outside world again. The lion's share of our efforts would now be concentrated on delivering these important conference days. Once again, it was a joy to share this new venture with Ann, not least because many engagements would be over a weekend. It would also prove extremely helpful to have a spare pair of hands for admin, manning the bookstall and unexpected emergencies, of which there were a number!

The aim was a worshipful, visual, interactive, bible-based, and practical day anywhere across the UK as well as Baptist House. Details were sent to every Regional Team, and via social media, inviting either a joint response among churches or for individual churches to host a conference. After a slow start, momentum built and we reached right across the UK, even fulfilling our last engagement in Stirling a few weeks after retiring!

As we expected, we were addressing a significant issue, both for churches and 'Third-Age' retirees. Time and again we were told, 'I am so relieved somebody thinks like me, I thought I was the only one.' It was sad to discover that very few churches were offering a challenge to retirees that was in line with their mindset and youthfulness as opposed to the traditional view of retirement featuring slippers, pipe, and easy-chair! Nothing is further from the reality of a third-age mindset. Over time, it was encouraging to hear of several churches exploring ways to inspire and challenge third-agers.

59

HOLY COWS AND SUPER NANNIES

It was during our Fresh Horizons tour across the UK that we began to pray and talk about where we should be living and serving in retirement. There was a small matter of a home. Ann's mum had left us a lovely legacy in her will, and a note that encouraged us to use some of it to travel, but there was not enough to buy a house! Contrary to so many ministers, who settled quietly to the 'South Coast Costas', our DNA is urban. Not simply because we had spent fifteen years in inner city Liverpool, but because we recognised the many advantages of living in, or near, a vibrant city. Lots of 'free' interest in museums, concert halls, art galleries, annual events, shopping options, free transport - including ferries! Access to renowned libraries, world class hospitals - so vital for Ann - gyms, cinemas, theatres, not to mention churches and housing options. It didn't take us long to discern that a return to Liverpool was on our, and God's, radar.

Two of our Fresh Horizons tour venues were in Liverpool, around eighteen months before retirement in March 2009. We were now actively searching and praying, with friends, about the right area and house. As we motored into Liverpool, on our way to Maghull, we were about to pass the Liverpool Cricket Club when Ann shouted, somewhat abruptly, 'turn left here!' With apologies to the driver behind, I made an un-indicated and rapid swerve into Riversdale Road. Ann explained that she had completed a shorthand-typing refresher course at Riversdale College some years ago. It was a divinely inspired shout! The college and grounds had been purchased by Wimpey Housing in 2004, the college demolished and a new estate, with apartments, social housing, and a range of upmarket 2-6 bed houses built.

As we entered the River Oaks Estate, we had that deep sense of peace promised in scripture. The peace that is meant to guide us in the decisions we make. However, we also laughed! The houses were clearly out of our league and we logged the experience away. Six months later we were back in Liverpool and decided to take another trip to River Oaks. As we drove past the, almost derelict pond area in the middle of the estate, we noticed a house for sale in a close of twelve houses adjacent to the pond. Somehow, we had missed the smallest houses on the estate on our previous visit! Inner peace remained, but the price was still beyond our means - but not beyond God's intervention.

Shortly after our return home to Didcot, we received a phone call from Stewart Green, the Administrator of the Retired Baptist Ministers Housing Society (later 'Organisation'). RBMHS trustees had been considering the possibility of their first ever 'equity' scheme. They believed it was right and Stewart began to discern who to contact. We were his first contact! Following his explanation about 'equity,' he said, 'we thought of you!' My reply was equally short, 'Stewart, you don't know what you have just done.' I explained our visits to River Oaks and the peace we felt about No 5 Chatbrook Close. He asked us to proceed with the estate agents and send him details.

At the same time, close friends, Brian & Angela Benford, had been praying earnestly for a home for us. They had been part of the team who had supported, prayed, encouraged, and given so much practical help during our time in Toxteth, not least in paving the way for Stepping Stones Restaurant by planning the lay out, encouraging staff and considering the menu. 'Whenever we pray for you, and this may seem weird,' Angela said, 'we see cows!' We laughed and muted the possibility of Jersey, Milton Keynes, Hereford, or the Dutch Frisian Islands. Was God leading us elsewhere?

The clincher was 'Supernanny' on TV. One of the episodes was being filmed on Otterspool Promenade, minutes from the house in Chatbrook Close. I was at a conference and Ann, who loves Supernanny, was watching the programme. As the camera panned along the prom a huge red sculpture of a bull filled the screen! Ann burst out laughing and realised that the bull was just down the road from River Oaks! If God can speak to Balaam via an ass, (Numbers chapter 22 verses 21-38), then he could speak to us through a red bull! The dye was set.

We agreed with Stewart to proceed with the purchase of the home at £181,000. RBMHS would own 51% and we 49%. The divine transaction simply followed the same faith-pattern we had previously experienced. The money we had was enough for our 49% share, with some spare for building work in the future. We, and others, had prayed, and the Lord provided a way where there seemed to be no way. One of the most amazing periods of our life and witness, now well over fifteen years, was being shaped for our retirement work.

60

TIME TO SAY GOODBYE

I love chocolate, in fact, I am a paid up addict! When certain staff members regularly deposited tins of Quality Street on the Mission Dept tables it was impossible to resist. As March 2004 drew near, the Mission Team were working hard at ensuring I would overdose! Secretive plans were afoot, designed to confuse me. A convoluted trip around Birmingham could not dislodge my expectations – 'Cadbury's World' it was. I am proud to report that I was very circumspect with the offerings. The sight of endless streams and fountains of chocolate may well have proved counter-productive. However, it was a special day, followed up by my leaving day.

Most of Baptist House staff gathered at the Mission Dept along with my wife Ann. Staff had been very creative with a 'mystery' barrel full of goodies, a CD of Willy Wonka and the Chocolate Factory with my head superimposed to great effect. A beautifully prepared, quality cardboard pouch - 'hand made for you with TLC' - was the crowning glory. I can guess who was responsible, but it was truly a team effort, with creatively chosen photos, cheeky quotes, thoughtful words, and wise advice such as, 'I'd give up chocolate – but I'm not a quitter.' 'Life is uncertain … eat dessert first', and a picture suggesting I might compromise with ice cream or custard on my rhubarb crumble! Clearly, they had missed the 'cream!' To the uninformed, the 'Terry' is now a specialist dessert in many a restaurant. PS, just say 'all three please' when they ask, 'do you want cream, custard or ice cream on your crumble?' Wait three seconds and log the waiter's incredulous response!

Inside the outer pouch was an inner pouch, a tear-jerker to be carefully considered at home. This precious treasure documented my time in pastoral ministry and mission department. There were more poignant photos, humorous insights, and very kind comments from just about everyone in Baptist House. A special thank you to my first Head of Department, Rev Derek Allan, a wise and supportive mentor, friend, and guide. He had moved on before I retired but had shaped all aspects of my time in Didcot.

I trust you will forgive me a little indulgence – well, there's not much you can do! It will ruin my humble reputation, but may also be a blessing. It misses all my weaknesses, doubts, failings, and mistakes. Below is a post from the Rev Ian Bunce, Head of Mission Department on my retirement. Ian had some difficult decisions to make about the direction of my work, some of which were disappointing but necessary given financial constraints. However, during my final two years, he embraced the Fresh Horizons vision with enthusiasm and encouragement. Fifteen years into retirement, that work continues in a different form, with a group of Third-Age retirees, under the banner of AWAM (Age with a Mission). This work is not my doing but one we have both embraced, supported, and are blessed by. I have always felt that the work of Fresh Horizons was incomplete and it is my hope that AWAM may well fill in a lot of missing pieces. Thank you all for the very kind comments packed into the pouch. Please accept my apologies for noting just one out of the many I could have included.

Rev Ian Bunce

What are we going to miss when you retire?

'A Pastor, who would always be there for people and spot the needs the rest of us missed. A passionate Prophet

who always spoke for the powerless, oppressed, and marginalised. A Pioneer who can see the emerging things of God and catch the crest of God's wave and surf it. We could say much more, but what we will miss most is a friend, a brother, and a true man of God. Thank you for all you have given'.

To have received such a glowing tribute is humbling, and precious, but it would never have been possible without a truly amazing wife. Because you have persevered this far in reading our story, you will know the challenges, trials, frustrations, and pain Ann has endured for a large part of her eighty years. She has done so with immense grit, determination, stubbornness, and resilience. I could not have asked for a more beautiful, wise, loving, and supportive wife. She has an inner beauty that is careful to listen well, respond with due diligence, and attractive to those who need empathy. It invariably draws others to her. She has supported me through thick and thin, guided me when I was making foolish decisions and kept me from numerous disasters. She is a wonderful mum and grandmother, home-maker, friend, lover, prayer-partner, and faithful wife. I love her deeply and give grateful thanks for our life together, the complimentary gifts she has exercised in ministry, and the family she has loved, nurtured, and consistently prays for.

As staff drifted away, there was one more unexpected blessing and one that would help to shape the next stage of our lives. Occasionally, I prayed with Linda Holder, a solicitor in the legal department. As we packed up to leave, she came to me with two prophetic words:

'Don't waste your time on that which is unfruitful' and *'Loiter in Jesus name.'* Linda, if you are still around, 'thank you.' Those words would be crucial, both in early decisions at River Oaks and over the next fifteen years.

61

FAMILY DYNAMICS

One of the most difficult aspects of life, as a nomadic tribe of 'Joneses', is the distance that occurs between family and the loss of close relationships forged in one place - a common challenge for so many today. In the RAF we had thirteen homes in twelve years, at least together as a family. In Christian Ministry it was a little easier with just four homes, given our two long pastorates and five years in Didcot. Now in retirement just one home, and all three children are spread North in Sunderland, South in Shepperton and eight thousand miles away in Peru! Add in the mix two divorces, and the dynamics that occur with access to grandchildren and their own life choices, and ties soon get stretched.

Andy eventually settled with a new partner, Sharon, and enjoyed his twenty-two year unbroken job with Sunderland FC in the ticket office. Over that time, he developed and retained a very wide circle of friends via the common denominator of football and the regular requests, 'any spare tickets Andy?' It was a shock to him, and other employees, when Sunderland plunged two divisions in succession and many staff were made redundant. As ever, he rolled up his sleeves and found other work quickly, always giving 100%. Lately he has developed two passions – working at becoming a super-chef and a green bowls star. Andy's son, Ben, now 30, has had a tough ride with health and work. His Type 1 diabetes is hard to control and he battles weight, both of which, and his mental health, have left him unemployed.

Tim retired from the Fire Service in 2018, having completed 32 years. He retains close friendships with previous colleagues and loves tackling rugged places with them each year on walking trips. Like Andy, he found another partner, Katherine. They have developed a lovely home in Shepperton, near London Airport, with Kathy's daughter Georgia. Katherine has a flourishing salon business, and Tim bought out a fellow firefighter's window-cleaning business which keeps him busy and fit! He has a wonderfully generous and caring nature, always working hard to keep the family together, part of which was the renting, in 2021 and 2022, of two amazing villas in Crete. This meant that most of the family could holiday together, including provision for Sharon to come over from Peru!

Granddaughter Tierney has just been promoted from Staff-Nurse to Sister in a paediatric ICU in Telford, a huge responsibility, and very stressful, but a job she loves. She and partner Tom are fitness fanatics and have just started a niche gym in Shrewsbury! Grandson Aaron found a partner, Chloe, in a queue at Alton Towers! They both share a passion for scary rides, so much so that Aaron has taken a job at Alton Towers! They recently bought a home in Chloe's home town of Stoke, where she works as a very caring carer.

As we expected, when Sharon settled at St Hilda's School, following our move to Liverpool, she flourished, despite some bullying and the challenges of living in Toxteth. Following a Geography Degree at Sheffield University, she failed to get on any PGCE courses, probably due to a complete lack of any experience with kids! At twenty-one, the day after moving back in with us after university and a year out working, she attended a mission service in a local gym and, following an appeal, confessed Jesus as her Saviour and became a Christian. She had been lacking peace for a while and knew that what was missing was a relationship with God.

God had already been putting some new plans in place, and in 1999 she was accepted on to a PGCE course at the Urban Learning Centre in London, which included practical placements in East London schools. A challenging role, given the large ethnic diversity in those areas with over twenty languages spoken at the school she worked in. If time in Toxteth had given Sharon a love for the poor and the inner city, living in Tower Hamlets would only cultivate that further. On completion of her PGCE she was offered a post at Brampton Primary School in Newham, where she remained for the next six years.

Once settled in London, after a year attending St Helen's in the city, she joined Urban Expression church in Tower Hamlets led by two Baptist Pastors, Jim & Juliet Kilpin. (UE's goal is to begin new Christian groups and churches in inner city areas and urban estates). In summer 2005, after being given the word, '*leaving*' from some visitors to the church, her vision for overseas mission work grew. Her prayer became, 'Lord, anywhere in Spanish speaking Latin America, as long as it's city and poverty.' In September 2006 she began serving with Latin Link, a mission organisation working in Latin America and Europe. Latin Link offers different options for mission:

Step teams, who share God's love with Latin American communities in tangible ways, over three weeks to three months.

Stride, which is a program for six to twenty-four months. Sharon did this between 2006-2008 before studying for two years at All Nations Christian College, enabling her to return to Peru with Latin Link on their Stay route.

Stay is for those desiring to make a longer-term commitment and work for lasting change.

It has been an amazing 'roller-coaster' ride for Sharon. Working with families and children in three different shanty towns – places of immense struggle, pain and despair, but also of life, hope and blessing. From the shanty towns she has moved into developing and publishing books for Sunday School, leading Christian Education courses, writing Holiday Bible Clubs, and promoting the prevention of child sexual abuse. Her work, alongside the team she has trained, takes her across Peru and, on occasions, other Latin American countries.

62

THE LANE AND RIVER OAKS - CHURCH AND COMMUNITY

I have always advised families or individuals, who are planning to move to a new town or city, 'find your church then your home'. Clearly, Liverpool was not new for us, so we had a clear idea of where we would start looking long before our home was settled. Our first port of call was Long Lane Church which we knew about and had two friends there, Steve and Brenda Taylor. Steve had worked on the Tab electrics and Brenda had been one of our playgroup teachers and leaders.

What we didn't know was 'The Lane's' recent history. Just a couple of years prior to our arrival they had called their first ever Pastor, Nick Johnson. A past punk-rocker, serious biker and 'pierced in the ear'- physically with his ring, and spiritually in his passion for Jesus. Originally a Brethren Assembly, The Lane was now an evangelical/charismatic community church, not that they weren't passionately evangelical before the change! It felt like home for us.

When we first settled, the congregation fitted comfortably into the building on Long Lane, just a couple of miles from our home, but growth was clearly happening. Contrary to our expectation to visit a few churches and discern where God would have us settle, at the end of that first visit we had no doubt this was where we should stay. Nick's preaching was refreshing, powerful, anointed and earthed. The worship was spiritually uplifting, Christ exalting and prayerfully prepared. It was a thriving family church with a great mixture of ages and very welcoming. It was also local, which was very important to us.

The only important matter I needed to share with Nick was our clear call to 'loiter in Jesus' name' on our estate. We would happily do anything asked of us at church, but a lot of our passion, energy and prayer would be invested right where the Lord had planted us at River Oaks. Once again, that has proved to be vital and, over many years, fruitful in our work of creating community and caring for the environment. It's not by chance that River Oaks Pond is affectionately called by some, 'Pond Church.' 'Not quite church as you know it Jim', to pinch, and alter, a common 'space' quote, but fulfilling much of what church should fulfil. We would also want to honour the way, especially at the beginning, that The Lane supported us prayerfully and practically in our vision for transformation at River Oaks.

Regarding our new home, apart from being a little bit small, it was perfect with beautiful views over the River Mersey towards the Wirral Peninsula. Further on, in Wales, Moel Famau, bordering Denbighshire and Flintshire, part of the Clwydian Range and an area of outstanding natural beauty. Two minutes away, Otterspool Promenade stretches six miles into the city centre bordering the river most of the way. This was tailor-made for Ann's mobility scooter and my bike rides. Our kitchen and bedroom look down on the pond at the centre of the estate and over the large expanse of field that is now part of River Oaks Charity land. There is a small garden at the front and a larger one at the back so just about manageable for a classic third-ager!

The surprise element occurred when signing off some documents for the Baptist Housing Manager. We discovered the plot of land adjacent to our two car parking spaces was also ours! The small plot is overshadowed by an enormous beech tree but had potential as a small garden or veg plot. Over time, all these gardens and plots would undergo significant transformation. Adding a lovely conservatory at the rear, and smaller side one for storage, has aided the usable space, with a large garage doubling as a store for charity stuff as well as our own.

It didn't take long for me to connect Linda's prophetic word about loitering within the pond arena. Every time I worked on, or visited the pond, I got to know more and more people, both from the estate as well as visitors from elsewhere. Hanging about, with time to chat, began to forge friendships and make connections. In the early days we managed to draw together volunteer teams to clean the woodland, maintain the toddler's play area and generally keep the area clean. However, it became clear that, if we were to progress our work and set a vision for the future, we needed a formal status.

One year after arriving, and dozens of community newsletters distributed, we formed RORA - River Oaks Residents Association – in 2010. This gave us access to grant funding opportunities as well as Gift Aid on donations. Nine trustees were appointed, including both myself as Chair and Ann as a trustee. Our first, and most important task, was to assess the cost of installing a fountain, meter cupboard and power source at the pond, with the primary aim of aerating and cleansing the water. Once agreed, I produced another newsletter and proceeded on my hour long visit around the estate houses. Gradually, I got to know every resident and family by name.

One of the first responders on the estate, was a surprise, and unexpected visitor to our door. Ann opened it to find Ricky Tomlinson in his overalls! I had never met him but knew of him via the Royale Family series on TV. Regarding the idea of a fountain, Ricky didn't wait long to lend his support, 'Great idea, 'er's me cheque, don't know who to make it out to.' I was tempted to say, 'me', but suggested RORA! Several more visitors turned up and thrust cash into my hand! I rapidly asked their names, stating, 'I need to account for these gifts.' The outcome was putting a name to a face and addressing them personally when taking Ann's beautifully crafted 'Thank You' cards to their homes. After fifteen years, she has supported so many families with a range of cards noting births, deaths, birthdays, anniversaries, new resident's welcome cards and fund-raising efforts, just one of her many contributions to 'creating community.'

On many occasions, the hour posting newsletters turned into hours as I shared conversations with residents. Ann quickly became a 'pond-widow' as I became an 'unofficial' Pastor. Thus began a caring ministry with an unorthodox pond-church! The loitering activity allowed me to serve families in a host of ways, whether accompanying those grieving, taking funerals, sharing births, planting shrubs, and sourcing plaques to celebrate an event or remember someone. Often it was praying for someone passing by as they stop and share their needs. Neutral space, beyond a church building, is so helpful at such times.

One of our personal objectives was to introduce 'community events.' It was a long shot, but we decided a small Easter Egg Hunt might work around the pond and in front gardens, with an egg-cup prize and easter eggs for the children provided by residents and members of Long Lane Church. Around twenty parents and children turned up and so enjoyed the hunt that fifteen years later, it has grown to well over one hundred residents and friends. It has also gained 'legendary' status; highly organised, annual theme changes, split into three teams, lots of prizes and eggs, and so competitive. It's the adults who dominate as they strive to lead their teams in the points race, so gaining the much-coveted Easter Egg Trophy – forget the little egg-cup!

At Christmas we've linked with residents, and our church, to provide carols with a small music group, hot meals such as scouse, curry, and pizza, along with drinks. Later we would move to mobile hog-roasts, drinks, and pizza vans. This allowed everyone to relax and enjoy the event rather than the pressure of providing all the food and drinks. The joy for us is knowing we have a community that is vibrant, inclusive of all, and a lot of fun for those who attend. A repeated phrase from visitors and newcomers is, 'you don't find anything like this too often.'

In the summers we worked on linking into national events such as Jubilee, World Cup and Olympics. At times we simply had sports days and food. Later, when we replaced the rotting toddler's play area, we arranged annual Teddy Bear's picnics to celebrate the charity's achievements. Bring your picnic and Teddy, camp alongside the new play area, and connect with other families.

To move our vision on, I used my years of grant funding experience in Toxteth to send out a range of grant applications with the aim of raising around £10,000 for the work required at the pond. It was a very stressful time, not least over the building of the meter cupboard and power installation, which had to connect with local housing cables some distance away and under one of the pond pathways! Halfway through the meter cupboard build, our workman left for a police cell! One day before the grand opening and switch on of the fountain, the power company told us we were responsible for digging the hole to unearth the main power supply. Think amateurs with large pick-axes! Once we had unearthed the main supply cable, and, hopefully survived a death-inducing voltage, their engineer would jump in the hole, plug in the cable, and jump out again - around an hour's work for almost £2000! Then to be told we could fill the hole four hours later!

At one point, with three power company vans parked up, and around ten workmen standing idle as they watched me wielding a pick-axe, I had to walk away. I was boiling with anger and might well have faced a manslaughter charge! In the end a 'digging team' arrived from the power company - you could not make it up. Suffice to say I stood aside and watched them finish Le Hole!

Steve Taylor, our electrician, had assembled the fountain and fully kitted out the meter cupboard in readiness for the initial switch on scheduled for the next day. Mercifully, a trial run was successful and the fountain fired up with a mighty 'whoosh.'

63

FOUNTAIN, FRIENDSHIPS AND FLOWERS

On Good Friday April 22nd 2011, at 1pm, over 100 adults and children gathered around the pond for a picnic, no doubt swelled by the news that Ricky Tomlinson would be counting down the fountain opening. As Baptists and water are never far apart, I chose a text from John's gospel chapter 7 verse 38, 'He who believes in me, as the Scripture said, from his innermost being will flow rivers of living water.' The fountain is a visual symbol of a spiritual experience. The receiving of God's Holy Spirit releasing the life of Jesus into our lives – a new life, cleansing and refreshment.

Ricky followed up, striking the right note and knowledge of his audience. He spoke about, 'this oasis of peace and quiet.' and the effect the Resident's Association has made to life on the estate. His classic word, on community relationships has resonated over the years, 'some people don't know their neighbours, and some people don't want to know their neighbours, but I love living here.' The work of RORA had intentionally, and at times unintentionally, created more community spirit and greater connection with neighbours, alongside a willingness to work together across the estate.

The moment of truth, about the effectiveness of our meter installation and cabling, was about to be publicly tested! Steve, our 'Tec-Elec', knelt in the cupboard, ready for my signal, as Ricky counted down from 10 to 1. As we held our breath, the 'whoosh' of water shot into the air. Ricky was the most excited participant as he held his hands high in the air at the sight of a plume some three metres high!

The cleansing had begun.

Within a year, the water was clean and ready for the introduction of fish. Around the perimeter we began a planting regime of daffodils and small Spring flowers. One of the most inspiring of ideas was the planting of roses in two of the barren borders, along with personalised plaques. Residents and visitors were encouraged to plant a rose and install a plaque with no more than seven words, celebrating an event, memory, birth, anniversary or just because they wanted to add to the rose border. The idea took off and within a year the borders were full and we moved to offering pots and containers.

As a neighbourhood we are indebted to the work, skill and time given by Colin and Carole Myers, not only among the first trustees, but passionately committed and extremely able gardeners, not least with respect to roses! The care of all borders attracted many more visitors to the pond. Over the next three years we added more fish, planted marginal pond plants, and introduced a range of shrubs and trees in the remaining two borders.

As the habitat improved, so the pond life thrived, with frogs, large and small dragonflies, damselflies, and other insects. Harry the heron is a daily visitor, lurking in the reeds and feeding on the smaller fish. More and more families were turning up to feed the fish and spot the pond insects. As for me, I simply hung around, built relationships, and responded to need where I could.

64

SEFTON PARK PALM HOUSE –
GOLDEN WEDDING ANNIVERSARY

In 1844, Richard Turner constructed the first ever 'super-sized glasshouse' in Sefton Park, Liverpool. Following extensive winter storm damage, and subsequent vandalism, the building was closed to the public in the 1980s. Our first visit to the park, following our arrival in 1989, was a sad occasion. A significant number of the three thousand, seven-hundred and one panes of glass were missing or badly broken. Precious plants were dead, dying, or open to the elements. After years of campaigning, £3.5 million was raised to begin the restoration and it was finally re-opened in 2001. June 29th 2013 was our Golden Wedding Anniversary. Given the numbers of people we wanted to invite, we needed a big venue and opted to explore the possibility of hiring the Palm House.

One humorous moment, when we visited the office, to check availability and cost, was a question from one of the younger admin team, 'Golden Wedding – how many years is that?' When we replied, 'fifty years,' it became obvious that the expectation of surviving fifty years married was not on her radar. In fact, the rest of the office staff were equally fascinated and could not recall a previous Golden Wedding Anniversary! We were honoured, and praised, for our marital longevity!

We duly signed up, determined to make it a fantastic evening. One hundred and ten family, friends, and neighbours arrived from across the country, to a truly stunning sight. The Palm House filled with exotic plants and fragrance. Every corner lit up with coloured lights. A very versatile singer, David

Marshall, welcoming each guest with an array of musical genres, then went on to serenade us personally with a large cornetto and a rendition of 'O Sole Mio!' Each of the fourteen tables represented a country we had visited from Peru to Alaska, Cyprus to the Virgin Islands, Canada to the USA. Sharon worked hard, and creatively, producing large gold-rimmed hearts with the national flag of each country and name of each guest, as well as a world map, with smaller hearts, enabling guests to identify their table on arrival. Together, Ann and Sharon assembled centre-piece flower arrangements. Large Lazy Susans on each table allowed the waiters to supply our up-market buffet. A Ceilidh Band, with a patient and clear caller, enabled almost everyone to join the dancing party! Our eldest son Andy did us proud, in his inimitable and humorous way, as he led the toast and tributes. As an ice-breaker, Sharon had prepared a few sentences for guests to complete, including, 'You are a … couple.' 'How did we meet?' 'You made me laugh when …' 'From you I have learnt …' 'My top tip to improve a fifty-year-old marriage is …'.

Shouting 'bastards' in a sermon featured in numerous responses, several of whom quoted it in the 'you made me laugh when …' question! My wearing of red trousers, over several decades, also came out frequently. (Denise, I still have them in pristine condition, but would never get them near my waist; offers from under 30-year-olds would be considered!) Suffice to note our supreme spirituality dominated, but best to skip over that one! One we particularly like, and try to emulate is, 'never, ever, become old.' Finally, but nowhere near exhausting hundreds of comments, 'Listen to your wife' is one I will continue to refine!

The Ceilidh would be the last time Ann was able to stand for just a short time on the dancefloor and enjoy a few twirls from me. Her lifetime physical limitations meant we could never safely dance or enjoy long walks together, but we have done the best wherever and whenever possible. Even a two minute twirl together is a special moment! I, of course, could manage several attempts at Ceilidh group dances, but with a certain sadness that Ann had to sit them out.

One of the downsides of endless movement is the loss of deeper relationships. One of the upsides of a significant anniversary celebration is the reminder that so many relationships have stood the test of time. Guests at the Palm House ranged across fifty years of marriage, twelve years in the RAF, but also more than sixty-four years of life. Family from Jersey, Southend, Manchester, Liverpool, and Chichester, and two of the couples from our Youth Club days, Rick & Vivian Owen and David & Pam Windsor. We have remained best friends for over sixty-four years and prayed for each other through joy and pain, crisis and challenge. A huge thank you to all who made our Golden Anniversary such a wonderful occasion.

65

VOLUNTEERING

As well as investing in our local community we both had a passion to explore how we might invest in the city. The Council had a 'City Stars' scheme which enabled volunteers to welcome visitors, service city assets - such as St George's Hall and the Town Hall – and provide support at major conferences and sports events in the new exhibition and arena centres. I applied and was accepted to join various small and large teams anywhere across the city. What a privilege and joy to welcome a new generation of visitors to a city now well into a renaissance of rebuilding its infrastructure, recovering its dignity, and reinventing itself as a premier tourist destination. To see cruise ship passengers, from across the world, coming to a city you would not want to fly over in the 1980's was a special joy. In the low season I also volunteered as a City Hall Ambassador, manning Christmas events in the Town Hall and St George's Hall plateau on the annual Remembrance Day parade.

Fulfilling as these opportunities were, I was keen to move on to volunteering at the cruise terminal. More and more ships were berthing in Liverpool and I was eager to share the city sights and hidden gems with world travellers. Having researched the history of Liverpool in two degrees I had sufficient knowledge to apply. The selection process was thorough, but relatively stress-free. I was duly accepted and presented with my third volunteer uniform! Following an introduction to the terminal and staff, I gradually got to know the drill and connect with other cruise ambassadors. Over the past eight years, I have loved every shift. The buzz of putting a smile on the faces of passengers is always my aim as they arrive up the gangway and enter the terminal. With very large maps of the city, on movable boards, as well as maps to pass on, ambassadors work hard at connecting all the city has to offer with the requirements of passengers. Occasionally we go the extra mile to help in a crisis, such as, 'I left my passport at home in Leeds,' or 'I cannot walk to the hop-on-hop-off bus stop.' We aim to solve every problem, and usually do! Almost all the ambassadors have a string of anecdotes and stories of maidens in distress or men trying to find Abbey Road! (For the record, it's in London not Liverpool as commonly believed by cruise ship visitors.)

It was a very special day for me, and clearly for Ann, when the Cruise Terminal staff agreed to take Ann on as their first disabled ambassador. Many disabled people either embark or arrive in the city, yet the Cruise Terminal did not have a disabled ambassador to help them either way. I advocated for such a volunteer, knowing that the sight of someone who is disabled welcoming a disabled visitor tells them we care about inclusion and empathy. For some years, I had asked whether Ann could join the team. She has a good knowledge of the city and would quickly pick up new information from me or other ambassadors. We have all been in that situation of not knowing an answer to a question, but we do know someone else on the team who will, and if all else fails we have Google!

Ann has loved every single shift, and consistently tells friends, she would volunteer for every one! She started in her wheelchair but has since progressed to a nippy scooter which makes for a swift crossing of the terminal when appropriate. Few people would appreciate the effort it takes, and the pain she goes through, to get going on an early morning shift. Nevertheless, she would not stop volunteering for all the tea in China! Time and again she is commended for her time with visitors and regularly asked for a picture! The cream on the cake, for all ambassadors, is when visitors return and make a point of saying, 'your guidance was perfect,' or, 'I had no idea Liverpool was such a beautiful city, I/we are determined to come back and explore more.'

As I write all ambassadors are in limbo. The cruise terminal has passed from public to private ownership and the ambassadors have not been welcomed back by the new owners, Global Port Holdings. Nobody is entirely sure of why, or when, but we are trusting for a swift resolution. We come free, with a vast knowledge of the city and a passion to welcome, serve and make every passenger smile as they enter the terminal.

PS: We are delighted to add, 'we are back!' Having switched to supporting and servicing the 'Seafarers Centre' as they care for crew members, in early July 2024 we received news of our reinstatement, just in time for this inclusion!

66

RIVER OAKS CHARITY AWARDS

In 2013 we entered the Britain in Bloom 'In Your Neighbourhood' competition for the first time. There are five certificate levels and we had expected to start at Level 1 or 2. It was a lovely surprise to gain Level 4, 'Thriving', at our first attempt. Our most exciting, totally unexpected, and prestigious award, was waiting in the wings and forged out of the art of grant funding in Toxteth. I had learnt many important lessons about grant funding, one of which is the art of discerning the difference between 'small crumbs' and 'a loaf,' and knowing when to apply for which one. Trustees of grant making bodies are experts at spotting greed, exaggeration, and lack of integrity. I learned to ask for exactly what we needed.

We applied to Biffa Awards 'small grant category' with a limit of £10,000. We needed £1970 for two pergolas and a quality bench seat. The amount was 'short-change crumbs' in funding terms, but carefully costed and transparent. We duly received the grant and had fun assembling and installing the pergolas at two of the pond arena entrances. The seat took pride of place on our large decking area overlooking the pond. Months later we received a letter from Biffa informing us that RORA had been shortlisted for their annual prize-giving in the Greenwich Maritime Museum in London. Hundreds of projects are considered, in different categories, ranging from a few thousand pounds to over a million! The excitement level heightened when we made the final four, in our 'small grants' category, at the award ceremony in London!

A hotel was booked, and a very excited couple set off by

car for Greenwich. We arrived at the museum, stood in awe of the buildings, history, and splendour of the hall, and searched for our table. We sat with the other three representatives of projects in our category, along with finalists from other projects. Among an array of gifts from Biffa was the booklet summarising the prize categories for each of the awards. We both reached eagerly for our books to read our write-up and see who we were up against. Our disappointment was palpable. All the other three projects had gone for the full amount of £10,000 and all had professional staff members. RORA just had volunteers. To compound our plunging joy, there were three prizes and four projects! We sat back, enjoyed a wonderful lunch, and consoled ourselves with the knowledge that we, at least, had beaten hundreds of other small projects to get to the final.

With lunch over, the master of ceremonies worked his way through the different categories, finally announcing the prize winners in the small grants section. In our minds we had a glimmer of hope that we might just sneak into third place. When the third and second place prizes were announced, and RORA was not selected, we just sat back, musing, 'well it was a good day.' The 'Master' began his introduction to the winner, 'now about this small project in Liverpool!' We could hardly believe it was us. He followed up with two statements. 'We were very impressed with the RORA application. They asked clearly for exactly what they wanted, whereas all the other three projects went for the maximum amount.' He then made everyone laugh, 'do you realise, the prize we are giving RORA today is more than the grant we gave them!' We received £2,000 plus a smart glass trophy engraved with 'River Oaks Residents Association - Best Community Project 2014!'

I suddenly realised that I would now have to go to the front, with Ann, and give a five-minute acceptance speech!

Ann, despite her disabilities, shot out of her chair like an Exocet missile and I frantically searched my pockets for my prepared speech! Although a lifelong Evertonian, I opened with Bill Shankley's drawling Scottish response when receiving a prestigious award, 'aye … ah deserve it!' I don't know how the poor couple, from the last of the 'big' projects was feeling, but they must have seen themselves as winners! Sometimes it's all about appreciating crumbs!

Following that magical day, the next Thursday we were present at the Liverpool Garden Competition. Once again, against dozens of other gardens across the city, we came out winners. No money, but another glass pyramid trophy and certificate for - 'Best Community Garden' in the city! We were getting used to winning and wondered how long it might continue! In 2015 we entered the Liverpool Echo/ United Utilities 'Environment Awards' and, against all the odds, with some notable opposition, we came out winners as 'Best Community Project' and received a carved wooden trophy and certificate. In 2015 we also received, the first of an eight year run, Level 5 'Outstanding' awards in the North West Britain in Bloom 'It's Your Neighbourhood' category. Our pond awards board was beginning to run out of space! The RHS 'Certificate of Distinction' award followed in 2018, along with the biggest cup, and most prestigious award, 'North West in Bloom Liverpool City Trophy.'

A funny moment occurred a year later in 2019. The Liverpool Trophy had never been given to the same project twice. Knowing that, near the end of the proceedings with just three awards left, we donned our coats and said goodbye to the other remaining participants on our dinner table. As we reached the exit, the 'Master' announced the Liverpool Trophy winners. To our amazement, he said, 'River Oaks Charity!' We had to race back to our table, lay down our coats and rush to the front, accompanied by applause and laughter! What a way to end a memorable day. As we have already changed our awards board twice, we decided to halt all competitions in 2024 and take a breather! (The transition from RORA to ROC features in the next chapter.)

Whilst Ann and I had the privilege, and pleasure, of attending all the award ceremonies, a special tribute is due to the tireless work of trustees, residents, volunteer teams and individual 'specialists' who have partnered with us over the past fifteen years. Also, a huge thank you to the different grant funding bodies and charity donors, who have generously supported the work of RORA/ROC: Biffa Awards, Duchy of Lancaster Foundation, Veolia Environmental Awards, Torus Foundation, P.H.Holt Foundation, Coop, Tesco, Lottery Community Fund, Liverpool City Council, Ricky Tomlinson, Timothy Jones, and a host of small grant funders whose contributions have enabled ROC to keep going and maintain a sizeable vision to 'Create Community and Care for the Environment.'

67

BATTLES

It was clear from our first attempt to clean the pond, that the maintenance company had no intention of maintaining the whole of River Oaks land, apart from minimal expenditure. Lying and procrastination were embedded in their programme. I, along with trustees and residents, began an eight year battle of attrition, challenging their stance with phone calls, trustee letters, emails, letters from residents, Council interventions, Councillors letters, along with a letter from our MP Louise Ellman. Being an avid poet, I also appealed, in tender verse, to any 'soft-side' they might possess. Finally, I resorted to threats of legal action. Nothing phased them. They had recourse to money and a powerful legal team. We had slender resources. I also discovered they had many 'class' actions against them across the UK, all featuring the lack of maintenance on their multiple sites. Throughout this time, I had regularly prayed for a change of attitude.

In 2016, on a cruise to Alaska, I received an email from one of the trustees, Dan, who said, 'you are not going to believe this.' He had received an email suggesting we get our solicitor ready as they were willing to pass all land, freehold, to RORA! This was both a breakthrough but also a challenge. To receive land, we had to be a charity. On return from Alaska, I began the process of moving from an Association to a Charity.

Like so many visionary projects, battles precede breakthroughs. The Charity Commission dismissed our first application, believing we were just a small, perhaps insular, and exclusive group, not worthy of becoming a charity. Eight years on from beginning our work we were anything but small, insular, or exclusive. Year on year we had attracted more and more visitors to the pond and our 'legendary' annual events. Volunteer teams from outside the estate joined in our cleaning and maintenance work. We had gained multiple and prestigious awards. Copious commendatory letters from residents had been part of our application. I wrote again to the Charity Commission but received the same negative reply. This meant we had one last chance on appeal. This time I decided to gather commendations from outside the estate as opposed to internal commendations. Previous Charity Commission responses had taken months, our appeal took just forty-eight hours! The mass of commendations from across the city may well have been the clincher. For me, it was also the power of prayer. Our status as a charity was confirmed and we were about to move from RORA to ROC!

Since the excitement of hearing the maintenance company's change of heart, six months had passed. When we informed them that we now had charitable status and negotiations could begin, we didn't receive a reply for three months! Had they hardened their stance again? Had all our effort been in vain? In the intervening months we had raised £48,000 to install a completely new toddler's play area in place of the rotting and dangerous one owned by the 'mis-management' company – and still the landowners! No agreement with the play equipment company could be signed and an installation date secured until the land was ours. Just when we were out of ideas, and angry at the landowner's stubbornness, early in 2017 the final breakthrough letter came, 'we are ready to pass the land, freehold, to ROC!'

Amazingly, it must be a rare occurrence for over twenty acres of land to be passed, free and freehold, to a new owner! The only charge we paid was their Solicitor's fees, amounting to around £2000. My long-term relationship with the Duchy of Lancaster Foundation enabled us to gain a grant to cover this cost. They had been very supportive in all our work over many years and always considerate to the many challenges we faced in securing the land at River Oaks. In March 2017, after a tense wait throughout the day, at 4pm we received news from our solicitors that everything was complete! Following my ecstatic 'woop' of delight and relief, I emailed the trustees, then rang the play equipment company and arranged a date for installation!

From the early days in 2009, when we discovered we were dealing with a company whose primary intention was to hoard the cash received from Wimpey to maintain the whole site, it was our intention to do all we could to gain the land. Now, eight years later, we had achieved our goal. What a journey it had been – prayer vital, perseverance essential, shrewd moves wise, constant focus on the goal, and a belief that could withstand dashed hopes, regular frustration, changes of strategy, and consistent appeals to the 'mis-management' company.

The reality, of course, was this very small charity now owned almost nineteen acres of woodland and field, a toddler's play area and a multi award-winning pond, plus a triangle of grass thrown in, all of which required regular and strategic maintenance! Significant grant funding applications were now on the ROC agenda.

68

WOODLAND ISSUES

Within months of arriving at River Oaks, I discovered the endemic issues associated with Mersey Road Woods (now River Oaks Woodland). Residents informed me they would not take their children through the woods, even though the houses were originally advertised, on the Wimpey brochure, as 'adjacent to a beautiful woodland adventure playground for your children!' I decided to do some research. It became clear that the woods had been a meeting place, primarily, but not exclusively, for male sexual acts for over sixty years. At night, the parking area adjacent to the Otterspool Promenade and Mersey Road, alongside the woods, was a significant meeting area for dogging. Web sites in Europe identified this area, should you be visiting Liverpool! It was common practice to have car headlights flashing at night, for anyone visiting, or returning home to the estate via Mersey Road. Successive Chief Constables had been informed of the activity, with little effective action, or no response at all.

To put it mildly, the woodland was a rubbish tip. An accessible fly-tipping dumping ground, and a ruined, but potentially stunning, habitat. A significant part of the problem, and ruination of the habitat, was the openness of the woods, especially from the sizeable car park. Five well worn paths allowed anyone to enter from the car park as well as two primary entrances from Mersey Road and via the estate field.

Our first response was to organise woodland cleaning teams. Fortunately, we had two extremely supportive, and hands-on Councillors, Emily Spurrell and Patrick Hurley, who joined our teams and supplied, via the Councillor's Fund, a sizeable skip. The skip was filled within hours. Fridges, washing machines, motorbikes, and cycles were commonplace, along with hundreds of condoms, wet wipes, magazines, drink bottles and cans. It was not uncommon, even in the middle of winter, for those who did venture through the woods, to encounter men in a state of undress. Families, whose new houses bordered areas of the wood, were complaining that their kids could pull back their curtains and see the sexual activity among the trees. When the college was on site, the woods were well hidden and nobody was affected by the antisocial activity. It was a different situation once the estate was finished.

Our second response, regarding restoration of the habitat, was to put in a grant application for £30,000 to Veolia Environmental Trust. This would enable us to erect palisade fencing along the car park openings, and areas of the field border, where fencing had rusted or been demolished. It was a complicated and lengthy application but worth it when it was granted. A 'heavy duty' volunteer team spent days clearing the fence line of fallen trees, bushes, and weeds in preparation for the fencing.

I also posted notices informing visitors of our plans. I was not surprised when I received threats, both from individuals and dogs. As I was tying a set of notices on one occasion, a guy you would not want to mess with, accompanied by two fierce XL Bullies, came over to read the notice. He told me to 'F*** off', as, in his words, 'this is our f****** woods.' Given his aggressive stance and language the dogs began to pull hard on their leads. I really believed he was about to set the dogs on me – a very scary moment I would not like to face again. Redeeming land for better purposes rarely comes without a fight.

Another issue, which would help to encourage more bikes,

wheelchairs, scooters, runners, and walking groups, to occupy the woods and deter anti-social behaviour, was the repair of the pathway. In many places it had eroded from two metres wide to well under a metre. Another application to Veolia ET secured £38,000 to install a one metre wide rhino-pave pathway across the field and through the woodland. Over a short period of time the footfall increased, with a noticeable drop in antisocial behaviour and less fly-tipping and rubbish. The historic pattern of behaviour has not been eradicated but certainly much reduced.

Just as the restoration of the pond was a ten year project so it will be with the woodland. We have made a great start, completed a survey to give us future guidance, worked on partnerships that will make the woodland accessible and safe for all. We have also had the joy of seeing our first 'Forest School' days with a trained teacher. Several have now been completed and very well attended. We are also in contact with Palmerston Special Needs School - a school I have had contact with for many years. They are keen to start a midweek Forest School for their students. Such activity also helps in terms of taking ownership of the woodland space which then deters antisocial behaviour.

After twelve years chairing the Resident's Association and charity, I retired - well almost, in 2022. I have had the privilege of working with several trustee groups over twelve years and the last three years as ROC Ambassador, doing what I can to support from a distance. Thank you all for sharing our journey of transformation together. For believing and participating in a wonderful rollercoaster journey. You are priceless, and often, unsung volunteers, without whom ROC could not have achieved a fraction of the transformation we have seen since 2009. On behalf of all residents, friends, visitors, and supporters, thank you.

69

ON THE EDGE

Being able to fulfil a promise is always a special occasion. The disappointment of leaving Ann sick in Las Vegas, while I marvelled at the South Rim of Grand Canyon, was about to be remedied. For the third time we flew into Las Vegas and enjoyed a short stay at the Trump Tower! (Honestly, we knew nothing about Donald and his infamous reputation.) Visits to the Bellagio fountains were a must, with meals, carefully considered, at St Mark's Square in the Venetian complex. Food poisoning to be avoided at all costs!

From Las Vegas we made our way, by car, to the Canyon and a return to the Imax Cinema to see the first navigation of the Colorado River and discovery of the Grand Canyon. We had booked a small cabin, literally a couple of hundred metres from the edge of the South Rim. This time Ann would stand with me and experience the emotion associated with seeing the awe-inspiring breadth and depth of the seventeen mile vista across to the North Rim. Contrary to my quick dash, on our second visit, our three day stay gave us ample time to explore so much more of the twists and turns of the canyon's edge and take excursions in the car to some of the extremities both West and East of the Canyon Village. Early morning trips, to see the sunrise, gifted us with amazing colour changes to the rock formations. Other early morning visitors had saddled horses and were heading down the narrow canyon paths to the canyon floor, then making their way across the desert paths to the North Rim. I confess to being as scared watching the horse-train skirting the edge of a narrow and rocky path as some of the riders must have been! However, the horses must have done it hundreds of times without sending anyone over the cliff edge! Having rejoiced at finally getting Ann to the South Rim it was time to say goodbye to one of the great scenes on earth and one I would never tire to see again. Little did we know it would not be our final goodbye!

From Las Vegas we motored to Sequoia National Parks. We had read about the giant Redwoods and the 'drive-through tree' options. We were so eager and excited to explore new vistas and adventures. The Redwoods did not disappoint. Towering like skyscrapers, they were simply awesome. The biggest in the world, 'General Sherman', is around 2,500 years old and 275 feet high. Not the tallest, but with a circumference of 101.5 feet and weighing in at 6,167 tons, it's not easy to steal! We found the giant 'Chandelier Tree,' hollowed out in the middle for cars to pass through! Half way in, I heard a scraping noise that sounded as if the car doors were being dented! The repair bill for the hire car flashed across my mind, followed by intense relief when I discovered, on exit, that it was rubber buffers each side of the tree that prevented such dents! A short distance further on we encountered a giant Redwood that had fallen across the road decades ago. Instead of sawing it up, and opening the road, it had been shaped into a mini-tunnel and was much wider than our previous 'Chandelier' adventure so no problem in getting through! From Sequioa we took a detour to King's Canyon. The journey along the meandering and bubbling King's River was a driver's dream, with sun bouncing off the water and canyon walls. A narrow gorge, endlessly twisting and turning, with high granite cliffs, spectacular waterfalls, and ever-changing vistas. Well worth the short detour on route to Yosemite.

The 'must-see' destination in Yosemite was El Capitan. A 2,308 metre granite monolith rock formation on the north side of Yosemite Valley in the Sierra Nevada range. This monolith is the free-climbers Everest, so no easy jaunt. Like Everest, it takes lives and can take up to a week to climb due to its forty-one different stages. A handful of people have completed it in under twenty-four hours, with just one woman, Emily Harrington, in 2020. The adjacent and famous Horsetail Waterfall was not in full flow but still spectacular as it tumbled in stages towards the valley floor.

From Yosemite we made our way directly to San Francisco on the West Coast. With just a few days there, we managed most of the tourist attractions; Lombard Street, known as the most crooked street in the world, and possibly one of the most attractive with its stunning flower beds. Fishermen's Wharf, with its seals, trendy shops, and copious restaurants. The Golden Gate Bridge, and views high above the Northern peninsula, mercifully free of the frequent fog banks. The ferry trip around the notorious Alcatraz prison, where we mysteriously picked up a mass of flies which breed and thrive in the abandoned infrastructure. Sadly, after standing in a queue for one of the famous trams, Ann could not make it up the high steps so we had to give that experience a miss.

From the city we began our much anticipated journey down the West Coast from San Francisco to Monterey, one of the top scenic drives in the US. A one hundred and thirty mile stretch of the senses, from magnificent Redwood Forests in the 'Big Sur,' to breathtaking vistas over the Pacific. The Nuevo State Park with its huge Elephant Seals and the smaller seals dotted along the rugged coastline. McWay Falls where the plunging water falls on to the beach and into the Pacific. A view that can be seen from the road. Not a large fall, but unusual.

At Monterey we stayed in a pretty boutique cabin adjacent to the famous 'Pebble Beach' golf course which can be visited when quiet - fortunately it was. As Monterey is a prime spot for whale and sea otter watching, we booked a trip out. It wasn't as spectacular as hoped, but we saw enough from a distance to evoke a chorus of 'oohs and aahs!' However, it was the otters in the harbour who stole the show as they floated by, wrestling with the kelp, and amazingly balancing their young on their tummy. The rest of the day was spent at the aquarium on Cannery Row Pier with its living kelp forest, sharks, penguins, and sea otters. From Monterey we made our way to Morro Bay, which still today is our favourite place on Route 1. The Estero Inn was a small boutique hotel situated right alongside the inlet of water from the Pacific. As our window faced the water we were treated to a steady flow of otters and babies passing up and down the inlet. Just around the bay, we overdosed on dozens of Otter families who had gathered to breed and play in the kelp. A magical experience for us.

As the forests and hills gave way to multi-lane highways and ever bigger towns, we popped in at Santa Barbara then Ventura for a night. Sadly, the railway ran alongside the hotel with large and lengthy goods-trains blowing their ultra-noisy horns all night. Sleep was in short supply! We skirted Los Angeles, glad to survive the twelve-lane freeways and arrive at the beautiful and sophisticated town of Laguna Beach. Another stunning boutique hotel, full of sea-related Redwood sculptures, was a delight to enter and relax in, before heading off for our evening meal in a restaurant perched high on a cliff overlooking the Pacific, where we were treated to a red-hot sunset and stunning sky.

We were now at the end of our foray along Route 1 and heading inland towards the extreme heat of Palm Springs, in the Sonoran Desert, Southern California, known for its hot springs, stylish hotels, and mid-century modern architecture. Our first port of call was the enormous swimming pool in our hotel, and a chance to cool down. Just one hurdle to overcome before arriving back in Las Vegas – the Mojave Desert. Ann was not looking forward to driving through, as we knew we could go miles before seeing another car! 'What if we breakdown,' was Ann's constant mantra - not a nice prospect, given the searing heat. There would be no cover and no protection from rattlesnakes! We had planned one stop in Mojave, which was home to Rutan Airport, a storage facility for hundreds of commercial aircraft and home to Richard Branson's 'Virgin Galactic' test centre. The town was a reminder of the Wild-West with a main street bordered by wooden shops, cafes, and a smattering of motels. Our motel was basic but sufficient for a rapid overnight stop. As the extreme heat had swollen my ankles, I emptied the ice machine and stood in the bath! As there was little to see, other than sand, we took a short trip out to the airport to check out the plane graveyard, one of a number that exist in the Mojave Desert. The dry air being the reason for storing all manner of aircraft, some to be stripped for parts and others stored for potential use in the future. Just one leg of our amazing trip was left as we navigated the rest of the Mojave Desert and made our way to Las Vegas.

One thing occupied our minds as we battled the heat – the Planet Hollywood Hotel pool! As we booked into the hotel, we became acutely aware of our age. It was jammed with 18-30's, which means we were almost fifty years older than every other guest! We had clearly missed the online comments about PH being for anyone under thirty! Also, being a Sunday it was packed with hunky Marines and bikini clad girls. We had no idea how bad it would be until we arrived at the pool and failed to see more than a bucket of water to swim in! The pool was standing room only! Dozens of Marines and girls holding bottles of beer occupying every inch. We looked in vain for two loungers until some kind souls took pity on us and offered us theirs! Swimming was out of the question. We eventually retreated to our air-conditioned room and vowed to keep clear of any Planet Hollywood Hotels in the future!

Our flight home the next day was in the evening, so, after breakfast, we took a punt on the pool and were amazed to find just a handful of Marines and girls chilling on the loungers and recovering from Sunday parties. We literally had the pool to ourselves. Time for our favourite pool pastime. Ann was not able to move easily but she could catch a mean ball! We would stand several metres apart, with a hard sponge ball the size of a cricket ball. We would then fling the ball as hard as possible to one another. We have been known to reach fifty or more throws without dropping the ball! As we progressed, we gathered a small audience of marines who were mesmerised by this older couple's antics and proficiency! Eager to get in on the action, they asked if they could join us. How cool was that! Lads in their twenties queueing up to play with the dudes in their seventies! Just one problem - they were totally useless. Over time, we had mastered our art, they had never thrown our type of ball! After failing consistently, they simply melted away as we added insult to injury by continuing to fling the ball faster and faster! (Our sincere apology to the US Marine Corp). We arrived home in triumph!

70

EXPANSION

You may not have heard of the 'Harrod's Sale Syndrome'. It is my theory that shoppers can be lured into buying something they don't need or want. They see other frantic shoppers grabbing items at the sales and believe they will miss out on a bargain - whatever is on sale. They join the crush and grab what is available, even without inspecting the goods.

I have seen similar signs on first-time 'look-see' visitors faces when they enter a church that already looks full. Minor panic sets in as they rapidly scan the seats for vacancies. That increases anxiety in line with the number in the family. At five to eleven, or whatever time your church begins, certainly true for us at Long Lane, multiple seats together become scarce. That's positive, given the belief that 'church' will be extinguished soon! However, for first-time visitors, it can feel awkward, slightly embarrassing, and a focus of attention as they scan the rows. A canny and sensitive church, of course, will have stewards or members who understand the dilemma and make sure the visitors don't feel awkward. When a church reaches a critical mass, around 80-90% of capacity, a revolving door situation begins. A reluctance to face embarrassment, or a belief that it's too big, may end by going elsewhere. The only way that a church can grow numerically is to provide more space. As it has been said, 'you don't fill the space you don't provide.' PS: other ways to grow are also available!

In 2011 the Lane faced an important decision. To facilitate growth, they would need to move to bigger premises. The relatively new, and first ever full-time pastor, Nick Johnson was a breath of fresh air and the Lane began to rapidly grow and outgrow the church building. After prayer and discussion, the church began the search for a bigger space and landed on a local site. In September 2010 the old schools of St Benedict and New Heys Comprehensive amalgamated and became ESLA (Enterprise South Liverpool Academy) situated on Horrock's Avenue but within a mile of the Lane and still in Garston. In October 2011, the congregation celebrated their first morning service in ESLA's old buildings. Within two years, ESLA were celebrating a completely new, and very shiny building. As the school moved in, so the congregation also moved to the shiny new building, holding the first service on March 24th 2013, which just happened to be my birthday, so a double celebration! Nick was delighted, four years later, when ESLA reverted to an Anglican school and was named St Nicholas Academy or 'St Nick's'!

Such a move of church services from an established site to a public building did not come without challenges; constant shifting of equipment and set-up early on a Sunday morning. A host of other major and minor challenges, can easily sap energy and zeal. Despite the challenges and changes, the church has tripled in size, now has four pastors, a CAP (Christians Against Poverty) centre and manager, and is presently considering how to engage with another area of Garston – a church plant, church move or something in between?

71

SURPRISE!

In marriage, or any other union, leaving room for surprises has been my advice when taking marriage preparation courses or sharing generally with couples. In April 2016 I sprang yet another of my many surprises on Ann, one that I had never tried before! I took her across the Mersey to New Brighton, on the Wirral, for a meal out. We found a table and, as Ann sat down, I remained standing. 'I have got something to tell you.' The look on Ann's face indicated a serious shock was coming. It was either divorce, cancer, or our exciting holiday in the US with daughter Sharon and missionary colleague Sarah had been cancelled.

The plan was to return to Saddlebrook Resort, courtesy of Denis and Linda Cole, and enjoy five days together before picking up Sharon and Sarah from Orlando Airport. We would stay another week at Saddlebrook, allowing the girls to unwind before flying on to Las Vegas for three nights at the Westin Hotel, then a hire car drive to the Grand Canyon and a stay in cabins near the edge of the rim. From the canyon to Lake Havasu where Sarah would leave us for Las Vegas and her return to Peru. We would drive once again across the scary Mojave Desert, visit San Diego then up Route 1 to Los Angeles and San Francisco. Sharon would fly back to Lima from San Francisco. As we had never been to Oregon, I had booked two nights in a boutique hotel overlooking the Pacific. We would then fly back home from San Francisco.

I began my surprise element. 'You know we have those two nights in Oregon before flying back home from San Francisco?' Ann replied, 'yes.' 'Well, we're not', I responded. 'We have a leisurely eleven days driving up the Oregon Coast into Kingston, a ferry across to Seattle, then a couple of days before we cruise to Alaska!' Ann burst into tears! No divorce, no cancer, no cancellation!

Liverpool-Dublin-Orlando

We had never considered this route before, but really pleased we did. Not least because you clear US customs security in Dublin and walk straight out of your US airport! Three hours after landing we were, once again, checking in to Saddlebrook Resort, just eighty-two miles away, and ready for bed. At 6am we were watching dawn break over the lake and spotting small and large Egrets along with a Blue Heron. Our personal alligator, Fred, recalled from previous visits, was in residence. We chilled in the apartment pool, all to ourselves, followed by shopping in a posh Publix Super market, then a lazy lunch on the patio. In the evening, we had a great meal at Cracker Barrel – a favourite destination on previous stays. Sadly, on a visit later in the week, Ann fell over and bruised her shoulder, adding to the numerous injuries suffered in falls over the years. The rest of the week we explored the resort, swam in the biggest pool in Florida and marvelled again at the extensive wildlife.

Saddlebrook maintains exceptionally beautiful natural corridors, which not only enhance your experience, but protect several plant and animal species indigenous to the area. This includes the Great Egret and the Bald Cypress Tree, two key endangered species of birds and trees that are fighting for a place in the wetland ecosystem. Alligators lurk in the pools, Ospreys nest, and masses of Great Egrets breed. The whole system is connected by a series of walkways, allowing visitors to interact with this stunning habitat.

One of the more humorous pastimes, for us, was the hidden danger, just lurking out of view on the banks of some of the raised golf greens. We would see 'Fred' sunbathing, out of the golfer's eyeline, and watch the flight of the golfer's ball. If it landed on the green and sped over the edge, it would often settle a few feet from Fred and his habit of lurking on the bank to sunbathe. The unsuspecting golfer would cross the green and peer down the bank, looking for his ball. It was a brave player who didn't make an immediate and swift u-turn! British golfers take note!

Hugs, tears, and excitement

The toughest moments for us, having a missionary daughter over eight thousand miles away was saying goodbye, knowing we might not see her for three years. Now we were on our way to Orlando in emotional reverse. Five days after arriving in Florida we were about to welcome Sharon and Sarah on their flight from Lima. Nothing beats a long hug, plenty of good tears and the excitement of sharing an adventure together. The girls were straight into our apartment pool, followed by salad on the patio, and a long catch up before bed.

Hawks, snakes, and fish

In all our previous visits to Saddlebrook, we had never seen a snake, nor a Red Shouldered Hawk. We were lazing around the pool and spotted a hawk perched on a pergola. Suddenly it swooped across our loungers and into a corner of the pool area. We immediately became aware of a commotion behind a small hedge on the patio, just feet away. The hawk had a long Indigo snake in its mouth and a dual between them was in full swing. Sharon grabbed her camera, shouted 'wow,' and captured an amazing video of the tussle. As we approached, the hawk looked us straight in the eye determined not to let his prize go. The hawk won and Sharon's media post became a hit with over 255,000 views. Suffice to say, we were much more alert to the possibility of snakes as we walked about the resort!

We did watch a further scary encounter as another Indigo snake made its way through a hedge behind us as we sat by the pool. Ann watched in a sort of 'fascinated-horror' as the snake pushed its head through the middle of the hedge and rose about two feet in the air! As it disappeared, the scarier part, for Ann, was second-guessing where it had gone! As for 'Fred' we were party to the devouring of a huge fish and a turtle!

Paying on

One of our more interesting culinary moments was in a '2 Minute Diner' in Zephyr Hills, just a few miles down the road. (You might recall my infamous 'Hooters' moment at First Baptist Church Zephyr Hills!) The 'Western' theme was prevalent with John Wayne featuring on every wall. As we scanned the menu, a guy on the next table lent over and suggested the chicken steak. We duly obliged. Halfway through our meal, the rugged builder was leaving and stopped at our table. 'It's all taken care of' he said! At first, I wasn't sure what he meant, but he was saying goodbye and had paid our bill! So began our own desire to 'pay-on' so that other customers might be blessed. We left $40 with the cashier and asked that it be reserved for any 'needy' customers. In Vancouver, on a subsequent holiday, we were sitting outside a café having a meal when I spotted a family in a café across the square. It was clear from their clothing that they were poor. The pinched and white faces of the kids reminded me of some of the youngsters in Toxteth. It was also evident that the parents were battling over ice creams and having to consistently say 'no.' I knew I should help. I simply went over and said 'for you' and placed my gift on the table. The look on their faces was priceless and the joy in my heart was precious. At times, a little gift makes a massive difference. Also, it doesn't have to be money. We spotted a mum and young boy in a Vancouver market carrying bunches of flowers. As we moved towards them, I noticed they were stopping and handing over a bunch to passers-by. They were using the same two words I had used for the café family - 'for you.' As we passed by them, the mum extended a bunch to us and we responded with thanks. The only problem was we were embarking on a cruise and needed all hands for luggage. As we moved through the doors out of the market a young lady was passing and guess what! She received the bunch with a 'for you.' There is something beautiful and joyful in thinking of others in such a simple way.

Busch Gardens – Tampa

In typical fashion, everything was perfect for us. Free entry for disabled visitors, with carers half-price. Straight to the front of queues and the best views and seats at the shows, Wherever, in the US we travelled it was the same 5-star care and facilities for the disabled, except Idlewild Baptist Church disabled parking where we received a $109 parking ticket! Visitors beware, don't you dare park in a disabled space without the appropriate badge!

'They say,' whoever 'they' may be, that the fifth child is also the most adventurous - like jumping out of an aeroplane without a parachute! It has certainly proved true with Sharon and her passion for scary rollercoasters. Although, to be fair, both our boys have that gene, and our grandson Aaron works at Alton Towers! Busch Gardens had a host of scary rollercoasters and Sharon rode every one! We, on the other hand, took the pictures! The rest of the day was spent with animals from across the world. Exotic birds such as the Scarlet Ibis, toucans and cranes, then on the safari train through the vast park with its array of African wildlife. By

5pm, given the heat, humidity, and an intense rain shower while Sharon was on a roller coaster with drops hitting her like stones, we returned to Saddlebrook. Our remaining days, before heading off to Las Vegas, were spent on site, making the most of the two pools, sunbathing, games and avoiding snakes!

Las Vegas

Whilst we were making our fourth trip, it was a first for the girls. Contrary to our expectations, that they might not like the glitz, they both adapted quickly and were determined to make the most of our three day stay. The Venetian complex, with its grandeur, canals, and bustling St Mark's square, was our goal for the evening, followed by the Bellagio Fountains. Over the next two days we visited some of the key attractions. The Mirage hotel 'volcano' with fire and water intermingling. The zoo with white tigers, lions, leopards, and extremely playful dolphins. On to Treasure Island hotel for a quick-fire pirate show and the sinking, and raising up, of a large galleon! Mandalay Bay hotel with an aquarium the size of Lake Como, well, you know what I mean! Separate ways also for the girls who wanted to tour the Wynn Hotel while we wanted to be mesmerised for an hour by the Bellagio Lake Fountains.

Grand Canyon

8am start and a protracted argument with our hire car company, who didn't have the car we had paid for and insisted on palming us off with a smaller one which would not take four passengers plus all our luggage. We prayed, stood our ground and, as if by magic, they came up with a new Jeep! We packed and set off on our mega-adventure. Having flown over the Hoover Dam twice, it was interesting to view it at ground level and take in just how immense it is. Stopped at Ash Fork on Route 66, so

Sharon could take over driving and I could boast of our exploits by purchasing the obligatory and trendy Route 66 baseball cap! Although Sharon had not driven for a couple of years, she handled the large Jeep with ease and without scaring three passengers! Another pit-stop at Williams for lunch in a sparkly red diner, then the last leg to the Canyon.

After a seven hour drive, we relaxed at the IMAX cinema and the stunning production of the Canyon discovery, followed by settling into our cabins, and a quick dash to the rim. For me, on my fourth visit and Ann on her third, it was still very emotional. All of us gazed quietly, and in awe, at the sheer size, beauty, and magic of one of earth's amazing and breathtaking wonders. Early to bed with determination to get up and see the sunrise, followed by the dramatic changes in the canyon walls as the sun weaves its path through the day.

After breakfast, we walked along the rim in a chilly wind but full sun. Sharon's penchant for losing things popped up when leaving her rucksack at a viewpoint. Quite a way along the path she realised the lack of weight, retraced her steps and, mercifully, it was still at the 'Point'. After lunch we drove along Desert View Drive and back via Mather Point. It reminded us of the Icefields Pathway in Canada when the amount of stops we made was far beyond our expectation! Just so many new vistas with every twist and turn of the canyon walls, and we didn't want to miss a single photo opportunity.

One of the privileges of Ann's Blue Badge is unexpected access. One drive was prohibited, except for coaches - unless you have a Blue Badge. We were blessed with quiet viewing points and empty roads all the way. After our breathtaking day, we had tea in the rustic, and registered historic landmark, Bright Angel Lodge, followed by star-gazing along the rim. It was our final night before a quick, and stunning drive, to Hermitage Rest the next morning. At midday we said goodbye to the Canyon, with grateful thanks for all the visits and vistas we had seen over the years.

Our route towards the West Coast took us via an overnight stay at Lake Havasu, home of the 'London Bridge' since 1971, when it had been dismantled and transported from London. It was assembled on the desert floor, then flooded creating a huge lake for fishing and water sports! At 5am we said goodbye to Sarah, who was heading back to Las Vegas by bus, then flying to Lima. Our goal was San Diego, across the Mojave Desert, alongside the Colorado River Reservation, into barren shrub and boulder hills, before entering the lush scenery of Cleveland National Park with high mountains, canyon trails and beautiful waterfalls. Sharon enhanced her road trip mileage by driving most of the way, then passing the baton to Dad for the urban 'fast and furious' chaos of San Diego! It was good to complete our six hour trip from Vegas, through varied and contrasting scenes, and heavenly to plunge into the Holiday Inn pool!

The following day was 'Memorial Day' in San Diego. We had planned a visit to the Navy Docks but, after driving for miles along the bay, we gave up all hope of parking and made our way to the Point Loma peninsula. It was to be a very emotional visit as we stumbled across the Military Cemetery. Thousands of regimented white gravestones overlooking the vast harbour and navy ships, each stone decorated with a rose and a US flag. I could not hold back my tears – an experience I would repeat in the future when standing in the US cemetery at Omaha Beach in France. The attention to detail is impressive, but I gather, from talking to many ex-servicemen over the years, that the care of veterans is far less impressive. How easy it is to present an image of perfection that doesn't match reality.

In the evening, we drove to La Jolla beach, one of the most photographed in California, with its beautiful surf and controversial mass of seals who occupy, and staunchly defend, the 'children's pool' area! Left San Diego in the morning, on route to Laguna Bay and Newport Beach - favourite haunts from a previous visit. Extremely exclusive and expensive pit-stops, but the surf was beautiful in Laguna, and the 'house-spotting' at Newport put paid to any idea of buying a second home! Onwards to Los Angeles where we realised our small motel, just round the corner from Hollywood Boulevard, was about as basic as you could get and surrounded by vagrants and three hospitals! Believe me, the walk of fame is a walk of shame!

We would have gladly bypassed LA, but Sharon had her 'Pretty Woman' dress so we could not miss a trip to the Beverly Wilshire! I think Sharon said, 'what am I doing?' No doubt following hundreds of other ladies who have popped into the hotel in their brown and white polka dot dress! To redeem a thoroughly understated city centre visit, we took to the hills past the Hollywood sign and on to the white domed Griffth Observatory thus tipping our hats to science and culture!

For Sharon, the next leg would be her last before flying back to Peru from San Francisco. She chose, wisely, not to enhance her driving experience by tackling the twelve lane freeway out of LA - sheer, and very slow, chaos. It was a relief to leave LA behind and enjoy the more relaxed journey through Santa Monica and Malibu, once again a very disappointing experience, given the hype you pick up from the media about Malibu. We passed Santa Barbara and Pismo on route to the small, but special for us, Estero Inn, where we had stayed on our previous journey down Route 1. It was very misty over the sea inlet but we managed to spot a couple of sea otters with their young. The following day we drove around the bay, in clear sun, to see the breeding area for otters. It was teeming with youngsters, just twenty feet from the shore, frolicking in the kelp, hitch-hiking on mum's tummy, and endlessly washing their faces with two paws cupped together. A truly wonderful spectacle.

Just a short distance from Morro Bay we stopped at the Piedras Blancas Elephant Seal Rookery, six miles of 'Blubber and Bloody Battles' - nobody swimming! Moved on to our overnight stay in a lovely suite at Monterey as we looked forward to our Pacific excursion in search of whales, more sea otters, harbour seals and dolphins. We managed four whales, a host of small dolphins, sea otters cracking shells on the side of boats in the harbour, a few harbour seals and, for our trouble, a good soaking in the Pacific swell! Back to hotel to dry out and on to Fishermen's Wharf and the famous aquarium, the only one in the world to hold a Great White Shark, but only for 178 days! Yet more sea otters up close in the sanctuary, as well as the enormous aquarium. We never cease to wonder at the natural world nor underestimate the privilege we have had to visit such places and see that world up close.

Finally, after exhausting all our previously visited attractions in San Francisco with Sharon, though this time I did manage a ride with her on a tram, it was time for another tearful parting. It had been another wonderful US experience, not without a few trials, tears, and disappointments along the way, but one of gratitude as we stood in awe and wonder together at the natural beauty of our world.

72

UNSPOILT VISTAS

It was time to hand back our trusty Jeep at the airport and pick up a smaller Hyundai for our journey into virgin territory. My surprise promise to Ann, in the Wirral Harvester, was about to be fulfilled. We left SF around 9am on Route 1, across the Golden Gate Bridge and into Oregon. A 115 mile journey, through Redwood and Pine forests, to Gualala (pronounced 'Wa-la-la') on the Pacific Coast. The Seacliff Motel was situated on a bluff overlooking the sea. A 'second-honeymoon' location! The view over the Pacific was breathtaking through the large lounge window. No whales in sight but a stunning sunset. Following a wacky Mexican restaurant evening meal we simply chilled on the decking, treated ourselves to a gin and tonic and relaxed in silence. Other details are not available!

After so many one night stays, it was lovely to take a leisurely breakfast and chill on the iconic US rocking chair as we scanned the Pacific for any sign of whales or dolphins. A lazy trip up the coast to Port Arena, coffee in a quirky coffee house and chat with a guy who had just returned from Peru! Lovely evening meal at Sandbanks accompanied by clear blue skies. Possibly a bit more G&T…!

As we waved Wa-la-la goodbye, we began a lengthy journey along the unspoilt and forest laden coast to Fortuna, stopping at Ferndale for lunch in a Victoriana Inn. What a contrast the Oregon Coast is from California – quiet roads, quaint coastal towns, uncommercialised and stunningly different, with its log-laden beaches, coves, and endless rock sculptures. More lazy ramblings up the coast, coffee at Eureka, rebel Elk encounter on the road, arriving at Brookings Harbour midday. Stunning beach for lunch, checked in to Ocean Suites overlooking the harbour - the busiest recreational maritime port on the Oregon coast, (we just love wandering around harbours). A wonderful sunset at Harris Beach, with its amazing rock structures, completed yet another awesome day. So much of what we really appreciate – sea-vistas, waterfalls, rivers, rocks, harbours, and awesome sunsets - and didn't cost a dime to appreciate!

Next stop, Salmon Harbour. According to previous reviews, the 'most unsightly harbour on the Oregon Coast!' Well, they'd cleaned it up by the time we arrived! The 'Victorian' theme prevailed again in our small but beautifully decorated cabin not far from the harbour. The area is a dune-buggy paradise and we seemed to have arrived in the middle of a major racing event. Free seats at the Grand Prix for yours truly! Stunning views of the sea and fresh fish on the harbour side so no complaints on our review. A good night's sleep which might have been our last ever!

Left early for the Sunset Surf Motel at Manzanita. Ten miles into the journey a yellow warning light appeared on the dashboard. Being a man, I dismissed it as nothing. However, as the miles passed and the light stayed on, Ann insisted we stop and get help, as it signals 'engine warning!' I gave in and stopped at the first auto-repair garage. They didn't know the problem and suggested I rang Budget Car Hire. Budget told me to go to Eugene. Eugene is not where I wanted to go! It was miles out of our way and my whole schedule went out of the window. After a serious air of marital tension, I decided to carry on to Manzanita. I finally stopped in Newport for a coffee and the waiter directed me to a garage not far away. Five minutes later, after a plug-in computer search, the mechanic said, 'faulty light, no problem, and no cost.' I gave him a tip for sparing us an unnecessary trip back to Eugene, and saving my marriage! We were back on speaking terms!

As I headed away from the garage, and back towards our route, I became more and more aware that we were going in the wrong direction! After a mile into the wilderness, I made a sudden decision to do a u-turn - without checking my mirror! Half way round the turn I sensed the presence of a large truck making a desperate swerve around my rear! By the grace of God, and several angels, it just missed and carried straight on! Another of life's motoring miracles. We didn't speak for a couple of hours! Several years later, I noted Ann's comment in her diary, 'God watching over us!' It was a relief to arrive at Sunset Surf Motel on the beach, turn my baseball cap so the peak was at the back and pretend I was forty years younger!

On the road at 8am as we said goodbye to Oregon and hello to Washington. A long trip to Forks, our last stay on a memorable 900 mile road-trip from San Francisco. Endless stunning lakes, huge forests, double rainbows and a wild mixture of sun and heavy showers. According to Google, Forks is a city with a population of under 4,000! More like a British village but the motel was comfortable, if a little basic. We needed to remind ourselves we were about to enter a floating palace, on route to Alaska, with more people than Forks!

Our final day on the road, as we headed out early for the 118 mile trip to Kingston Ferry and the thirty minute crossing to Edmonds. Just a twenty minute wait then a pleasant sunny crossing, always scanning the Puget Sound for any sight of orcas and whales! Lunch was at Edmonds Marina followed by a major shopping expedition for suitable 'cruise' and 'Alaska' clothing, along with an unexpected new camera and Ipad at bargain prices! A slightly frustrating period as it took us two hours to find our overnight stop at the Holiday Inn. It was good to get a rest after a busy day on the road and at the local mall!

Welcome lie in, then breakfast before a short hop to Seattle to return the hire car and head for the cruise terminal. Great service from the Budget guy who insisted on driving us to the terminal. Sheer 'cab-chaos' on entry, but we edged our way forward and finally made it on board Royal Caribbean Explorer of the Seas. By one thirty we were sitting in 'Dizzys' having our lunch, followed by a rest in our cabin on Deck 14. It was certainly the most stunning ship we had boarded and the largest disability access cabin. At five thirty we arrived at our dinner table for eight. All our table guests were very pleasant and we soon built good relationships. We did however, try and keep off Mr Trump, as two of our new friends on the table were ardent supporters!

The cruise retraced most of our 40th Wedding Anniversary stops, on Holland America Veendam, back in 2003, but it was still a magical Alaskan journey. Sometimes it is a mistake to return to memorable destinations, but I doubt a dozen cruises to Alaska would ever exhaust its breathtaking vistas. Many more 'blows and flukes' from whales this time round. An amazing 'ice show', an informative lecture on Alaska from Park Rangers, five ice-carvings at Dawes Glacier, large brown bear on shore and a wander up Tracey Arm fiord and the 'Terror Wilderness Area'. A first-time visit to Victoria, on Vancouver Island, the capital of British Columbia. Indicators of our colonial past everywhere in architecture, signs, and the stunning gardens. Another 'pay-on' couple treated us to coffee following a casual chat! All too soon we were back in Seattle and feeling the ground beneath us constantly move! Toured Pike-Place market, enjoyed a short cruise around the harbour, didn't bump into President Obama who was visiting Seattle. I imagine he was devastated to miss us!

Our last night before flights from Seattle to San Francisco, Dublin then Liverpool. So glad we could navigate straight back home and avoid a long and tiring car journey on landing. Wow, what an amazing trip. The free pleasures of Las Vegas without a single pull of a slot-machine. The awesome grandeur of Grand Canyon with its constantly shifting vistas as the sun drenches the multicoloured rock strata. The scary Mojave Desert littered with military, aeronautic, and space sites. Route 66 with its iconic musical, biker, and wild west connections. Route One, snaking for hundreds of miles up the West Coast and offering endless Pacific vistas, giant forests, and tourist attractions. The unspoilt bays of Oregon with its quaint and quirky fishing ports, lazy lifestyle, fascinating rock structures, and giant Redwood Forests. The breathtaking wilderness of Alaska, where creation endlessly shouts out and touches our heart with the importance of a connection with the Lord of all creation. 'Greatly blessed' doesn't do justice for the privilege we have had to explore such a beautiful world.

73

COVID

I imagine everyone has a 'Covid' story. Many were truly heartbreaking, horrendous, and terrifying. Following the lifting of the restrictions, countless lives were changed either for good or bad. Some changed their whole lifestyle, others changed their jobs, while many pondered the future with a degree of dread. Pandemics disturb life across the globe. It was so for us, but the disappointment also led to joy and blessing.

One of the most vital, important, and key publications our daughter Sharon has produced in Peru is 'Aurora' – the prevention of sexual abuse of children. The importance of this publication was highlighted in Mexico by key global regional directors and the then international director of CLC (Christian Literature Centre). Following Sharon's presentation they responded, 'we know of no other work in the world like this.' The European Director, now International Director, Gary Chamberlin, asked Sharon if she would travel to Poland to present the material to regional directors at a book rights conference and then deliver training in three Spanish cities. Slightly running ahead of the game, he began to speak of many other nations that Aurora could be taken to. Sharon responded positively to Gary's invitation - he would work on the venues.

In March 2020 Sharon was flying out of Lima. Somewhere over the Amazon, or the Atlantic, an email pinged on her phone. Her first access was at Schiphol Airport Amsterdam. It was from Gary, 'sorry Sharon, but all presentations have been cancelled due to Covid regulations.' It was a heavy blow for her and for us as we had booked to meet up with her in Spain. On the plus side she made her way home and here she stayed for nine months! It was an unexpected blessing as we would normally see her once every three years. Had the email arrived a few hours earlier she would not have been on the flight!

Sadly, Peru's per-capita death rate was the highest in the world, with over 222,000 deaths - twice the per-capita rate of the USA. The lockdown regulations in Peru were also among the world's toughest. Had Sharon stayed in Peru she would have experienced a tough battle, given her personality, sociable nature, and creative mind. At least here she could concentrate on her hobbies, learning to make polymer clay earrings as well as develop her photography. Both featured well over the months, with 'doortraits' (door-step portraits), and email orders for her earrings. It was fun to chauffeur her around and watch the interaction on the street and at the door. Pyjamas featured a few times in door-step pictures! It was also an uninterrupted time to concentrate on new material for future publications. Our conservatory became a creative studio for trying out visual effects for Bible stories, which would then feature in live broadcasts! Disappointments and delays feature regularly in all our lives. The key is transforming setbacks into blessings, making the most of unexpected interruptions and navigating obstacles in fresh ways. Sharon was able to do that in spades!

Having multiple gardens to tend, I was not short of options to keep me sane, whilst Ann had card making, knitting, and making the most of Sharon's unexpected stay! Tim could keep on cleaning windows! Andy found it much more difficult as working from home. With limited contact, he was the one family member who suffered most. His extrovert personality, which thrived with human connections, was severely tested. Support from friends was a very special lifeline.

Covid also allowed the birthing of Zoom in a way previously not experienced. Church was online for everything; Sunday broadcasts, prayer meetings, vision evenings, life groups, family connections, even games together! It has been interesting to see a significant increase of people, not necessarily connected with church but tuning in to the Sunday morning service. Locally the River Oaks Charity Trustees started on zoom and have continued. It saves organising a home, maybe putting kids elsewhere and disrupting family life. It's all about creativity, flexibility and efficiency, but nothing beats personal contact!

74

CRETE & CRUISING

When families are spread, it is a special joy to have them all together in one place. In 2019 Tim spent many hours researching villas that would be suitable and accessible for Mum and eight of the family. He eventually settled on an amazing villa in Crete, overlooking Rethymnon. A three storey palace with infinity pool, well equipped games room and cinema, lift to all floors, walk in showers and a stunning kitchen and lounge overlooking the sea. Flights and accommodation all paid, including flying Sharon back from Peru! It was a brilliant week with everyone on the shopping and cooking rota – except Dad and Mum! Very few arguments and lots of hilarity in and out of the pool and hot tub. Andy was master of ceremonies with regards to games, so no shortage of activities! I won't mention Andy's favourite pasttime of trying to get a small golf ball into a crazy-golf hole! After twenty strokes the whole gang were in stitches! Love you son. It was also special time to spend more time with Tierney, and Aaron's then partner, Philippa, who was relatively new to the family. Sadly, Tim's partner Katherine had to stay behind to manage her beauty and tanning salon.

An extra bonus for us, later in the year, was a UK cruise on Royal Caribbean Anthem of the Seas. At the time of booking, we expected to share the ship with 3,000+ but once boarded we were told it was just 900! Covid memories were far too raw, so confined spaces were still 'no-go zones' for many. We joked about having our own pool and restaurant, and sometimes it felt that way! The ship was the biggest and best we had sailed on, with every single care taken to ensure disabled passengers had access without hassle. Automatic opening on all doors, not least in the toilets which can be tricky at times. By staying on board in Liverpool, we managed to get an extra trip up the aerial viewing pod, a 360 degree viewing arm that travels up and down whilst in port but also moves out to sea when sailing. The entry for Ann, on her scooter, was seamless and the view at the top spectacular. The ship also had an ice rink and bumper cars, gaming centres, and an extra-large lit-up swing in the front lounge which was Ann's favourite!

One of our longstanding 'bucket list' entries was to sail into Liverpool and wave to our Cruise Ambassador friends. It was a magical experience as we sailed up the River Mersey and berthed alongside one of the most iconic and stunning skylines in the world. The 'Three Graces' - Royal Liver, Cunard, and Port of Liverpool Buildings - dominate the horizon and make a spectacular backdrop to the cruise terminal. The Cunard Building is the spiritual home of Cunard Shipping Line, where cruising began in July 1840 when the Brittania sailed from Liverpool to Boston. May 2015 was a landmark occasion as Liverpool celebrated the 175th anniversary of Cunard Line's maiden transatlantic voyage. Over one million people gathered on the banks of the Mersey to welcome the 'three Queens' - Queen Mary 2, Queen Elizabeth, and Queen Victoria. A magical pirouette of these giant cruise ships took place in the centre of the river – no mean feat at low tide!

Further celebrations took place on June 3rd 2024 as the latest Cunard vessel, Queen Anne, arrived for her naming ceremony. Thousands gathered to enjoy the festivities at the Pier Head, with the Royal Liverpool Philharmonic Orchestra leading the musical tributes and Andrea Bocelli touching the heart with his penetrating voice. As volunteers on duty for the day, we were privileged to serve at the terminal and presented with two Cunard Posters of Queen Anne and two magnets celebrating the occasion. I guess the posters will be worth a fortune … in a hundred years! The 'naming' was very much Liverpool's domain, with noted local celebrities speaking the lines and thousands of people in the crowd responding with the same words. The city truly 'owned' the occasion. The sail-away, as darkness fell and the ship moved out into the river, was spectacular and way beyond the obligatory display that occurs when vessels are making their first visit to Liverpool. Cunard may be owned by the USA, and do most of its cruises out of Southampton, but its history will always be owned by its birthplace – the great port City of Liverpool. When on Cruise welcome duty, I suggest passengers tip their hat when passing the Cunard's Building!

In 2022 Tim repeated the villa blessing with another Crete location a few more miles out of Rethymnon. This time we paid our own flights, apart from Sharon's from Peru! As it is normally difficult for us all to be together in December, Andy secretly planned a Christmas celebration - three months early! He began by giving us all Christmas cards and reindeer T-shirts. A small Christmas Tree appeared, along with decorations and ingredients for a full Christmas meal! Sadly, UK customs confiscated the Christmas crackers - no doubt seen as offensive weapons! Andy and Sharon Bell did us proud and we all produced our favourite tipple. Crete gave us some precious moments, lots of fun and a time to deepen our relationships and share some honest and open conversations - mainly in the hot tub after drinks! Thanks to Tim for amazing generosity, endless planning, and making it possible for almost all the family to spend quality time together again in a stunning location.

75

AWAM - AGE WITH A MISSION

In November 2020 we received an invitation from friends Brian and Angela Benford, to share our Fresh Horizons experience, regarding third-age retirees, with a small group in the South of England who met regularly for prayer. The group were very ably serviced by David Henderson, whose ability to recall prayer requests and pass them to members of the group is legendary! Covid put paid to meetings in homes and they had, like thousands of others, moved to Zoom meetings. Some of the group had shared experiences of being unsettled, excluded, or isolated in their church; their life experience, gifting, and passion for Jesus meant they were all eager to serve, pray and share their faith. Sadly, the opportunity was not given and they had found new hope by joining together for prayer with others in the same situation.

Having met many retirees, at the Fresh Horizon's Day Conferences, who shared similar experiences, I was well aware of the sense of isolation and discouragement that marginalisation brings. Although it has not been my experience, I felt it was important for Ann and me to invest as much time and prayer with this group as possible. After meeting together for some time, the Lord spoke clearly to Derry, one of the prayer group, about the age equivalent of YWAM (Youth with a Mission). Whilst praying and listening to the Spirit of God, she received the word AWAM; a prophetic moment warmly accepted by the group. Taking this title was checked with YWAM before being announced more widely. An addition was the need for a logo. I suggested our daughter Sharon, given her creative design skills, and, after prayer and consideration, she came back with the image of a large oak tree. The key component was a square lined box covering many of the tree branches, with some of the branches breaking out of the lines and beyond the box. AWAM's task would be to serve the heart of the church but also to break beyond traditional and conventional boundaries with branches outside the box.

One of the key aims promoted by AWAM is the support we might give to other churches, groups, or individuals. Among those who meet regularly is Rev Jonathan Martin, previously an Anglican Minister, now a bereavement counsellor and chaplain to the Royal Navy. Jonathan had accepted an invitation to pastor, part-time, a small Baptist Church in Poole, Dorset - Buckland Road BC. In human terms, this church had no future; few people attending, few wage earners, a small building, and some important issues to address. Jonathan asked the AWAM group for support. As we were returning from a cruise to Norway in April 2022, and would be disembarking around 8.30am on a Saturday, we offered to make a short detour to Poole and share our story with the friends at BRBC before motoring back home. It was the first visit from AWAM members, followed by others in the team of fervent prayer partners, who brought a range of gifts to the table and laid a good foundation for the work to prosper. BRBC was certainly support outside the box! What a joy to meet a receptive and varied group of disciples and interact together on the challenges facing this small band of believers. From everyone's perspective it was an important time together, with a fruitfulness over time, that is encouraging, exciting and full of hope. It is this model of being friends to small churches and encouraging retirees to engage in mission that fits well into the AWAM vision.

Jonathan very graciously penned this wonderful summary of our short time spent with BRBC. I must underline, that while we were the first responders, others, far more capable, swiftly followed. Each has left insight, wisdom, prayer, and practical support.

Buckland Road Baptist Church – Initial visit

- Terry's storytelling of drug caches in Liverpool, his ability to set people at their ease, along with Ann's willingness to let people push her around the patch, gave 'Buckers' people a sense of belief, that these folk are not so different to us, if they can do it, maybe we can.

- Hospitality appreciated by Terry and Ann. They encouraged BRBC to develop hospitality across the board. This has led to the church gaining confidence to provide 2 to 3 course meals to lots of visitors, open the church for two days a week and provide homemade cake every Sunday.

- Terry encouraged us to think that we didn't have to strive to be what we weren't, but that we could become a centre for loving change within our own community. This felt possible, and lifted a weight off our shoulders. Other 'AWAMers' visited bringing similar and different skills, all of which enhanced our sense of confidence; we had a purpose and place in God's plan.

- Constant and consistent prayer, together with the gift of unconditional prayerful and practical support, are a welcome prop on which new foundations have been laid.

- More recently Terry and Ann's daughter, Sharon, visited on her way back to ministry in Peru. The church had been encouraged by some of her teaching in the past and were blessed by her presence. The awareness that someone special wants to visit us was such a blessing. It was great!

- So, there is a sense in which Terry and family, along with other 'AWAMers' are built into the re-laid foundations of the church.

*****

It is together that we have left a small legacy that BRBC has embraced and acted upon. There is also so much more BRBC have accomplished including hosting a Ukrainian Church, providing a 'warm space' and a gardening club. Early days but much to give thanks for.

One of the overflows of AWAM monthly prayer meetings is the personal touch. The ability to merge visionary prayers beyond the box for AWAM, with prayer for each other, our wider family and involvement in mission and ministry in our locality and beyond. I had been aware for some years that my colleague from college, batch leader and former boss in the Baptist Union Mission Department, Derek Allan, had been supporting Javea International Baptist Church in Spain. He and Sally, his wife, would travel to Spain and spend several months preaching, guiding and pastorally caring for this community. The congregation are largely British expats with the occasional member from other countries, not least Ukrainian refugees following Russia's invasion. Given the limited conditions for a stay, now that Britain was out of the EU, Derek required several other leaders to fill the gaps throughout the year.

In 2021 Derek wrote and asked whether we would consider a period of three weeks in Javea in June 2022. We had previously spent two villa holidays in Javea with our family, so knew and loved the area. We talked and prayed together and had peace that we should go. I also believed that teaching from the book of Nehemiah would be helpful, given the uncertainty relating to JIBC's future tenancy and the need for a fresh vision. I also informed Derek that a member of AWAM, Rev Jonathan Martin, would be suitable and willing to play a part in supporting JIBC.

We chose to drive rather than fly to Spain, thus tagging the journey on to our stay and giving us space to explore the country. As we both love ships, the route from Plymouth to Santander, with Britanny Ferries, would be a chance to enjoy the Bay of Biscay. Normally, you would expect something of a rollercoaster crossing in the Bay of Biscay. We enjoyed flat calm with not a white-top in sight! Given Ann's disabilities and limitations, we could not have asked for a more perfect cruise! Our plan was to drive halfway across Spain to Zaragoza, stay overnight, arriving at Javea late in the afternoon. It worked well and allowed us time to enjoy the varied landscapes without tackling the 830 kms in a day! We were warmly welcomed by the church, with time to move into their apartment and settle, followed by a breakfast gathering the next day at a local golf club. I was aware of tensions among the congregation very quickly. When there is a new vision or challenge regarding a new building and location, it is common to face conflicting opinions. Is our task to serve the church or evangelise the locality? Should we be looking at what the church needs or what the community needs? Is our priority internal or external?

I became aware over the three weeks that all was not well. As the preaching became more challenging, the atmosphere altered. It was a little cooler and polarised with regards to the next move; protect what we have or launch out into a fresh vision for JIBC? Some preachers are called, occasionally, to plough ground before a fresh batch of seed is sown and a new harvest is reaped. I had a distinct feeling of ploughing! Mercifully, it was not for me to decide the outcome, but be faithful to the word I had received and preached. I was very sure that I would not be returning in 2023!

The almost immediate blessing, on return, was the news that Derek had been in discussion with Jonathan and he would be following my footsteps to Javea in 2023 and 2024. It's June 1st 2024, and, as I write, Jonathan is making his return visit. Another AWAM branch extending beyond the box! My prayers are for wisdom, guidance, freedom, and clear direction for JIBC.

76

COMPLICATIONS

Over the years we had anticipated ongoing issues and concerns regarding Ann's mobility and embraced ways to minimise accidents, make life as comfortable as possible, and still make valuable contributions to church, community, and city. Many people remarked on our youthful outlook and zest for active life, whether accompanied by mobility scooters or walking frames! When referring to Ann's medical history, I often quote, 'Ann has undergone more operations than the SAS, with x-rays to match that should light her up at night!' However, she had never had an x-ray of her ankles in seventy-seven years.

2021 would bring a significant change. It was clear, over a couple of years, that Ann was experiencing more pain and limitations when trying to move around the house, especially ankle pain. Though very familiar with operations and visits to Wrightington Orthopaedic Hospital, where she had undergone a revision on her left hip and a replacement on her right hip, we were into new territory with her ankles. The Consultant, Mr Davenport, was yet another specialist in the long line of consultants who had supported us over decades. When Ann's x-rays were displayed on his screen, he turned, with a degree of shock, and said to Ann, 'I have no idea how you are walking. Your pain threshold must be off the scale. You have completely the wrong bones in your ankles.'

The lack of paediatric doctors in 1944 not only resulted in missing the hip complications but the emerging formation of a rare ankle bone abnormality. Instead of forming pivotal joints, she has ball and socket joints, now completely shot and pressing her ankles out on each foot. At a later consultation Mr Davenport informed Ann that she was, possibly, one of only five people he knew of, in the UK, who had this deformity – a real celebrity, but bone on bone is no picnic when taking full body weight!

We were now faced with a difficult decision. Ann was already on the list for surgery on both knees. Now, ankles would require total fusion. It would be one knee operation, one ankle fusion, followed by the other knee and ankle. Given that Ann is 80, and her recovery time from previous operations worked out much longer than uncomplicated surgery, we could be looking at up to ten years of hospitalisation, surgery, clear dangers, and recovery. All dependent on perfect success along the way and her hips requiring no interventions.

We talked and prayed with respect to the pre-op discussion with Mr Hemmady at Wrightington. Having performed two operations on Ann's hips, he was aware of the complications she faced. On arrival, it was Mr Hemmady's registrar we saw first. He was excellent and walked us carefully through the first knee op and the extra complications given Ann's history. Our key prayer was centred around 'peace' and how vital it is to have this peace when making decisions, not least decisions of such magnitude. Colossians chapter 3 verse 15, 'The peace that Christ gives is to guide you in the decisions you make; for it is to this peace that God has called you together in the one body.'

Following the registrar's extensive explanation, he presented the consent sheet. As Ann was about to sign, he suddenly suggested he bring Mr Hemmady in from the next office. He duly arrived and sat on the edge of the desk. He then reiterated the registrar's comments, in even greater detail, stressing the dangerous procedures involved given Ann's complications. He ended by looking at us carefully and said, 'you know, surgery is not always the answer!' It was an unexpected statement, especially from a renowned Surgeon, that resulted in peace. We had really questioned whether Ann would have any better quality of life over such a long period of hospitalisation and recovery, knowing that the fusion of her ankles would give her freedom from pain but little benefit in walking and balance. We opted for a pathway of pain control and apologised to the registrar, who promptly tore up the consent agreement. We left with thankful hearts and peace, but certainly aware, that without a miracle, the battle with pain would not be easy.

The peace Christ gives is not the absence of problems, suffering or challenges, it is a deep sense of receiving the right wisdom at the right time for the best possible outcome. When we stayed in Henley, against all the odds we had peace and waited for God to provide. When we took on the pastorates at Ashford and Toxteth, we had peace that houses and finance would follow. When we searched for a retirement home, on an estate we knew we couldn't afford, we let peace guide us and waited for the provision – it always arrived on time.

It has been the same practically, regarding Ann's limitations. 'Motability' have provided cars every three years for thirty years. Denis Cole made available, several times, a beautiful apartment in Florida. The RAF Benevolent Fund provided a new, large, mobility scooter. The Retired Baptist Minister's Housing Organisation provided equity for our home and a wetroom for ease of access to a shower. Son, Tim, bought mum a nippy little scooter that folds up and fits in the car boot. 'Jehovah Jireh' is one of the many names for the Lord, 'The Lord our provider', fitting the missing jigsaw pieces into place as we trust and wait for his timing.

For Ann, and me, as I look on and seek to be the support

she needs, the last few years have not seen the diminishing of pain, the reduction of greater limitations or the absence of constant frustrations, but a belief that we made the right decision at the right time. We are vulnerable but blessed, and hope that our struggles will help others in their need. We endeavour to remain positive, young at heart, useful and grateful. Our love is strong, patient and, we trust, kind. We are always finding ways to overcome the physical and emotional limitations, enabling us to express our love to one another.

Many times, in ministry, when I revealed my failure, weakness, and vulnerabilities, I had people, sometimes queueing, for a conversation. Success without vulnerability is cold comfort and often keeps others at a distance. Ann is a perfect example of someone living with serious limitations and vulnerabilities - it is like a magnet attracting others to her. She is such a wise listener and perceptive counsellor. It is harder to develop an ordinary friendship, given her physical needs and, at times, the 'Reverend' and 'Pastor's wife' tags can lead to certain assumptions about us fitting into 'everyday' life! Believe me, we are far more earthy and ordinary than you would ever imagine!

77

DIAMOND WEDDING ANIVERSARY - 29TH JUNE 2023

'It was the best of times - it was the worst of times' to quote Mr Dickens. We could not afford the grand Palm House venue we enjoyed for our Golden Anniversary, so trawled a few hotels and the Royal Liver Building 'Balcony' rooms. These were either too expensive or fully booked. We had toyed with the Liverpool Marina Restaurant, but I wasn't very keen. Having visited several times in the past I remember the room as rather dinghy and small. However, as we were running out of options, we decided to pay a visit early on a Saturday morning. We were in for four surprises. The first was the renovation, which was amazing with new lighting, seating, décor, and space for over 100 guests. The second was the size. It struck us as much bigger than our previous visits. The third was the cost, so much cheaper than anywhere else we had explored. The fourth was the owner's story which he freely shared – although we now believe it was not quite the whole story.

He told us he had made a fortune in business and lost it over a divorce settlement that didn't go his way. Destitute, and sleeping on a Spanish beach, he was spotted by a Christian Pastor who stopped and listened to his story. The Pastor then shared the good news of Jesus love, mercy, and forgiveness, and invited 'B' to accept Jesus as his Lord and Saviour. They prayed together and 'B' felt a weight lift from his body. He returned to the UK, started up once again, and had taken over the Marina Restaurant in Liverpool. He had also remarried.

All the time 'B' shared his story, he had no idea we were

Christians! When he had finished his testimony, I said, 'there is something we would like to do for you.' He responded, 'What do you mean?' I said, 'We would love to pray for you.' 'Are you Christians?' he said. I told him a little of our story to faith. We had no inkling that his story might be a sham, or at least a half-truth. He was very emotional, as we prayed. We then asked about dates that were vacant. We could not get the exact date of our anniversary but opted for June 24th, just five days prior. We duly booked a band, DJ, and met the two event managers. 'B' would not be at the event as he was opening another restaurant and nightclub in Southport. Everything appeared to be perfectly fitting into place.

The first signs of chaos appeared on the morning of the celebration. We went to prepare the room with flowers for the tables and seating plans for our guests. Tables were stacked against a wall and a guy was washing the floor from the previous night's party. He forbade us to walk on the floor until it was dry. The event lady with all the tableware arrived and was asked to stay away also. Over an hour later, it was still not dry! As the table lady was desperate to get away, as unknown to us she was struggling with a bereavement in the family, we refused to wait any longer. Tables were quickly prepared and we finished set up – two hours later than expected.

The second sign of chaos was in the evening. We arrived early to ensure all was well - it wasn't. No Events Manager, no bottles of red and white wine on the tables, no juice, and no glasses! It was a very warm evening so the bar was packed with visitors. Trying to get the bar manager to appreciate our concerns was a battle of voices! As the bar was separate from our anniversary it was not the manager's job to sort out our event! Finally, the table lady turned up for a quick check and together we ferried all the missing drinks and glasses from the stockroom. Guests were now arriving as we raced around the tables with wine and glasses!

Amidst all the chaos, I am running around like a madman trying to explain to a young DJ his role with songs, as the booked DJ was otherwise engaged and had not passed on our clear instructions re the order for the evening! The replacement DJ was oblivious to the play tracks we had carefully worked out. Meanwhile the band turned up and began their set up for playing later in the evening. I tried to keep my stress level down and not reveal the problems before guests. I was finally told, by the table lady, that the Events Manager had been in hospital for several days and had undergone an operation. Nobody informed us. The chaos was compounded when the stand-in Events Manager, our 'table lady', could not stay for the event! There was nobody at all who could assist us should a problem arise – and boy it did! I tried to remain calm and carry-on! Eventually, somewhat shredded with nerves, I welcomed everyone and thanked them for coming.

We planned to renew our marriage vows prior to food and I was wrecked! Two more difficult moments were waiting in the wings! Fortunately, the renewal was very ably led by Rob McAvoy, one of our Pastors at church. After we had shared our vows, I knelt and slipped another, small diamond ring, alongside Ann's wedding ring. It was, for me, the best and most precious moment amidst the chaos. Ann later reminded me that I had never proposed sixty years ago, I simply had said, when joining the RAF, 'will you wait for me?' Kneeling and presenting a ring was my proposal – slightly late!

Following the vows, food was laid out and everyone relaxed into the evening. As the final tables were queuing for food, I was aware that very little food was left and two dishes we had paid for had not arrived. I went to the kitchen looking for the chef. The kitchen was empty! I had to go again to the bar manager, fight through the crowd and was eventually told, 'the chef left some time ago!' I felt angry, frustrated, and embarrassed for guests who may not have had a decent meal. The final battle was lurking!

The band finally had their opportunity to play. I had given clear instructions for songs and specifically asked for 'sound sensitivity' as some of the guests had not seen each other for decades and wanted to catch up without having to shout. It didn't take the band long to completely dismiss our request. When the decibel level reached a crucial milestone I watched the room empty outside, with just a few tables left with guests. I went to the band and asked if they could turn the sound down. The leader reacted with aggression, 'Do you want us to leave?' I was a whisker away from saying 'yes.' Instead of being there for us, they were clearly there to run their own agenda.

It was heartening to discover, later in the evening, that very few guests were aware of the battles that had preceded, or taken place, during the evening. Because we had paid for food we had not received, and had to work through some important issues, I wrote to 'B' expressing the catalogue of disasters and disappointment – to put it mildly! After several weeks and no reply, I finally managed to connect on the phone. He assured me that it should not have happened and it would be sorted. Several months later, I tried again and a story of family illness, his hospitalisation, and other factors meant he had not been able to consider resolving the complaint. I fell for all of it and suggested we leave it a few months and I would contact him again – not least as Christian brothers – so I thought.

It now appears, that almost all of it was a sham and a scam. The restaurant closed, and not a single bill had been paid. His debts ran to hundreds of thousands including £60,000 to the owner of the Marina site. It all left me so angry about his story in Benidorm, even more than the stress caused at our 60th Anniversary. Was there even a shred of truth amidst the lies and deception? I may never know.

78

THE MISSING PIECE

There is an obvious flaw in linking a jigsaw puzzle analogy with the jigsaw of life. A jigsaw may last a day or a month before every piece is in place. In life we find the pieces arrive over decades. We begin with just a few and try to make sense of these pieces as we grow. Over time we realise that some of the pieces we have don't fit. Moments of crisis, chaos and change require completely different pieces to make sense of the patterns and plans of our lives. As we tackle the issues, questions, trials, and mysteries of life we realise key pieces are missing. We become frustrated, angry, discontent, depressed and restless. We search for meaning and purpose, by collecting 'stuff', striving to make more money than we really need, working harder, slipping into addictions, and bowing to false gods. We strive for happiness and pile up 'happen-nings.' When the highs stop, the team gets relegated, the divorce or divide strikes, and the stuff doesn't satisfy, we ponder, if wise, the questions of meaning and purpose. 'What's it all for?' That elusive missing piece we thought we had, never quite 'fits the bill.'

The 'Good News' is that new life has the power to change everything. It certainly does when a baby is born! Finding the 'missing piece' of life has the power to change you and me. In a secretive encounter with Nicodemus, a very religious member of the inner-circle of the Jewish ruling court - the Sanhedrin, Jesus explains the 'missing piece' in Nicodemus life. John's gospel, in the Bible, tells us that Nicodemus came to Jesus 'at night' - John chapter 3 verse 2. He was searching for truth but keen to keep his search a secret. You can almost imagine him dodging from side to side in the darkness, a giant shawl protecting his identify. As Nicodemus had trailed Jesus, he saw in his life, words, and miracles, something beyond the natural. He wanted to know more. In his own words, Nicodemus expresses his awareness of God incarnate, God inhabiting the earth, God calling humanity to Himself - 'Rabbi, we know you are a teacher who has come from God. For no one could perform the miraculous signs you are doing if God were not with him.' John chapter 3 verse 2. God is wanting to place that 'missing piece' in Nicodemus's life – not religion but relationship.

Jesus immediately reveals a stark contrast, the difference between natural and spiritual birth. Nicodemus is confused and tries to imagine a grown man entering again into the womb. A challenge swiftly follows, 'You must be born again.' John chapter 3 verse 3. You were born naturally by an act of the flesh, a sexual act, but you must be born again spiritually, by a supernatural act, God's Holy Spirit giving you a new life. The first is the work of mankind, the second the work of God. The first is a physical relationship, the second a spiritual relationship.

Nicodemus knew everything about being 'religious', but little about a life-changing 'relationship' with God. Jesus explains how this is possible in John chapter 3 verse 16, 'For God so loved the world that he gave His one and only Son, that *whoever believes in him* shall not perish but have eternal life.' The 'whoever' means you, me, and everyone in the world has the invitation. Nobody is excluded from the possibility of being 'born again.' The key to this promise is 'whoever believes.' Believing is a verb, an action on our behalf that results in an action - 'new birth' – from God because of what Jesus did on the cross. Our 'action-response' is described in Romans chapter 10 verse 9, *'If you confess with your mouth, Jesus is Lord, and believe in your heart that God raised him from the dead, you will be saved.'* 'Saved' means you are forgiven, accepted and a child of God. You are adopted, by new birth, into God's family and into a personal relationship with the 'one true God.'

Several themes occur, and weave their way through our life story. They make up the multi-coloured jigsaw, but the most important has always been our faith in Jesus as Lord of our lives. To live without Jesus is to live without an eternal purpose and hope. It is to live without God, for Jesus is the only pathway, the only door to God, as declared simply in John chapter 14 verse 6, Jesus said, *'I am the Way, the Truth, and the Life. Nobody comes to the 'Father', except through me'.*

For me, life makes no sense, if it has no meaning beyond the grave. If all we have achieved and worked for dies in the dust. No reckoning for murderous dictators. No justice for millions of innocent people slaughtered without mercy. No accountability for the lives we have lived. It is Jesus who makes sense of life and our purpose within it, and the life beyond it.

Jim Elliot was one of five American missionaries who were martyred by Auca Indians on January 3rd 1956. They landed on a small island in the Ecuadorian jungle. Their hearts were set on bringing the Good News of Jesus to a notoriously dangerous tribe. They built a hut and waited for the tribe to approach them, having previously dropped gifts by air over a three month period. After three days waiting, contact was made with three Indians who accepted gifts. Members of the tribe returned and lanced all five missionaries to death. Jim had previously quoted words that had been used three hundred years before by the Father of Matthew Henry, a biblical scholar: *'He is no fool, who gives up what he cannot keep to gain what he cannot lose.'*

Have you found the missing piece? Have you anchored Jesus into your life's 'jigsaw?' May we urge you to be like Nicodemus and search for, long for and pray for the presence of the 'Living God' in your life and your family. That is our prayer for you, as you complete this story of our lives.

Acknowledgements

If you have persevered to the end, thank you.

It would be impossible, and foolish, to try and identify the many friends, strangers, colleagues, neighbours and, of course family, who have, over twenty-five years encouraged me to 'write a book.' The stories belong to a host of people, over my lifetime, who have invested their time, prayers and wisdom into my life, and those whose kindness, generosity and practical support and has enabled both Ann and I to invest a large part of our lives serving others. Thank you all.

Even at eighty, and given our limitations, we are both as eager as we have ever been to make a difference wherever we can. As we have been seeking to make that difference, since retirement in 2009, at River Oaks you might enjoy checking out:

www.riveroakscharity.co.uk

The menu will guide you to the history of the site from the 1800's, the role of Riversdale College and the reason why River Oaks Residents Association, then River Oaks Charity were formed. The gallery is packed with the transformation pictures over the past fifteen years.

I am sure every author hopes for an 'error' free book. I can state with certainty, you will find something that is not right, even after four revisions! I accept full responsibility - it was not deliberate! Please contact us if there is anything you would like to share, comment on, detect is wrong and needs correction.

toglyn@hotmail.co.uk annbytheriver@gmail.com

Acknowledgements

If you have persevered to the end, thank you.

It would be impossible, and foolish, to try and identify the many friends, strangers, colleagues, neighbours and, of course family, who have, over twenty-five years encouraged me to 'write a book.' The stories belong to a host of people, over my lifetime, who have invested their time, prayers and wisdom into my life, and those whose kindness, generosity and practical support and has enabled both Ann and I to invest a large part of our lives serving others. Thank you all.

Even at eighty, and given our limitations, we are both as eager as we have ever been to make a difference wherever we can. As we have been seeking to make that difference, since retirement in 2009, at River Oaks you might enjoy checking out:

www.riveroakscharity.co.uk

The menu will guide you to the history of the site from the 1800's, the role of Riversdale College and the reason why River Oaks Residents Association, then River Oaks Charity were formed. The gallery is packed with the transformation pictures over the past fifteen years.

I am sure every author hopes for an 'error' free book. I can state with certainty, you will find something that is not right, even after four revisions! I accept full responsibility - it was not deliberate! Please contact us if there is anything you would like to share, comment on, detect is wrong and needs correction.

toglyn@hotmail.co.uk annbytheriver@gmail.com

Have you found the missing piece? Have you anchored Jesus into your life's 'jigsaw?' May we urge you to be like Nicodemus and search for, long for and pray for the presence of the 'Living God' in your life and your family. That is our prayer for you, as you complete this story of our lives.